Ninja Foodi

Deluxe XL

Pressure Cooker Cookbook

Simple & Delicious Ninja Foodi Pressure Cooker and Air Fryer Recipes for Everyone

Janice Sottile

TABLE OF CONTENTS

Introduction

The Ninja Foodi is the most flexible and revolutionary kitchen appliance on the market today. It's the only appliance that can work as a slow cooker, sauté pan, electric pressure cooker, rice cooker, and even an air fryer in just one pot.

High tech kitchen appliances have brought much-wanted ease and comfort to everyone's life. The idea of a single pot, multi-style cooking has come into play with various multifunctional cooking devices. Ninja Foodi is one such leading name in the kitchen tech industry, which has garnered a good repute for its variant cooking functions and unique modes. The Ninja Foodi Multi-Crisp Cooker is nothing short of a revolutionary cooking appliance that has seemingly taken the whole culinary world by storm! If I am being completely short and precise, the Ninja Foodi is an all-in-one and extremely versatile appliance that is designed to function as a slow cooker, rice cooker, pressure cooker, rice cooker, and even an Air Fryer! The versatility of the appliance also means that using the Ninja Foodi, you will be able to craft all of your dishes from mains, desserts to yogurt and even baked goods! What's even more fascinating, is the fact that with the combined power of pressure cooking and Air Fryer, you will be able to prepare your meals almost 70% faster and with 75% less fat when compared to other traditional means of cooking. Unlike other devices of such sort, it combines all the basic modes of cooking rather than providing sub-modes or temperature settings.

And just in case you're wondering, with this amazing device, you're not only limited to making simple pressure cooker dishes. The versatility of this appliance will allow you to create anything from soups, stews, chilis, breakfast dishes, and desserts! Your imagination is the only limitation here. You can achieve any meal you desire from this multipurpose appliance.

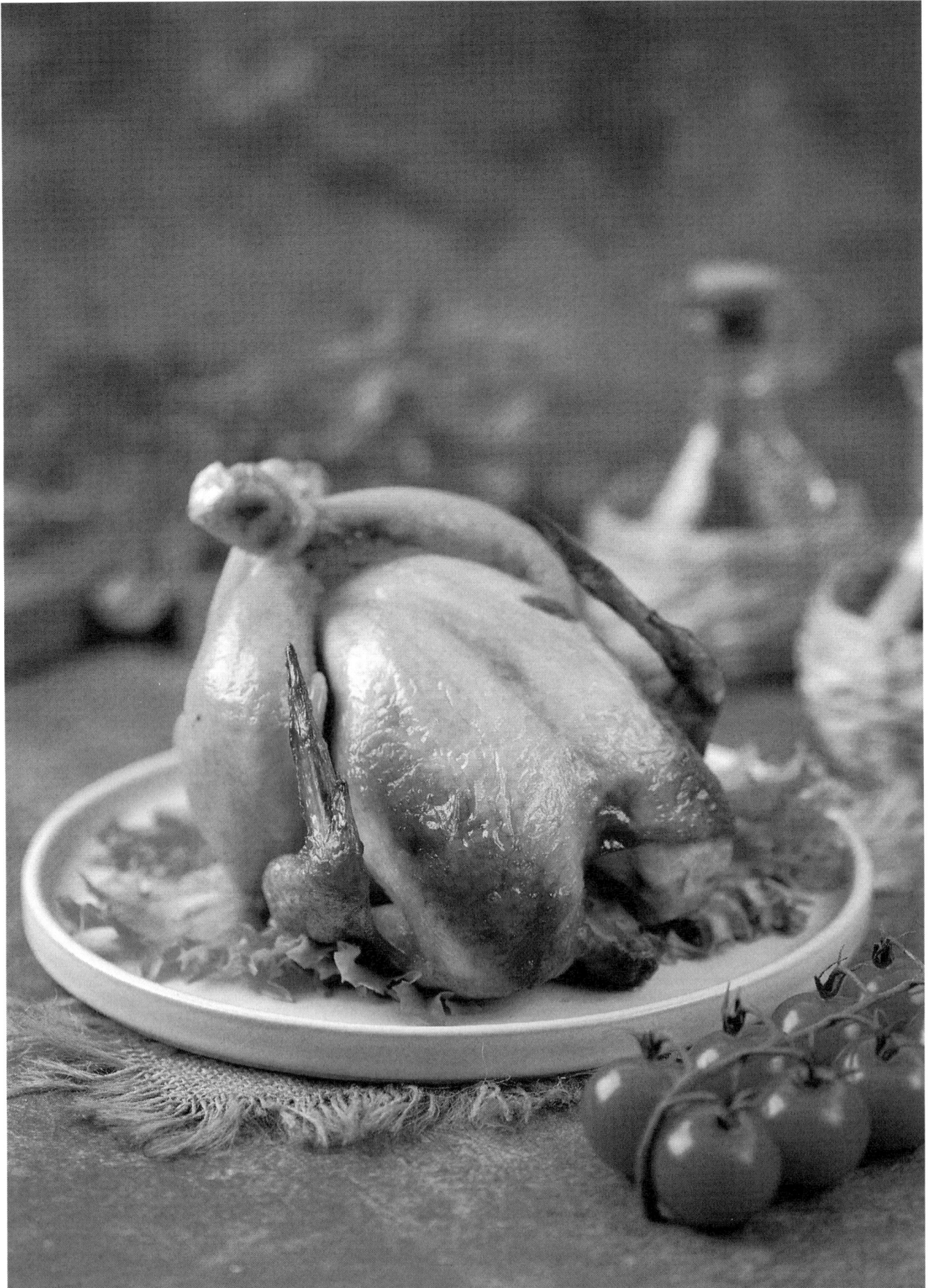

What is Ninja Foodi Deluxe XL Pressure Cooker?

The Ninja Foodi Deluxe XL Pressure Cooker is a modern pressure cooker that provides other cooking functions like oven, steamer, roaster, slow cooker, air fryer, and dehydrater. It makes the device one of its kind has developed a massive customer base across the world. It is made by Shark Ninja and gained the trust of thousands worldwide with the exceptional functions being offered in a single device.

The main theme is to provide the user with the state of the art TenderCrisp technology that is developed by Foodi Ninja and installed in the Ninja Foodi Deluxe XL Pressure Cooker. Furthermore, the device comes with two separate lids, i.e., each for a different purpose. One of the lids is the Pressure Cooking Lid which provides thorough tenderness to your food. The other cooking lid is the non-detachable Crisping Lid which, evident from its name, offers efficient crispiness to your food.

The Ninja Foodi Deluxe XL Pressure Cooker comes with many variants. The most advanced and competent variant of the Ninja Foodi Deluxe XL Pressure Cooker launched was the Ninja Foodi Deluxe 8-Quart. It was primarily released in 2019 and since then has dominated the market. It is made with refined and efficient stainless steel, which establishes its compactness and reliability. Furthermore, Ninja focused on improving the user interface efficiently by introducing an LCD with a central dial that controls the functions. Moreover, the cooking capacity is really catchy for people who have larger families. Additionally, there is a Yogurt Function button also available on the device.

With Ninja Foodi Deluxe XL Pressure Cooker you can pressure cook, slow cook, air crisp, bake and dehydrate all at once place. That is the feature which has made Ninja Foodi a much-wanted kitchen device of the day. In this cookbook, we shall discover the various ways this Ninja Foodi can be deemed perfect for cooking variety of healthy meals.

How does the Ninja Foodi Work?

The Ninja Foodi can pressure cook, slow cook, sauté, steam, and air fry your food. It also features Ninja's unique TenderCrisp Technology, a combination of pressure cooking and air frying that allows you to rapidly cook your food, leaving it with a crispy texture.

Owning a Foodi eliminates the need for you to own three separate appliances (a pressure cooker, a slow cooker, and an air fryer). Although it does take up more space than some of these appliances on their own, overall, it reduces clutter in your kitchen.

Since the Ninja Foodi's introduction, Ninja Foodi has released a few models with some tweaks, like the Ninja Foodi electric countertop grills and the Ninja Foodi Deluxe XL. The Ninja Foodi includes a pressure lid and a crisping lid, a cook and crisp basket, and a reversible cooking rack. It's simple to use for entrées, sides, desserts, or whatever else you can think to cook with it. Good Housekeeping magazine says the controls are straightforward and intuitive to use—great news if you're not a professional and simply want to follow the included recipe guide. The positions of the Ninja Foodi's pressure release valves are clearly labeled, and the control panel **features easy-to-use buttons with presets and custom settings.**

Prime Cooking Functions of Ninja Foodi Deluxe XL Pressure Cooker

The mighty Ninja Foodi comes with eight cooking smart functions, eliminating the need for multiple appliances in the kitchen. This makes it an 8-in-1 multipurpose deluxe food-making appliance. Aside from air frying and air crisping, there are six other cooking functions.

1. Pressure Cook
With the Pressure Lid and cooking pot, you can cook your meat in minutes rather than waiting for hours. The pressure valve/vent is specified in the pot for releasing quick/natural pressure.

2. Steam
You can steam your veggies and meat with the Foodi's two reversible racks. This function allows even steaming, meaning you don't even need to flip the food halfway through cooking.

3. Slow Cook
You can also slow cook your food if you're busy and want to spend less time in the kitchen. This function allows you to slow-cook healthy meals. You can make all kinds of recipes, such as chilis, pulled pork or beef, and soup.

4. Sear/Sauté
The Foodi can be used as a regular saucepan or frying pan, so you can also sear and sauté your food.

5. Air Crisp
Want to eat crispy but healthy, non-oily food? You can with the Ninja Foodi! It allows you to air fry and crisp up your food with its patented TenderCrisp Technology. Now you can have your guilt-free fried food any time you like.

6. Bake/Roast
The Ninja Foodi can bake and roast your meat and veggies. It can function as a compact conventional oven and bake/roast delicious meals. You can bake and roast chicken, meat, turkey, cutlets, as well as desserts and puddings.

7. Broil
The Ninja Foodi also allows you to broil meat and veggies. This means you can broil your food indoors without the need to burn any charcoal or produce any mess or smoke.

8. Dehydrate
Dehydration is required to make several forms of jerkies and other special food, therefore, this feature is specially added to the Ninja Foodi. Place a double layer Cook & Crisp basket in the Ninja Foodi cooking pot, then set the items over this rack. Press Dehydrate after closing the lid, and set the time and temperature, then press Start to initiate the program.

What Can You Get with the Ninja Foodi?

While many of the best cooking, baking recipes contain typically deep-fried foods, you can also use this appliance to roast vegetables, cook meat, and bake cookies.

- **Crispy homemade snacks and sides**

If you like to make your foods crispy without using any oil, the air fryer is a great option for making crispy homemade snacks and sides. You simply need to select the Air Crisp function. However, you can't make anything that uses a wet batter, such as cookies, cakes, and pancakes.

- **Tender and juicy meat**

You can pressure cook, bake, sear, air fry, crisp chicken, fish, or other meat. The result will always be tender, juicy, and delicious.

- **Scrumptious vegetables**

The Ninja Foodi allows you to cook, bake, and air fry vegetables without losing their essential nutrients. You can create anything from veggie chips to stews to soup. You can even cook rice to perfection.

- **Yummy desserts**

The Ninja Foodi also functions as a conventional oven. You can bake chicken, meat, and veggies as well as yummy desserts. The appliance is manufactured on the principle of even heating, so you'll get perfect results every time.

The Ninja Foodi Cleaning Guide

How to clean the Ninja Foodi before and after every use

Cleaning the Ninja Foodi is much easier than cleaning an Instant Pot. This is thanks to the coating on the inside pot and the easy-clean plastic exterior. The best part about the Ninja Foodi is that its removable parts are dishwasher-safe, making cleaning and washing even more convenient.

The inside cooking pot, reversible rack, detachable diffuser, Cook & Crisp Basket, and silicone ring can be washed and are dishwasher safe. Never immerse the Ninja Foodi base or any other components in water or other liquids, or wash them in a dishwasher.

The accessories are ceramic-coated to help with easy cleaning, so avoid using abrasive cleaning tools. The removable parts are easy to clean with warm soapy water, so don't worry if you don't own a dishwasher.

You'll need to keep your Ninja Foodi in tip-top shape, so clean the accessories after every use. After cooking, the Ninja Foodi will be hot. Leave the hood open after removing food so it can cool while you're eating. If washing the accessories by hand, use a cleaning brush.

The Ninja Foodi needs to be cleaned thoroughly after each use:

1. Always unplug the appliance from the wall outlet before cleaning it.
2. NEVER immerse the Ninja Foodi base in water, other liquids, or put it in the dishwasher.
3. When cleaning the Ninja Foodi base and control panel, wipe them clean with a moist cloth.
4. The inside cooking pot, reversible rack, detachable diffuser, Cook & Crisp Basket, and silicone ring can be washed in a dishwasher.
5. The pressure lid, anti-clog cap, and pressure release valve can be cleaned with water and dish detergent. NEVER clean the Pressure Lid or its parts in the dishwasher, and DO NOT take apart the red float valve assembly or pressure release valve.
6. After the heat shield cools, clean the Ninja Crisping Lid, take a damp cloth or paper towel, and wipe it down.
7. If leftover food is stuck on the inside cooking pot, Cook & Crisp Basket, or reversible rack, fill the inside pot with warm soapy water to allow soaking before cleaning. NEVER use abrasive cleaning pads. If you need to scrub, always use a non-abrasive detergent or dish soap with a brush or pad.
8. Let all parts air-dry after every use.

The Ninja Foodi's dishwasher-safe parts

- Inside cooking pot
- Cook & Crisp Basket
- Reversible rack
- Detachable diffuser
- Silicone ring

The Ninja Foodi's non-dishwasher-safe parts

- Ninja Foodi base
- Crisping Lid and heat shield
- Pressure Lid or any of its component

Nut-Packed Porridge

Prep Time: 10 minutes
Cook Time: 10 minutes
Serves: 6

Ingredients:
- 1 cup porridge
- 1 cup roasted pecans, halved
- 1 cup roasted cashew nuts, unsalted
- 4 tsp coconut oil, melted
- 2 cups water
- Fresh Mix berries (Optional)

Preparation:
1. Add 2 cups water along with 1 cup porridge with coconut oil in the Ninja Foodi cooker base.
2. Close the pressure lid, pressure cook for 4 minutes on High mode.
3. Quick-release the pressure.
4. Open the lid and mix the nuts in the porridge.

Nutritional Information Per Serving:
Calories 70; Fat: 6g; Carbs: 1g; Protein: 3g

Morning Buttery Pancakes

Prep Time: 10 minutes
Cook Time: 10 minutes
Serves: 6

Ingredients:
- 2 cups cream cheese
- 2 cups almond flour
- 6 large whole eggs
- ¼ tsp salt
- 2 tbsp butter, divided
- ¼ tsp ground ginger
- ½ tsp cinnamon powder

Preparation:
1. Take a large bowl and add the cream cheese, eggs, and 1 tablespoon of butter. Blend on until creamy
2. Slowly add the flour and keep beating.
3. Add the salt, ginger, and cinnamon and beat until fluffy.
4. Set your Ninja Foodi to SEAR/SAUTÉ mode and grease the stainless-steel insert. Add the remaining butter and heat it up.
5. Add ½ cup of the batter and cook for 2–3 minutes, flip and cook the other side.
6. Repeat with the remaining batter. Serve warm and enjoy!

Nutritional Information Per Serving:
Calories 432; Fat: 40g; Carbs: 3g; Protein: 14g

Crispy Spiced Broccoli

Prep Time: 5–10 minutes
Cook Time: 10 minutes
Serves: 4

Ingredients:
- 2 heads broccoli, cut into florets
- 4 tbsp soy sauce
- 2 tbsp canola oil
- 4 tbsp balsamic vinegar
- 2 tsp maple syrup
- Red pepper flakes and sesame seeds, to garnish

Preparation:
1. In a mixing bowl, whisk together the soy sauce, balsamic vinegar, oil, and maple syrup. Add the broccoli; toss well.
2. Take the Ninja Foodi, place it on your kitchen countertop, and open the top lid.
3. Arrange the Cook & Crisp Basket in the pot and close the top lid. Select AIR CRISP and then the temperature to 350°F. Adjust the timer to 10 minutes and then press START/STOP. The Ninja Foodi will start preheating.

4. The Ninja Foodi is preheated and ready to cook when it starts to beep. After you hear a beep, open the top lid.
5. Arrange the broccoli over the crisp basket.
6. Close the top lid and allow the broccoli to cook until the timer reads zero.
7. Divide the broccoli among serving plates.
Nutritional Information Per Serving:
Calories 141; Fat: 7g; Carbs: 14g; Protein: 4.5g

Delish Broccoli and Scrambled Eggs

Prep Time: 10 minutes
Cook Time: 5 minutes
Serves: 4
Ingredients:
- 1 pack (12 oz) frozen broccoli florets
- 2 tbsp butter
- Salt and pepper, as needed
- 8 whole eggs
- 2 tbsp milk
- ¾ cup white cheddar cheese, shredded
- Crushed red pepper, as needed
- Optional bacon strips

Preparation:
1. Open your Ninja Foodi lid and select SEAR/SAUTÉ mode. Add the butter and broccoli to the pot and stir well.
2. Season the mix with salt and pepper; adjust according to your taste.
3. Lock the lid and select PRESSURE mode. Cook on HI pressure for 10 minutes. Let the appliance release the pressure naturally.
4. Take a medium-sized bowl. Crack in the eggs. Beat them well, and then add the milk and stir.
5. Pour the egg mixture into the Ninja Foodi over the broccoli mix and gently stir.
6. Set the Foodi to SEAR/SAUTÉ mode and let it cook for 2 minutes.
7. Once the egg has set, add the cheese, and sprinkle with red and black pepper and salt.
Nutritional Information Per Serving:
Calories 184; Fat: 12g; Carbs: 5g; Protein: 12g

Spinach and Turkey Cups

Prep Time: 15 minutes
Cook Time: 23 minutes
Serves: 4
Ingredients:
- 1 tbsp unsalted butter
- 1 lb. fresh baby spinach
- 4 eggs
- 7 oz cooked turkey, chopped
- 4 tsp unsweetened almond milk
- Salt and ground black pepper, as required

Preparation:
1. Select the SEAR/SAUTÉ setting on the Ninja Foodi and place the butter into its inner pot.
2. Press START/STOP to begin cooking. Heat the butter for about 2–3 minutes.
3. Add the spinach and cook for about 2–3 minutes or until just wilted.
4. Press START/STOP to stop cooking and drain the liquid completely.
5. Transfer the spinach into a bowl and set it aside to cool slightly.
6. Arrange the Cook & Crisp Basket in the Ninja Foodi's pot.
7. Close the Ninja Foodi with the Crisping Lid and select AIR CRISP.
8. Set the temperature to 355°F for 5 minutes. Press START/STOP to begin preheating.
9. Divide the spinach into four greased ramekins, followed by the turkey.
10. Crack 1 egg into each ramekin and drizzle with almond milk. Sprinkle with salt and black pepper.
11. After the appliance has preheated, open the lid and place the ramekins into the Cook & Crisp Basket.
12. Close the Ninja Foodi with the Crisping Lid and select AIR CRISP.
13. Set the temperature to 355°F for 20 minutes. Press START/STOP to begin cooking.
14. When done, open the lid and serve hot.
Nutritional Information Per Serving:
Calories 200; Fat: 10.2g; Carbs: 4.5g; Protein: 23.4g

Pepperoni Omelet

Prep Time: 10 minutes
Cook Time: 5 minutes
Serves: 4
Ingredients:
- 4 tbsp heavy cream
- 15 pepperoni slices
- 2 tbsp butter
- Salt and pepper, to taste
- 6 whole eggs

Preparation:
1. Take a bowl and whisk in the eggs, cream, pepperoni slices, salt, and pepper.
2. Set your Foodi to SEAR/SAUTÉ mode and add the butter. Pour in the egg mix and sauté for 3 minutes. Flip the omelet over.
3. Lock the lid and select AIR CRISP mode for 2 minutes at 350°F.
4. When the omelet is done, transfer it to a serving plate and enjoy!

Nutritional Information Per Serving:
Calories 141; Fat: 11g; Carbs: 0.6g; Protein: 9g

Eggs in Avocado Cups

Prep Time: 10 minutes
Cook Time: 12 minutes
Serves: 2
Ingredients:
- 1 avocado, halved and pitted
- Salt and ground black pepper, as required
- 2 eggs
- 1 tbsp parmesan cheese, shredded
- 1 tsp fresh chives, minced

Preparation:
1. Arrange a greased square piece of foil in the Cook & Crisp Basket and place the basket in the Ninja Foodi's pot.
2. Close the Ninja Foodi with the Crisping Lid and select BAKE/ROAST.
3. Set the temperature to 390°F for 5 minutes. Press START/STOP to begin preheating.
4. Carefully scoop out about 2 tsp of flesh from each avocado half.
5. Crack 1 egg in each avocado half and sprinkle with salt, black pepper, and cheese.
6. When the appliance has preheated, open the lid.
7. Place the avocado halves into the Cook & Crisp Basket.
8. Close the Ninja Foodi with the Crisping Lid and Select BAKE/ROAST.
9. Set the temperature to 390°F for 12 minutes.
10. Press START/STOP to begin cooking.
11. When done, open the lid and transfer the avocado halves onto serving plates.

Nutritional Information Per Serving:
Calories 278; Fat: 24.7g; Carbs: 9.1g; Protein: 8g

Sausage and Bell Pepper Frittata

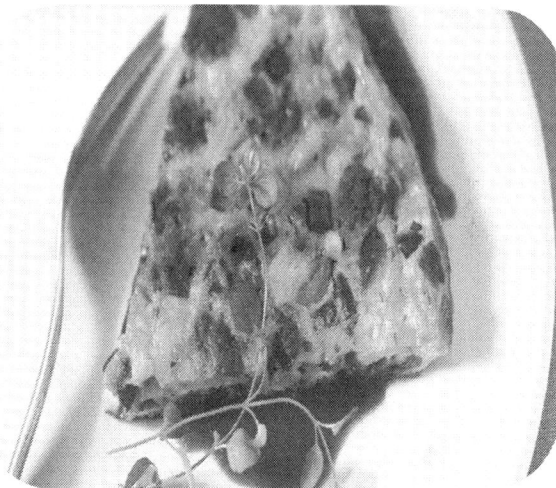

Prep Time: 15 minutes
Cook Time: 18 minutes
Serves: 2
Ingredients:
- 1 tbsp olive oil
- 1 chorizo sausage, sliced
- 1½ cups bell peppers, seeded and chopped
- 4 large eggs
- Salt and ground black pepper, as required
- 2 tbsp feta cheese, crumbled
- 1 tbsp fresh parsley, chopped

Preparation:
1. Select the SEAR/SAUTÉ setting of the Ninja Foodi and place the butter into the inner pot.
2. Press START/STOP to begin cooking and heat the butter for about 2–3 minutes.
3. Add the sausage and bell peppers and cook for 6–8 minutes or until golden brown.

4. Meanwhile, in a small bowl, add the eggs, salt, and black pepper and beat well.
5. Press START/STOP to stop cooking and place the eggs over the sausage mixture, followed by the cheese and parsley.
6. Close the Ninja Foodi with the Crisping Lid and select AIR CRISP.
7. Set the temperature to 355°F for 10 minutes. Press START/STOP to begin cooking.
8. Open the lid and transfer the frittata onto a platter.
Nutritional Information Per Serving:
Calories 398; Fat: 31g; Carbs: 8g; Protein: 22.9g

Western Omelet

Prep Time: 10 minutes
Cook Time: 35 minutes
Serves: 4
Ingredients:
- 3 eggs, whisked
- 3 oz chorizo, chopped
- 1 oz feta cheese, crumbled
- 5 tbsp almond milk
- ¾ tsp chili flakes
- ¼ tsp salt
- 1 green pepper, chopped

Preparation:
1. Add all the listed ingredients to a bowl and mix well. Take an omelet pan and pour the mixture into it.
2. Preheat your Ninja Foodi on BAKE mode at 320°F for 10 minutes.
3. Transfer the pan with the omelet mix to your Ninja Foodi and bake for 30 minutes, or until golden and the egg has set properly.
Nutritional Information Per Serving:
Calories 426; Fat: 38g; Carbs: 7g; Protein: 21g

Cowboy Casserole

Prep Time: 30 minutes
Cook Time: 30 minutes
Serves: 4
Ingredients:
- 1 lb. ground beef
- 1 bag frozen tater tots
- 1 small onion, chopped
- 1 can black beans
- 1 cup corn
- 1 can Ro-Tel tomatoes with chilies
- 1 tsp cumin
- 1 tsp chili powder
- 1 cup sour cream
- 1 cup cheddar cheese, shredded
- 3 slices cooked bacon
- Green onions, for topping (optional)

Preparation:
1. Turn your Foodi on to SEAR/SAUTÉ mode. Cook the ground beef on HI until no longer pink.
2. Add the onions and cook until they are soft, about 1–2 minutes, and then add the seasonings.
3. Stir in the beans, corn, and sour cream. Stir until well combined.
4. Top with the frozen tater tots.
5. Adjust the setting to AIR CRISP and place the Crisping Lid on the Foodi. Cook at 390°F for 20 minutes.
6. Remove the lid and place the cheese on top. Place the Crisping Lid again, select AIR CRISP at 390°F, and cook for an additional 5 minutes.
Nutritional Information Per Serving:
Calories 500; Fat: 30g; Carbs: 24g; Protein: 34g

Morning Pancakes

Prep Time: 10 minutes
Cook Time: 10 minutes
Servings: 4
Ingredients:
- 2 cups cream cheese
- 2 cups almond flour
- 6 large whole eggs
- ¼ teaspoon salt
- 2 tablespoons butter
- ¼ teaspoon ground ginger
- ½ teaspoon cinnamon powder

Directions:
1. Take a large bowl and add cream cheese, eggs, 1 tablespoon butter. Blend on high until creamy
2. Slow add flour and keep beating
3. Add salt, ginger, cinnamon
4. Keep beating until fully mixed
5. Select "Sauté" mode on your Ninja Foodi and grease stainless steel insert
6. Add butter and heat it up
7. Add ½ cup batter and cook for 2-3 minutes, flip and cook the other side
8. Repeat with the remaining batter. Enjoy.

Nutritional Values Per Serving:
Calories: 432; Fat: 40g; Carbs: 3g; Protein: 14g

Nutmeg Pumpkin Porridge

Prep Time: 15 minutes
Cook Time: 5 hours
Servings: 8
Ingredients:
- 1 cup unsweetened almond milk
- 2 pounds pumpkin, peeled and cubed into ½-inch size
- 6-8 drops liquid stevia
- ½ teaspoon ground allspice
- 1 tablespoon ground cinnamon
- 1 teaspoon ground nutmeg
- ¼ teaspoon ground cloves
- ½ cup walnuts, chopped

Directions:
1. In the Ninja Foodi's insert, place ½ cup of almond milk and remaining ingredients and stir to combine.
2. Close the Ninja Foodi's lid with a crisping lid and select "Slow Cook".
3. Set on "LO" for 4-5 hours.
4. Press the "Start/Stop" button to initiate cooking.
5. Open the Ninja Foodi's lid and stir in the remaining almond milk.
6. With a potato masher, mash the mixture completely.
7. Divide the porridge into serving bowls evenly.
8. Serve warm with the topping of walnuts.

Nutritional Values Per Serving:
Calories: 96; Fat: 5.5g; Carbs: 11.2g; Protein: 3.3g

Spinach Casserole

Prep Time: 10 minutes
Cook Time: 5 minutes
Servings: 4
Ingredients:
- 4 whole eggs
- 1 tablespoons milk
- 1 tomato, diced
- ½ cup spinach
- ¼ teaspoon salt
- ¼ teaspoon black pepper

Directions:
1. Take a baking pan small enough to fit Ninja Foodi and grease it with butter.
2. Take a medium bowl and whisk in eggs, milk, salt, pepper, add veggies to the bowl and stir.
3. Pour egg mixture into the baking pan and lower the pan into the Ninja Foodi.
4. Close crisping lid and Air Crisp for 325 degrees F for 7 minutes.
5. Remove the pan from eggs, and enjoy hot.

Nutritional Values Per Serving:
Calories: 78; Fat: 5g; Carbs: 1 g; Protein: 7 g

Brussels Sprouts Bacon Hash

Prep Time: 10 minutes
Cook Time:20 minutes
Servings: 4
Ingredients:
- ½ lb. brussels sprouts, sliced in half
- 4 slices bacon, chopped
- ½ red onion, chopped
- salt, to taste
- black pepper, to taste

Directions:
1. Toss all the ingredients into the Ninja Foodi cooking pot.
2. Secure the Ninja Foodi lid and turn its pressure handle to 'SEAL' position.
3. Select mode for 20 minutes at HI.
4. Once done, release the steam naturally then remove the lid.
5. Serve fresh.

Nutritional Values Per Serving:
Calories 121; Total Fat 9 g; Total Carbs 13.8 g; Protein 4.3 g

Apricot Oatmeal

Prep Time: 10 minutes
Cook Time: 8 hours
Servings: 8
Ingredients:
- 2 cups steel-cut oats
- ⅓ cup dried apricots, chopped
- ½ cup dried cherries
- 1 teaspoon ground cinnamon
- 4 cups milk
- 4 cups water
- ¼ teaspoon liquid stevia

Directions:
1. In the Ninja Foodi's insert, place all ingredients and stir to combine.

2. Close the Ninja Foodi's lid with a pressure lid and select "Slow Cook."
3. Set on "LO" for 6-8 hours.
4. Press the "Start/Stop" button to initiate cooking.
5. Open the Ninja Foodi's lid and serve warm.

Nutritional Values Per Serving:
Calories: 148; Fat: 3.5g; Carbs: 4.2 g; Protein: 5.9 g

Cashew Porridge

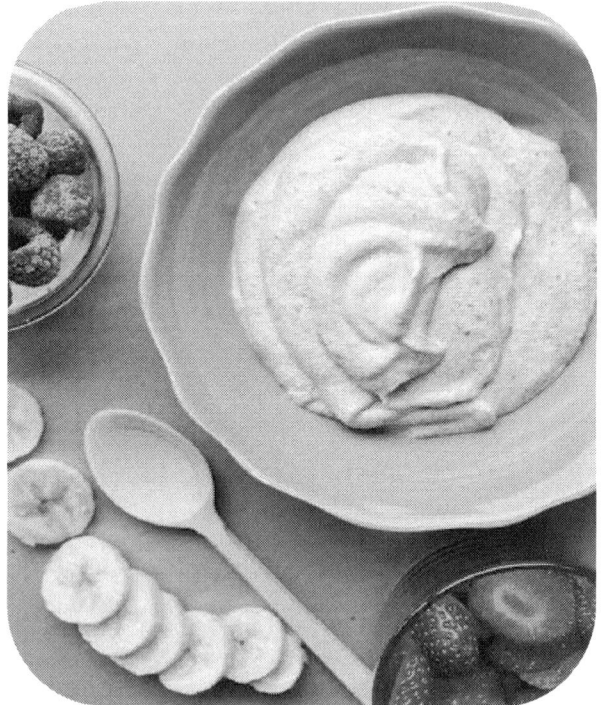

Prep Time: 10 minutes
Cook Time: 10 minutes
Servings: 6
Ingredients:
- 1 cup pecans, halved
- 1 cup cashew nuts, raw and unsalted
- 4 teaspoons coconut oil, melted
- 2 cups of water

Directions:
1. Add 1 and ½ cups of water and place a steamer rack in your Ninja Foodi.
2. Trim the core of the cauliflower head and cut it into florets.
3. Take a small bowl and mix with olive oil, salt, cumin, and paprika, then drizzle over cauliflower.
4. Close the Ninja Foodi's pressure lid. Turn the pressure release valve to the SEAL position. Set the unit to Pressure mode.
5. Cook for 4 minutes on Hi.
6. Quick-release the Pressure.
7. Garnish with cilantro.
8. Serve and enjoy.

Nutritional Values Per Serving:
Calories: 70; Fat: 6g; Carbs: 1 g; Protein: 3g

Chicken Omelet

Prep Time: 10 minutes
Cook Time: 16 minutes
Servings: 2
Ingredients:
- 1 teaspoon butter
- 1 small yellow onion, chopped
- ½ jalapeño pepper, seeded and chopped
- 3 eggs
- Black pepper and salt, as required
- ¼ cup cooked chicken, shredded

Directions:
1. Select the "Sauté/Sear" setting of Ninja Foodi and place the butter into the pot.
2. Press the "Start/Stop" button to initiate cooking and heat for about 2-3 minutes.
3. Add the onion and cook for about 4-5 minutes.
4. Add the jalapeño pepper and cook for about 1 minute.
5. Meanwhile, in a suitable, add the eggs, salt, and black pepper and beat well.
6. Press the "Start/Stop" button to pause cooking and stir in the chicken.
7. Top with the egg mixture evenly.
8. Close the Ninja Foodi's lid with a crisping lid and select "Air Crisp."
9. Set its cooking temperature to 355 degrees F for 5 minutes.
10. Press the "Start/Stop" button to initiate cooking.
11. Open the Ninja Foodi's lid and transfer the omelette onto a plate.
12. Cut into equal-sized wedges and serve hot.

Nutritional Values Per Serving:
Calories: 153; Fat: 9.1g; Carbs: 4g; Protein: 13.8g

Bell Pepper Frittata

Prep Time: 15 minutes
Cook Time: 18 minutes
Servings: 2
Ingredients:
- 1 tablespoon olive oil
- 1 chorizo sausage, sliced
- 1½ cups bell peppers, seeded and chopped
- 4 large eggs
- Black pepper and salt, as required
- 2 tablespoons feta cheese, crumbled
- 1 tablespoon fresh parsley, chopped

Directions:
1. Select the "Sauté/Sear" setting of Ninja Foodi and place the butter into the pot.
2. Press the "Start/Stop" button to initiate cooking and heat for about 2-3 minutes.
3. Add the sausage and bell peppers and cook for 6-8 minutes or until golden brown.
4. Meanwhile, in a suitable bowl, add the eggs, salt, and black pepper and beat well.
5. Press the "Start/Stop" button to pasue cooking and place the eggs over the sausage mixture, followed by the cheese and parsley.
6. Close the Ninja Foodi's lid with a crisping lid and select "Air Crisp".
7. Set its cooking temperature to 355 degrees F for 10 minutes.
8. Press the "Start/Stop" button to initiate cooking.
9. Open the Ninja Foodi's lid and transfer the frittata onto a platter.
10. Cut into equal-sized wedges and serve hot.

Nutritional Values Per Serving:
Calories: 398; Fat: 31g; Carbs: 8g; Protein: 22.9g

Broccoli Egg Scramble

Prep Time: 10 minutes
Cook Time: 5 minutes
Servings: 4
Ingredients:
- 1 pack, 12 ounces frozen broccoli florets
- 2 tablespoons butter
- Black pepper and salt, to taste
- 8 whole eggs
- 2 tablespoons milk
- ¾ cup white cheddar cheese, shredded
- Crushed red pepper to taste
- Optional bacon strips

Directions:
1. Open your Ninja Foodi lid and add butter, broccoli, and stir
2. Season the mix with black pepper and salt, adjust according to your taste
3. Lock and secure the Ninja Foodi's lid, then cook on "HIGH" pressure for 10 minutes
4. Release pressure naturally
5. Take a medium-sized bowl and crack an egg, beat well, add milk to the eggs and stir
6. Add egg mixture into the Ninja Foodi over the broccoli mix, gently stir
7. Set your pot to "Sauté" mode and let it cook for 2 minutes
8. Once the egg has settled in, add cheese, sprinkle red and black pepper
9. Season with salt
10. Serve and enjoy with some bacon.
Nutritional Values Per Serving:
Calories: 184; Fat: 12g; Carbs: 5 g; Protein: 12 g

Almond Quinoa Porridge

Prep Time: 10 minutes
Cook Time: 1 minute
Servings: 6
Ingredients:
- 1¼ cups water
- 1 cup almond milk
- 1½ cups uncooked quinoa, rinsed
- 1 tablespoon choc zero maple syrup
- 1 cinnamon stick

- Pinch of salt
Directions:
1. In the Ninja Foodi's insert, add all ingredients and stir to combine well.
2. Close the Ninja Foodi's pressure lid and place the pressure valve in the "Seal" position.
3. Select "Pressure" mode and set it to "Hi" for 1 minute.
4. Press the "Start/Stop" button to initiate cooking.
5. Now turn the pressure valve to "Vent" and do a "Quick" release.
6. Open the Ninja Foodi's lid, and with a fork, fluff the quinoa.
7. Serve warm.
Nutritional Values Per Serving:
Calories: 186; Fat: 2.6 g; Carbs: 4.8 g; Protein: 6 g

Flaxseeds Granola

Prep Time: 15 minutes
Cook Time: 2½ hours
Servings: 16
Ingredients:
- ½ cup sunflower kernels
- 5 cups mixed nuts, crushed
- 2 tablespoons ground flax seeds
- ¼ cup olive oil
- ½ cup unsalted butter
- 1 teaspoon ground cinnamon
- 1 cup choc zero maple syrup

Directions:
1. Grease the Ninja Foodi's insert.
2. In the greased Ninja Foodi's insert, add sunflower kernels, nuts, flax seeds, oil, butter, and cinnamon and stir to combine.
3. Close the Ninja Foodi's lid with a pressure lid and select "Slow Cook."
4. Set on "HI" for 2½ hours.
5. Press the "Start/Stop" button to initiate cooking.
6. Stir the mixture after every 30 minutes.
7. Open the Ninja Foodi's lid and transfer the granola onto a large baking sheet.
8. Add the maple syrup and stir to combine.
9. Set aside to cool completely before serving.
10. You can preserve this granola in an airtight container.
Nutritional Values Per Serving:
Calories: 189; Fat: 10 g; Carbs: 7.7 g; Protein: 4.6 g

Cheesy Eggs with Tomatoes

Prep Time: 15 minutes
Cook Time: 8 hours 25 minutes
Servings: 6
Ingredients:
- 1 tablespoon olive oil
- 1 medium yellow onion, chopped
- 2 garlic cloves, minced
- 1 jalapeño pepper, seeded and chopped
- 2 teaspoons smoked paprika
- 1 teaspoon ground cumin
- Salt, as required
- 1 26-ounce can dice tomatoes
- 6 eggs
- ¼ cup feta cheese, crumbled

Directions:
1. Select the "Sauté/Sear" setting of Ninja Foodi and place the butter into the pot.
2. Press the "Start/Stop" button to initiate cooking and heat for about 2-3 minutes.
3. Add the onion and cook for about 3-4 minutes.
4. Add the garlic, jalapeño, paprika, cumin, and salt and cook for about 1 minute.
5. Press the "Start/Stop" button to pause cooking.
6. Close the Ninja Foodi's lid with a pressure lid and select "Slow Cook."
7. Set on "Low" for 8 hours.
8. Press the "Start/Stop" button to initiate cooking.
9. Open the Ninja Foodi's lid and with the back of a spoon, make 6 wells in the tomato mixture.
10. Carefully crack 1 egg in each well.
11. Close the Ninja Foodi's lid with a pressure lid and select "Slow Cook."
12. Set on "High" for 20 minutes.
13. Press the "Start/Stop" button to initiate cooking.
14. Open the Ninja Foodi's lid and serve hot with the topping of cheese.

Nutritional Values Per Serving:
Calories: 134; Fat: 8.5g; Carbs: 8.1g; Protein: 8g

All Cheese Egg Bites

Prep Time: 10 minutes
Cook Time: 8 minutes
Servings: 4
Ingredients:
- 3 large eggs
- ¼ cup cottage cheese
- ¼ cup cream cheese
- ½ cup mix vegetables, chopped
- ½ cup cheddar cheese, shredded

Directions:
1. Whisk eggs with soft cheese and cottage cheese in a blender at medium speed until smooth.
2. Add chopped vegetables and shredded mozzarella cheese.
3. Divide this mixture into a greased silicone egg mold tray.
4. Pour 1 cup water in the Ninja Food pot and place trivet over it.
5. Set the silicone mold over the trivet.
6. Secure the Ninja Foodi lid and turn its pressure handle to 'SEAL' position.
7. Select Pressure mode for 8 minutes at 350 degrees F.
8. Once done, release the steam naturally then remove the lid.
9. Serve warm.

Nutritional Values Per Serving:
Calories 231; Total Fat 17.6g; Total Carbs 3.1g; Protein 15.7g

Cauliflower Meal

Prep Time: 10 minutes
Cook Time: 4 minutes
Servings: 4
Ingredients:
- 1 cauliflower head, florets
- ½ cup vegetable stock
- 2 garlic cloves, minced
- Black pepper and salt to taste
- ⅓ cup grated parmesan
- 1 tablespoon parsley, chopped
- 3 tablespoons olive oil

Directions:
1. Take a suitable and add oil, salt, pepper, garlic, cauliflower and toss well.
2. Transfer the mix to Ninja Foodi cooking basket.
3. Add stock and stir.
4. Lock and secure the Ninja Foodi's pressure lid, turn the pressure valve to SEAL position. Set the unit to Pressure mode. Then cook on "HIGH" pressure for 4 minutes.
5. Add parsley, cheese, and toss.
6. Serve and enjoy a healthy breakfast.
Nutritional Values Per Serving:
Calories: 120; Fat: 2g; Carbs: 4g; Protein: 3g

Ham Breakfast Casserole

Prep Time: 10 minutes
Cook Time: 10 minutes
Servings: 4
Ingredients:
- 4 whole eggs
- 1 tablespoons milk
- 1 cup ham, cooked and chopped
- ½ cup cheddar cheese, shredded
- ¼ teaspoon salt
- ¼ teaspoon black pepper

Directions:
1. Take a baking pan small enough to fit into your Ninja Foodi bowl, and grease it well with butter
2. Take a medium bowl and whisk in eggs, milk, salt, pepper and add ham, cheese, and stir
3. Pour mixture into baking pan and lower the pan into your Ninja Foodi
4. Set your Ninja Foodi Air Crisp mode and Air Crisp for 325 degrees F for 7 minutes
5. Remove pan from eggs and enjoy.
Nutritional Values Per Serving:
Calories: 169; Fat: 13g; Carbs: 1g; Protein: 12g

Deviled Eggs

Prep Time: 10 minutes
Cook Time: 10 minutes
Servings: 4
Ingredients:
- 8 large eggs
- 1 cup of water
- Guacamole
- Sliced Radishes
- Mayonnaise
- Furikake

Directions:
1. Add water to the inner insert of your Ninja Foodi.
2. Place the steamer rack inside the pot and set the eggs on top of the rack.
3. Lock pressure lid and cook on "HIGH" pressure for 6 minutes.
4. Release Pressure naturally over 10 minutes and transfer the eggs to a suitable full of icy water.
5. Peel after 5 minutes.
6. Cut in half and decorate with guacamole, sliced radish, mayo and enjoy.
Nutritional Values Per Serving:
Calories: 70; Fat: 6g; Carbs: 1g; Protein: 3g

Omelets in the Jar

Prep Time: 10 minutes
Cook Time: 8 minutes
Servings: 5
Ingredients
- 10 eggs
- ⅓ cup heavy cream
- ⅔ cup of shredded cheese
- 1 green pepper, chopped
- 1 ham steak, chopped
- ½ lb. bacon, cooked and chopped
- 5 mason jars or other jars

Directions:
1. Grease the mason jars with canola spray.
2. Whisk 2 eggs with 1 tbsp cream in a bowl then pour it into a jar.
3. Add 1 tbsp of ham, green peppers, and cheese to the same jar.
4. Repeat the same steps to fill remaining jars.
5. Pour 1 cup of water in the Ninja Food pot and place rack over it.
6. Set all the mason jars over the rack.
7. Secure the Ninja Foodi lid and turn its pressure handle to 'SEAL' position.
8. Select Pressure mode for 8 minutes at HI.
9. Once done, release the steam naturally then remove the lid.
10. Drizzle bacon and cheese over each jar.
11. Serve fresh.
Nutritional Values Per Serving:
Calories 111; Total Fat 8.3 g; Total Carbs 1.9 g; Protein 7.4 g

Glazed Carrots

Prep Time: 10 minutes
Cook Time: 4 minutes
Servings: 4
Ingredients:
- 2 pounds carrots, washed, peeled and sliced

- Pepper, to taste
- 1 cup of water
- 1 tablespoon butter
- 1 tablespoon choc zero maple syrup

Directions:
1. Add carrots, water to the Instant Pot
2. Lock and secure the Ninja Foodi's lid, then cook on "HI" pressure for 4 minutes
3. Quick-release Pressure
4. Strain carrots
5. Add butter, maple syrup to the warm mix, stir it gently
6. Transfer strained carrots back to the pot and stir
7. Coat well with maple syrup
8. Sprinkle a bit of pepper and serve
9. Enjoy.
Nutritional Values Per Serving:
Calories: 358; Fat: 12g; Carbs: 20g; Protein: 2g

Spinach Turkey Cups

Prep Time: 15 minutes
Cook Time: 23 minutes
Servings: 4
Ingredients:
- 1 tablespoon unsalted butter
- 1-pound fresh baby spinach
- 4 eggs
- 7 ounces cooked turkey, chopped
- 4 teaspoons unsweetened almond milk
- Black pepper and salt, as required

Directions:
1. Select the "Sauté/Sear" setting of Ninja Foodi and place the butter into the pot.
2. Press the "Start/Stop" button to initiate cooking and heat for about 2-3 minutes.
3. Add the spinach and cook for about 3 minutes or until just wilted.
4. Press the "Start/Stop" button to pause cooking and drain the liquid completely.
5. Transfer the spinach into a suitable and set aside to cool slightly.
6. Set the "Air Crisp Basket" in the Ninja Foodi's insert.
7. Close the Ninja Foodi's lid with a crisping lid and select "Air Crisp."
8. Set its cooking temperature to 355 degrees F for 5 minutes.

9. Press the "Start/Stop" button to initiate preheating.
10. Divide the spinach into 4 greased ramekins, followed by the turkey.
11. Crack 1 egg into each ramekin and drizzle with almond milk.
12. Sprinkle with black pepper and salt.
13. After preheating, Open the Ninja Foodi's lid.
14. Place the ramekins into the "Air Crisp Basket."
15. Close the Ninja Foodi's lid with a crisping lid and select "Air Crisp."
16. Set its cooking temperature to 355 degrees F for 20 minutes.
17. Press the "Start/Stop" button to initiate cooking.
18. Open the Ninja Foodi's lid and serve hot.
Nutritional Values Per Serving:
Calories: 200; Fat: 10.2g; Carbs: 4.5g; Protein: 23.4g

Swiss Bacon Frittata

Prep Time: 10 minutes
Cook Time: 23 minutes
Servings: 6
Ingredients:
- 1 small onion, chopped
- ½ lb. of raw bacon, chopped
- 1 lb. of frozen spinach
- 10 eggs
- 1 cup cottage cheese
- ½ cup half and half cream
- 1 tsp salt
- 1 cup shredded swiss cheese

Directions:
1. Preheat your Ninja Foodi for 5 minutes at MD:HI on Sear/Sauté Mode.
2. Add bacon, and onion to the Foodi and sauté for 10 minutes until crispy.
3. Stir in spinach and stir cook for 3 minutes.
4. Whisk eggs with cottage cheese, salt and half and half cream in a bowl.
5. Pour this mixture into the Ninja Foodi cooking pot.
6. Drizzle swiss cheese over the egg mixture.

7. Secure the Ninja Foodi lid and switch the Foodi to Bake/Roast mode for 20 minutes at 350 degrees F.
8. Serve warm.
Nutritional Values Per Serving:
Calories 139; Total Fat 10.1g; Total Carbs 2.3g; Protein 10.1g

Chorizo Omelet

Prep Time: 10 minutes
Cook Time: 30-35 minutes
Servings: 4
Ingredients:
- 3 eggs, whisked
- 3 ounces chorizo, chopped
- 1-ounce Feta cheese, crumbled
- 5 tablespoons almond milk
- ¾ teaspoon chilli flakes
- ¼ teaspoon salt
- 1 green pepper, chopped
Directions:
1. Add listed ingredients to a suitable and mix well.
2. Take an omelette pan and pour the mixture on it.
3. Pre-heat your Ninja Food on "BAKE/ROAST" mode at a temperature of 320 degrees F.
4. Transfer pan with omelette mix to your Ninja Foodi and cook for 30 minutes, or until the surface is golden and the egg has set properly
5. Serve and enjoy.
Nutritional Values Per Serving:
Calories: 426; Fat: 38g; Carbs: 7g; Protein: 21g

Pepperoni Omelets

Prep Time: 10 minutes
Cook Time: 5 minutes
Servings: 4
Ingredients:
- 4 tablespoons heavy cream
- 15 pepperoni slices
- 2 tablespoons butter
- Black pepper and salt to taste
- 6 whole eggs

Directions:
1. Take a suitable and whisk in eggs, cream, pepperoni slices, salt, and pepper.
2. Set your Ninja Foodi to "Sear/Sauté" mode and add butter and egg mix.
3. Sauté for 3 minutes, flip.
4. Lock and secure the Ninja Foodi's crisping lid and Air Crisp for 2 minutes at 350 degrees F
5. Transfer to a serving plate and enjoy.

Nutritional Values Per Serving:
Calories: 141; Fat: 11g; Carbs: 0.6g; Protein: 9g

Vanilla Banana Bread

Prep Time: 10 minutes
Cook Time: 50 minutes
Servings: 8
Ingredients:
- 2 cups flour
- 1 teaspoon baking powder
- ½ cup erythritol
- ½ cup butter softened
- 2 eggs
- 1 tablespoon vanilla extract
- 4 bananas, peeled and mashed

Directions:
1. Grease a 7-inch springform pan.
2. In a suitable, mix flour and baking powder.
3. In another bowl, add erythritol, butter, and eggs and beat until creamy.
4. Add the bananas and vanilla extract and beat until well combined.
5. Slowly add flour mixture, 1 cup at a time, and mix until smooth.
6. Place mixture into prepared loaf pan evenly.
7. In the Ninja Foodi's insert, place 1 cup of water.
8. Set the "Reversible Rack" in the Ninja Foodi's insert.
9. Place the pan over the "Reversible Rack."
10. Close the Ninja Foodi's lid with the pressure lid and place the pressure valve to the "Seal" position.
11. Select "Pressure" mode and set it to "High" for 50 minutes.
12. Press the "Start/Stop" button to initiate cooking.
13. Switch the pressure valve to "Vent" and do a "Quick" release.
14. Cut into desired sized slices and serve.

Nutritional Values Per Serving:
Calories: 336; Fat: 13.1 g; Carbs: 50.4 g; Protein: 5.4g

Ninja Foodi Coconut Cereal

Prep Time: 5 minutes
Cook Time: 8 hours 3 minutes
Servings: 3
Ingredients:
- ½ cup unsweetened coconut, shredded
- 1 cup water
- ¼ teaspoon ground cinnamon
- ⅛ teaspoon liquid stevia
- 1 cup unsweetened almond milk
- ¼ cup coconut flour, divided
- ¼ teaspoon vanilla extract

Directions:
1. Add shredded coconut, almond milk, half of the coconut flour, water and cinnamon in the pot of Ninja Foodi. Mix well.
2. Close the pressure Lid and select "Slow Cook".
3. Set on LOW TEMP for 8 hours and press the "Start/Stop" button.

4. Open the lid and add in the remaining coconut flour, stevia and vanilla extract. Mix until well combined.
5. Close the pressure Lid and cook for 3 minutes.
6. Open the lid and take out.
7. Serve and enjoy!
Nutritional Values Per Serving:
Calories: 102; Fat: 6.6g; Carbs: 9.6g; Protein: 2.1g

Avocado Cups

Prep Time: 10 minutes
Cook Time: 12 minutes
Servings: 2
Ingredients:
- 1 avocado, halved and pitted
- Black pepper and salt, as required
- 2 eggs
- 1 tablespoon Parmesan cheese, shredded
- 1 teaspoon fresh chives, minced

Directions:
1. Set a greased square piece of foil in "Air Crisp Basket."
2. Set the "Air Crisp Basket" in the Ninja Foodi's insert.
3. Close the Ninja Foodi's lid with a crisping lid and select "Bake/Roast".
4. Set its cooking temperature to 390 degrees F for 5 minutes.
5. Press the "Start/Stop" button to initiate preheating.
6. Carefully scoop out about 2 teaspoons of flesh from each avocado half.
7. Crack 1 egg in each avocado half and sprinkle with salt, black pepper, and cheese.
8. After preheating, Open the Ninja Foodi's lid.
9. Place the avocado halves into the "Air Crisp Basket."
10. Close the Ninja Foodi's lid with a crisping lid and Select "Bake/Roast."
11. Set its cooking temperature to 390 degrees F for about 12 minutes.
12. Press the "Start/Stop" button to initiate cooking.
13. Open the Ninja Foodi's lid and transfer the avocado halves onto serving plates.
14. Top with Parmesan and chives and serve.
Nutritional Values Per Serving:
Calories: 278; Fat: 24.7g; Carbs: 9.1g; Protein: 8.4g

Hashbrown Casserole

Prep Time: 10 Minutes
Cook Time: 20 Minutes
Servings: 6
Ingredients:
- 6 eggs
- 30 ounce bag frozen hash browns
- ¼ cup milk
- 1 tablespoon pizza sauce
- 2 tablespoons olive oil
- 1 medium-sized onion (chopped)
- 1 pound ham
- ½ cup cheddar cheese

Directions:
1. Turn on the Air Crisp Mode at Medium temperature on your Ninja Foodi Deluxe XL Pressure Cooker.
2. Add chopped onions and olive oil. Cook it till the color becomes translucent.
3. Add pizza sauce for that pop of flavor.
4. Then add the frozen hash browns to it. Add eggs on the hash browns.
5. Add the meat to the top of the pot.
6. Place Ninja Foodi Deluxe XL Pressure Cooker on Air Crisp Mode at 390° F for 10 minutes at least, or wait until the top turns golden brown and the eggs are done.
7. Add cheddar cheese on top, close the lid and let the cheddar cheese melt for about 1 minute!
Nutritional Values Per Serving:
Calories: 682; Fat: 8g; Carbs: 5g; Protein: 16g

Ninja Foodi Eggs with Spinach

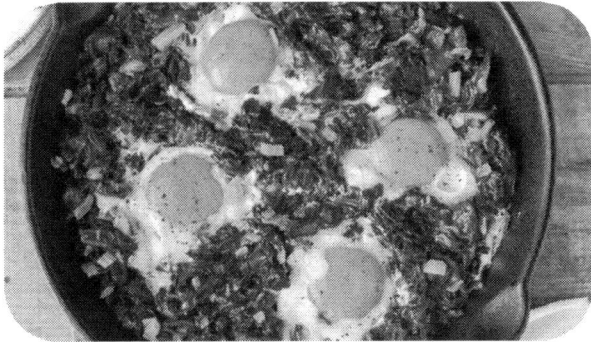

Prep Time: 10 minutes
Cook Time: 25 minutes
Servings: 4
Ingredients:
- 2 tablespoons olive oil
- 4 eggs
- ¼ cup scallion, chopped
- 10 cups chopped baby spinach
- Salt and black pepper, to taste

Directions:
1. Add oil and scallion in the pot of Ninja Foodi Deluxe XL Pressure Cooker and cook for 5 minutes with an open lid.
2. Add in pepper, salt and spinach and cook for 5-minutes.
3. Make fourwells in the mixture and crack eggs in each well.
4. Close the Crisping Lid and select "Bake".
5. Press the "Start/Stop" button and bake for 15 minutes at 400 degrees F.
6. Take out, serve and enjoy!
Nutritional Values Per Serving:
Calories: 142; Fat: 11.7g; Carbs: 3.5g; Protein: 7.8g

Ninja Foodi Ham Muffins

Prep Time: 10 minutes
Cook Time: 20 minutes
Servings: 4
Ingredients:
- 4 eggs
- ½ cup cooked ham, crumbled
- ½ cup red bell pepper, seeded and chopped
- 1 tablespoon water
- Salt and black pepper, to taste

Directions:
1. Add eggs, salt, pepper and water in a bowl. Mix well.

2. Now, add in red bell pepper and crumbled ham. Mix well and set aside.
3. Pour the mixture in greased muffin-tins and place them in the pot of Ninja Foodi Deluxe XL Pressure Cooker.
4. Select "Bake" and close the Crisping Lid.
5. Press the "Start/Stop" button and bake for 20 minutes at 350 degrees F.
6. Take out, serve and enjoy!
Nutritional Values Per Serving:
Calories: 95; Fat: 5.9g; Carbs: 2.1g; Protein: 8.5g

Ninja Foodi Cinnamon Tea

Prep Time: 5 minutes
Cook Time: 12 minutes
Servings: 2
Ingredients:
- 1 cup water
- 1 teaspoon black tea
- 2 cinnamon sticks
- 4 black peppercorns
- ½ cup fat-free cream

Directions:
1. Add water, peppercorns and cinnamon in the pot Ninja Foodi Deluxe XL Pressure Cooker.
2. Boil for about 10 minutes and add in cream.
3. Close the pressure Lid and select "Pressure".
4. Press the "Start/Stop" button and cook for about 2 minutes at LOW pressure.
5. Open the lid and strain the tea.
6. Serve hot and enjoy!
Nutritional Values Per Serving:
Calories: 62; Fat: 0.8g; Carbs: 5.4g; Protein: 8.5g

Ninja Foodi Baked Eggs

Prep Time: 12 minutes
Cook Time: 9 minutes
Servings: 3
Ingredients:
• 3 eggs
• 3 tablespoons low-fat parmesan cheese, shredded
• ½ cup fresh spinach, chopped finely
• 3 tablespoons heavy cream
• 3 tablespoons olive oil
• Salt and black pepper, to taste
Directions:
1. Grease three muffin tins with olive oil and add spinach in them.
2. Add in eggs and top them with heavy cream, parmesan cheese, salt and pepper.
3. Place the muffin tins in the pot of Ninja Foodi Deluxe XL Pressure Cooker and select "Bake".
4. Close the Crisping Lid and press the "Start/Stop" button.
5. Bake for 9 minutes at 400 degrees F and open the lid.
6. Take out, serve and enjoy!
Nutritional Values Per Serving:
Calories: 326; Fat: 29.9g; Carbs: 2g; Protein: 15g

Ninja Foodi Broccoli Pancakes

Prep Time: 5 minutes
Cook Time: 20 minutes
Servings: 2
Ingredients:
• ¼ cup chopped broccoli
• ¼ cup low-fat cheddar cheese, shredded
• ½ teaspoon dried onion, minced

• 1 egg
• ½ teaspoon garlic powder
• Salt and black pepper, to taste
Directions:
1. Add everything in a food-processor and pulse until a smooth mixture is formed.
2. Pour the mixture in the pot of Ninja Foodi Deluxe XL Pressure Cooker and select "Bake".
3. Close the Crisping Lid and press the "Start/Stop" button.
4. Bake for about 20 minutes at 400 degrees F and open the lid.
5. Take out and serve hot.
Nutritional Values Per Serving:
Calories: 95; Fat: 6.9g; Carbs: 1.7g; Protein: 6.8g

Ninja Foodi Arugula Omelet

Prep Time: 10 minutes
Cook Time: 5 minutes
Servings: 4
Ingredients:
• 6 eggs
• 2 tablespoons unsweetened almond milk
• 2 cups fresh arugula, chopped
• 4 scallion, chopped finely
• 2 tablespoons olive oil
• Salt and black pepper, to taste
Directions:
1. Add everything except olive oil in a bowl. Whisk well.
2. Now, heat olive oil in the pot of Ninja Foodi Deluxe XL Pressure Cooker and add in egg mixture.
3. Press the "Steam" button and close the pressure Lid.
4. Press the "Start/Stop" button and cook for about 5-minutes on low heat.
5. Open the pressure Lid and take out.
6. Serve and enjoy!
Nutritional Values Per Serving:
Calories: 163; Fat: 13.8g; Carbs: 2.1g; Protein: 8.9g

Gluten-Free Apple Crisps

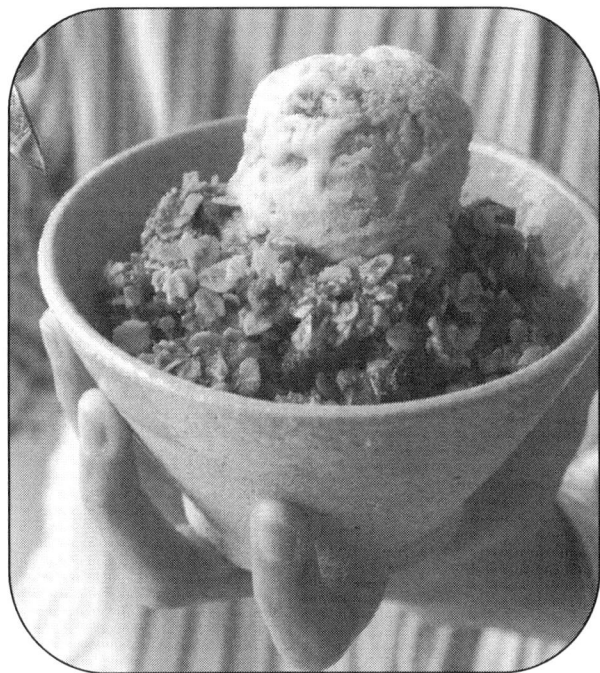

Prep Time: 15 Minutes
Cook Time: 40 Minutes
Servings: 10-12
Ingredients:
For Apples:
- 1 pounds thinly sliced apples
- ½ cup white sugar
- ½ cup gluten-free all-purpose flour
- ½ cup brown sugar
- 1 teaspoon nutmeg
- 1 teaspoon chia seeds
- ½ teaspoon nutmeg (ground)
- ½ cup water

For Topping:
- ½ cup gluten-free oats
- ½ cup all-purpose flour
- ½ cup of packed brown sugar
- ½ teaspoon of baking soda
- ½ cup of melted or softened butter
- Any flavored ice cream (optional)

Directions:
1. Place the thinly sliced apples in the Ninja Foodi Deluxe XL Pressure Cooker.
2. In a bowl combine the sugar, all-purpose gluten-free flour, cinnamon, and nutmeg powder.
3. Pour this mixture evenly on top of the apples.
4. Pour water over the apples.
5. Take another bowl and add oats, flour, brown sugar, baking powder, and baking soda. Mix in the butter. It should be a crumble mixture. Top up the apples with this mixture and close the lid.
6. Bake it for about 40 minutes at a temperature of 375° F.
7. Serve it warm with your favorite ice cream!

Nutritional Values Per Serving:
Calories: 444; Fat: 9g; Carbs: 5g; Protein: 2g

Breakfast pizza

Prep Time: 10 Minutes
Cook Time: 20 Minutes
Servings: 4
Ingredients:
For the Pizza Dough:
- 100 grams all-purpose flour
- 1 tablespoon sugar (granulated)
- 1 teaspoon baking powder
- ¼ teaspoon table salt
- Greek yogurt ⅔ cup

For Topping Purposes:
- ¾ slices of center cut bacon
- 4 beaten eggs
- 3 ounces cheddar/ mozzarella cheese (freshly cut)

Directions:
1. Mix all the dry ingredients including flour, baking powder, and salt in a container. Do this before adding the yogurt. Mix everything up with a spatula until crumbly. Now form a ball of the dough onto the flat surface.
2. Create a thicker edge for the crust than in the center. The diameter of the dough should be around 8. A rolling pin could be used as a good option here.
3. Give a Cook & Crisp Basket the oil spray before adding the crust. Brush a bit more cooking spray.
4. For 10 minutes start Air Crisp Mode at 390° F before flipping. Air Crisp for an additional 3 minutes at 390° F before adding the toppings.
5. While the crust is being cooked, over medium-high heat adds bacon strips to a non-stick skillet. Remove the skillet from the heat once fully cooked and then add eggs.
6. Stir to scramble the eggs and then add cream cheese once eggs are nearly fully done.
7. Now add the bacon and egg mixture to the crust. Top with cheddar cheese and let it melt completely for three to 4 minutes. After that, the pizza is done and you can enjoy it!

Nutritional Values Per Serving:
Calories: 313; Fat: 7g; Carbs: 12g; Protein: 19g

Ninja Foodi Pancakes

Prep Time: 10 minutes
Cook Time: 25 minutes
Servings: 2
Ingredients:
- ¼ cup fat-free milk
- ½ tablespoon canola oil
- ¼ teaspoon ground nutmeg
- ¼ cup all-purpose flour
- 1 egg
- 2 tablespoons sugar

Directions:
1. Add milk, ground nutmeg, all-purpose flour, egg and sugar in a large bowl. Whisk properly.
2. Pour egg mixture in the pot of Ninja Foodi Deluxe XL Pressure Cooker and close the Crisping Lid.
3. Select "Bake" and press the "Start/Stop" button.
4. Bake for 20 minutes at 400 degrees F and open the Crisping Lid.
5. Take out, serve and enjoy!
Nutritional Values Per Serving:
Calories: 177; Fat: 5.9g; Carbs: 25.7g; Protein: 5.4g

Fruit Pancakes

Prep Time: 7 Minutes
Cook Time: 20 Minutes
Servings: 2
Ingredients:
- ½ cup of pancake mix oats

- 2 eggs
- ¼ cup regular milk
- 1 teaspoon melted butter
- 2 drops of Vanilla essence
- 1 date
- ½ teaspoon cinnamon
- ½ cup of any fresh fruit of your choice
Directions:
1. In a mixing bowl mix together the pancake mix or oats, eggs, melted butter, cinnamon, dates, vanilla essence, and milk until a thick batter is prepared.
2. Gently mix in available fresh fruit, it can also be any thawed fruit.
3. Spray the Ninja Foodi Deluxe XL Pressure Cooker's cooking pot with spray oil. Non-sticky canola spray could also be the best option.
4. Preheat your Ninja Foodi Deluxe XL Pressure Cooker to 375° F on the Bake option.
5. After that, pour in the batter and it should be spread with even consistency throughout the Ninja Foodi Deluxe XL Pressure Cooker.
6. Close the crisping lid of the Ninja Foodi Deluxe XL Pressure Cooker and set the time of cooking to 12 to 15 minutes. 15 minutes are considered ideal for a perfect turnout of the pancake.
7. Lastly, serve it with any fruit or toppings of your choice.
Nutritional Values Per Serving:
Calories: 227.5; Fat: 8.5g; Carbs: 18.5 g; Protein: 10.5 g

Ninja Foodi Hard-boiled eggs

Prep Time: 8-10 Minutes
Cook Time: 15 Minutes
Servings: 6
Ingredients:
- 12 eggs
- 1 cup water
Directions:
1. Place the Multi-purpose pan filled with one cup of water inside Ninja Foodi Deluxe XL Pressure Cooker.
2. Be very careful while placing the eggs in the Ninja Foodi Deluxe XL Pressure Cooker.

3. Secure the pressure lid and turn the valve to Seal. Set the Ninja Foodi Deluxe XL Pressure Cooker to High Pressure for 5 minutes. Press START/STOP.
4. While the eggs are being done, take a bowl, add ice cubes and water.
5. After 5 minutes, turn valve for Quick Pressure Release. Then take eggs out.
6. After taking out the eggs, put them in that ice bath for 5 minutes at least.
7. Peel and serve, the eggs are ready. They can also be stored in the fridge for up to a week!

Nutritional Values Per Serving:
Calories: 155; Fat: 11g; Carbs: 1g; Protein: 6g

French Toast Bites

Prep Time: 10 Minutes
Cook Time: 15 Minutes
Servings: 1
Ingredients:
- ¼ loaf of French bread
- 2 eggs
- 2 tablespoons milk
- ½ teaspoon cinnamon
- 1 mashed banana

Topping
- 1 tablespoon brown sugar
- 1 tablespoon honey
- ½ teaspoon cinnamon

Directions:
1. Cut the French bread into cubes and add it to a container.
2. In a separate small bowl, combine eggs, milk, mashed banana, vanilla, and cinnamon.
3. Pour mixture over the bread cubes and mix it all well till it's equally coated.
4. In a greased Ninja Foodi Deluxe XL Pressure Cooker Basket, add bread pieces in a single layer.
5. Sprinkle brown sugar and cinnamon on top of it.
6. Then select Air Crisp at 390° F for 10 minutes. Keep tossing or mixing halfway through.
7. When the golden-brown color appears, drizzle the honey, bites are ready to be served!

Nutritional Values Per Serving:
Calories: 302; Fat: 6g; Carbs: 21g; Protein: 13g

Breakfast Oats Bowl

Prep Time: 3 Minutes
Cook Time: 8 Minutes
Servings: 2
Ingredients:
- 1 cup oats
- 1.5 cup milk
- 1.5 teaspoon ground cinnamon powder
- Water as required

Optional Toppings:
- Flax seeds
- Honey
- Granola mix

Directions:
1. Add all the ingredients in the Ninja Foodi Deluxe XL Pressure Cooker Pot.
2. Oats should be fully submerged in water. Secure the pressure lid and turn the valve to Seal. Set the Ninja Foodi Deluxe XL Pressure Cooker to High Pressure for 5 minutes.
3. After 5 minutes turn the valve off and let the oats sit for about 5 minutes after being fully cooked and all pressure to release.
4. Serve with your favorite toppings!

Nutritional Values Per Serving:
Calories: 162; Fat: 4.8g; Carbs: 12g; Protein: 9.3g

Egg rolls

Prep Time: 5 Minutes
Cook Time: 20 Minutes
Servings: 4
Ingredients:
- 2 teaspoons olive oil
- ½ cup chopped sliced cabbage
- 1 small carrot (thinly sliced)
- 1.5 cup boiled and shredded chicken
- 1.5 tablespoon vinegar
- 1.5 tablespoon soy sauce
- 1 tablespoon grounded herbs
- Ginger garlic as required

For the sauce:
- 1 tablespoon mustard sauce
- 1 tablespoon chili garlic sauce
- 1.5 tablespoon vinegar
- 1.5 tablespoon soy sauce

For Egg Roll Making:
- 4 wrappers
- 1 beaten egg
- 1 tablespoon olive oil/ sesame oil

Directions:
1. Slice up the vegetables; carrots and cabbage. The frozen vegetable mix could also be used here. The quantity should be about three to four cups to make four egg rolls.
2. Peel ginger garlic and grate it.
3. Now turn on the Roast function of Ninja Foodi Deluxe XL Pressure Cooker and set the temperature on High. Add in the cabbage mix and olive oil. Add the shredded chicken.
4. After that, add in vinegar, soy sauce, ginger, and garlic paste. Stir it and steam in Ninja Foodi Deluxe XL Pressure Cooker for three to 5 minutes or until you get your desired texture.
5. Remove the pot from heat and let it cool for a bit.
6. In Ninja Foodi Deluxe XL Pressure Cooker for 5 minutes on Air Crisp Mode at the temperature of 390° F add the filling into an egg roll wrapper, brush its edges, and roll. Brush lightly with oil and place it on a rack in a high position in Ninja Foodi Deluxe XL Pressure Cooker.
7. Air Crisp it for a period of ten to 15 minutes, keep flipping it every three seconds to ensure its crispiness.
8. Remove it after it's done and serve it with the dipping sauce!

Nutritional Values Per Serving:
Calories: 286; Fat: 9.5g; Carbs: 16g; Protein: 22g

Egg Bites

Prep Time: 8 Minutes
Cook Time: 12-15 Minutes
Servings: 2
Ingredients:
- 3 egg whites
- ½ cup whipping cream
- ¼ teaspoon salt
- ½ cup chopped mushrooms
- ½ cup tomatoes
- ¼ cup green onions
- 1 tablespoon cheddar cheese
- Water per requirement

Directions:
1. Take a container and whisk eggs, cream (heavy), salt, and pepper together well.
2. Add up the remaining ingredients and again mix well.
3. Prepare the mold and spray with olive oil or use any greased baking tray.
4. Fill half of the mold with the mixture. Place its cover.
5. Place the Ninja Foodi Deluxe XL Pressure Cooker Rack in the Low position. Put the covered mold onto the rack. In the Ninja Foodi Deluxe XL Pressure Cooker Pot, add two cups of water. Place covered mold on the rack.
6. Set the timer of the Steam option to 12 minutes.
7. Once ready, pop-out the egg bites of the mold!

Nutritional Values Per Serving:
Calories: 140; Fat: 9.3g; Carbs: 2.5g; Protein: 3.8g

Cheese Stuffed Dates

Prep Time: 5 minutes
Cook Time: 7 minutes
Serves: 7
Ingredients:
- 6 oz parmesan cheese, grated
- 8 oz ripe dates
- 1 tsp garlic, minced
- 1 tbsp sour cream
- 1 tsp butter
- ½ tsp ground white pepper
- 1 tsp oregano

Preparation:
1. Remove the stones from the dates.
2. Combine the garlic, sour cream, ground white pepper, and oregano, and stir the mixture. Add in the parmesan. Blend the mixture until smooth.
3. Stuff the dates with the cheese mixture and place them in the Ninja Foodi's cooking pot.
4. Set the Ninja Foodi to PRESSURE mode.
5. Add the butter and close the Pressure Lid. Cook for 7 minutes.
6. When the cooking time ends, remove the dates from the Ninja Foodi, let them rest briefly, and serve.

Nutritional Information Per Serving:
Calories 203; Fat: 7.6g; Carbs: 28.3g; Protein: 8g

Breadsticks

Prep Time: 25 minutes
Cook Time: 10 minutes
Serves: 8
Ingredients:
- 1 tsp baking powder
- ½ tsp erythritol
- ½ tsp salt
- 1 cup warm water
- 2 cups almond flour
- 5 oz parmesan, grated
- 1 tbsp olive oil
- 1 tsp onion powder
- 1 tsp basil

Preparation:
1. Combine the baking powder, erythritol, and warm water in a mixing bowl.
2. Stir the mixture well. Add the almond flour, onion powder, salt, and basil.
3. Knead the dough until smooth.
4. Separate the dough into 10 pieces to make long logs. Twist the logs into braids.
5. Preheat the Ninja Foodi on BAKE mode for 10 minutes at 325°F.
6. Place the twisted logs into the baking pot of the Ninja Foodi.
7. Sprinkle the logs with the grated parmesan cheese and the olive oil, and close the lid.
8. Bake the breadsticks on BAKE mode for 15 minutes at 325°F.
9. Leave the breadsticks for 10 minutes to rest.

Nutritional Information Per Serving:
Calories 242; Fat: 18.9g; Carbs: 2.7g; Protein: 11.7g

Herbed Cauliflower Fritters

Prep Time: 15 minutes
Cook Time: 13 minutes
Servings: 7
Ingredients:
- 1-pound cauliflower
- 1 medium white onion
- 1 teaspoon salt
- ½ teaspoon ground white pepper
- 1 tablespoon sour cream
- 1 teaspoon turmeric
- ½ cup dill, chopped
- 1 teaspoon thyme
- 3 tablespoons almond flour
- 1 egg
- 2 tablespoons butter

Directions:
1. Wash the cauliflower and separate it into the florets.
2. Chop the florets and place them in a blender.
3. Peel the onion and dice it. Add the diced onion to a blender and blend the mixture.
4. When you get the smooth texture, add salt, ground white pepper, sour cream, turmeric, dill, thyme, and almond flour.
5. Add egg blend the mixture well until a smooth dough form.
6. Remove the cauliflower dough from a blender and form the medium balls.
7. Flatten the balls a little. Set the Ninja Foodi's insert to" Sauté" mode.
8. Add the butter to the Ninja Foodi's insert and melt it.
9. Add the cauliflower fritters in the Ninja Foodi's insert, and sauté them for 6 minutes.
10. Flip them once. Cook the dish in" Sauté" mode for 7 minutes.
11. Once done, remove the fritters from the Ninja Foodi's insert.
12. Serve immediately.

Nutritional Values Per Serving:
Calories: 143; Fat: 10.6g; Carbs: 9.9g; Protein: 5.6g

Cheesy Egg Bombs

Prep Time: 10 minutes
Cook Time: 10 minutes
Servings: 8
Ingredients:
- 6 ounces puff pastry
- 1 teaspoon salt
- 8 ounces mozzarella pearls
- 1 egg
- ½ cup coconut flour
- ¼ cup of coconut milk
- ½ teaspoon oregano
- 2 tablespoons butter

Directions:
1. Roll the puff pastry using a rolling pin. Add the egg to a mixing bowl and blend it using a whisk.
2. Add coconut milk and salt and whisk the mixture until the salt is dissolved.
3. Cut the rolled puff pastry into medium-sized squares.
4. Put a mozzarella pearl in the middle of every square and wrap the dough around each one to make the balls.
5. Sprinkle the egg mixture with the oregano and mix well.
6. Dip the puff pastry balls into the egg mixture, then dip the balls into the coconut flour.
7. Add the butter to the Ninja Foodi's insert and melt it.
8. Place the puff pastry balls in the Ninja Foodi's insert and Close the Ninja Foodi's lid.
9. Cook the dish in the "Pressure" mode for 10 minutes.
10. Once done, release the pressure completely and remove the lid.
11. Transfer the dish to serving plates.

Nutritional Values Per Serving:
Calories: 269; Fat: 19.4g; Carbs: 14.1g; Protein: 8.5g

Dill Butter

Prep Time: 10 minutes
Cook Time: 5 minutes
Servings: 7
Ingredients:
- 1 cup butter
- 1 teaspoon minced garlic
- 1 teaspoon dried oregano
- 1 teaspoon dried cilantro
- 1 tablespoon dried dill
- 1 teaspoon salt
- ½ teaspoon black pepper

Directions:
1. Set "Sauté" mode and place butter inside the Ninja Foodi's insert.
2. Add minced garlic, dried oregano, dried cilantro, butter, dried dill, salt, and black pepper.
3. Stir the mixture well and sauté it for 4-5 minutes or until the butter is melted.
4. Then switch off the cooker and stir the butter well.
5. Transfer the butter mixture into the butter mould and freeze it.

Nutritional Values Per Serving:
Calories: 235; Fat: 26.3g; Carbs: 0.6g; Protein: 0.4g

Broccoli Turmeric Tots

Prep Time: 15 minutes
Cook Time: 8 minutes
Servings: 8
Ingredients:
- 1-pound broccoli
- 3 cups of water
- 1 teaspoon salt
- 1 egg
- 1 cup pork rind
- ½ teaspoon paprika
- 1 tablespoon turmeric
- ⅓ cup almond flour
- 2 tablespoons olive oil

Directions:
1. Wash the broccoli and chop it roughly.
2. Put the broccoli in the Ninja Foodi's insert and add water.
3. Set the Ninja Foodi's insert to "Steam" mode and steam the broccoli for 20 minutes.
4. Remove the broccoli from the Ninja Foodi's insert and let it cool.
5. Transfer the broccoli to a blender. Add egg, salt, paprika, turmeric, and almond flour.
6. Blend the mixture until smooth. Add pork rind and blend the broccoli mixture for 1 minute more.
7. Pour the olive oil in the Ninja Foodi's insert.
8. Form the medium tots from the broccoli mixture and transfer them to the Ninja Foodi's insert.
9. Set the Ninja Foodi's insert to "Sauté" mode and cook for 4 minutes on each side.
10. Once the dish is done, remove the broccoli tots from the Ninja Foodi's insert.
11. Allow them to rest before serving.

Nutritional Values Per Serving:
Calories: 147; Fat: 9.9g; Carbs: 4.7g; Protein: 11.6g

Crispy Onion Rings

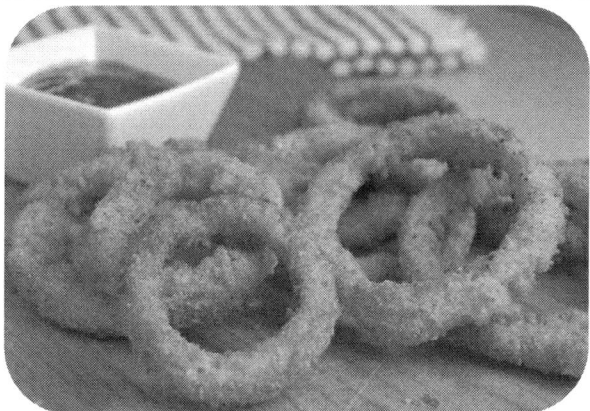

Prep Time: 10 minutes
Cook Time: 8 minutes
Servings: 7
Ingredients:
- 1 cup coconut flour
- 1 teaspoon salt
- ½ teaspoon basil
- 1 teaspoon oregano
- ½ teaspoon cayenne pepper
- 3 eggs
- 5 medium white onions
- 3 tablespoons sesame oil

Directions:
1. Combine the coconut flour, salt, basil, oregano, and cayenne pepper together in a mixing bowl.
2. Stir the coconut flour mixture gently. Add the eggs to another bowl and whisk them.
3. Peel the onions and cut them into thick rings.

4. Separate the onion rings and dip them into the egg mixture.
5. Pour the sesame oil in the Ninja Foodi's insert. Preheat it on the "Pressure" mode.
6. Dip the onion rings in the flour mixture. Transfer the onion rings to the Ninja Foodi's insert.
7. Sauté the onions for 2 minutes on each side.
8. Transfer the cooked rings to the paper towel and rest briefly.
9. Season with salt while hot and serve.
Nutritional Values Per Serving:
Calories: 180; Fat: 10.1g; Fiber 7.5g; Carbs: 6.8g; Protein: 5.6g

Glazed Walnuts

Prep Time: 5 minutes
Cook Time: 4 minutes
Servings: 4
Ingredients:
- ⅓ cup of water
- 6 ounces walnuts
- 5 tablespoon Erythritol
- ½ teaspoon ground ginger
- 3tablespoons psyllium husk powder

Directions:
1. Combine Erythritol and water together in a mixing bowl.
2. Add ground ginger and stir the mixture until the erythritol is dissolved.
3. Transfer the walnuts to the Ninja Foodi's insert and add sweet liquid.
4. Close the Ninja Foodi's lid and cook the dish in the "Pressure" mode for 4 minutes.
5. Remove the walnuts from the Ninja Foodi's insert.
6. Dip the walnuts in the Psyllium husk powder and serve.
Nutritional Values Per Serving:
Calories: 286; Fat: 25.1g; Carbs: 10.4g; Protein: 10.3g

Avocado Deviled Eggs

Prep Time: 10 minutes
Cook Time: 5 minutes
Servings: 6
Ingredients:
- 6 eggs
- 1 avocado, peeled
- 1 tablespoon cream
- ½ teaspoon minced garlic
- 1 cup water for cooking

Directions:
1. Place the eggs in the Ninja Foodi's insert and add water. Close and seal the lid.
2. Cook the eggs on High-pressure mode for 5 minutes.
3. Then use natural pressure release for 5 minutes more.
4. After this, blend together avocado, minced garlic, and cream.
5. Once the mixture is smooth, transfer to the mixing bowl.
6. Peel the cooked eggs and cut them into halves.
7. Remove the eggs yolks and transfer them to the avocado mixture.
8. Fill the boiled egg whites with the avocado mixture.
9. Serve.
Nutritional Values Per Serving:
Calories: 133; Fat: 11g; Carbs: 3.4g; Protein: 6.2g

Garlicky Tomato

Prep Time: 10 minutes
Cook Time: 5 minutes
Servings: 5
Ingredients:
- 5 tomatoes
- ¼ cup chives, chopped
- ⅓ cup garlic clove, minced
- ½ teaspoon salt
- ½ teaspoon black pepper
- 1 tablespoon olive oil
- 7 ounces Parmesan cheese

Directions:
1. Wash the tomatoes and slice them into thick slices.
2. Place the sliced tomatoes in the Ninja Foodi's insert.
3. Combine the grated cheese and minced garlic and stir the mixture.
4. Sprinkle the tomato slices with chives, black pepper, and salt.
5. Then sprinkle the sliced tomatoes with the cheese mixture.
6. Close the Ninja Foodi's lid and cook the dish in the "Pressure" mode for 5 minutes at LO.
7. Once done, remove the tomatoes carefully and serve.

Nutritional Values Per Serving:
Calories: 224; Fat: 14g; Carbs: 12.55g; Protein: 13g

Shallots with Mushrooms

Prep Time: 15 minutes
Cook Time: 30 minutes
Servings: 7
Ingredients:
- 9 ounces shallot
- 8 ounces mushrooms
- ½ cup chicken stock
- 1 tablespoon paprika
- ½ tablespoon salt
- ¼ cup cream
- 1 teaspoon coriander
- ½ cup dill, chopped
- ½ cup parsley
- 1 tablespoon Erythritol

Directions:
1. Slice the shallot and chop the mushrooms.
2. Combine the chicken stock, salt, paprika, cream, coriander, and Erythritol in a mixing bowl.
3. Blend the mixture well. Chop the dill and parsley.
4. Pour the cream mixture in the Ninja Foodi's insert.
5. Set the Ninja Foodi's insert to" Sauté" mode and add sliced shallot and chopped mushrooms.
6. Blend the mixture using a wooden spoon. Close the Ninja Foodi's lid and sauté the mixture for 30 minutes.
7. Chop the parsley and dill. Once the dish is done, transfer it to serving plates.
8. Sprinkle the cooked dish with the chopped parsley and dill.
9. Do not stir again before serving it.

Nutritional Values Per Serving:
Calories: 52; Fat: 1g; Carbs: 10.2g; Protein: 3g

Zucchini Muffins

Prep Time: 15 minutes
Cook Time: 15 minutes
Servings: 6
Ingredients:
- 1 cup coconut flour
- 1 medium zucchini, finely chopped
- 1 teaspoon baking soda
- 1 tablespoon lemon juice
- ½ teaspoon salt
- ½ teaspoon black pepper
- 1 tablespoon butter
- ⅓ cup of coconut milk
- 1 teaspoon poppy seeds
- 2 tablespoons flax meal

Directions:
1. Place the chopped zucchini in a blender and mix until smooth.

2. Combine the salt, baking soda, lemon juice, poppy, coconut flour, butter, black pepper, and flax meal together.
3. Add the milk and blended zucchini.
4. Knead the dough until smooth. It can be a little bit sticky.
5. Place the muffins in the muffin's tins and transfer the zucchini muffins in the Ninja Foodi's insert.
6. Cook the muffins on the" Steam" mode for 15 minutes.
7. Once done, check if the dish is done using a toothpick.
8. If the muffins are cooked, remove them from the Ninja Foodi's insert and serve.
Nutritional Values Per Serving:
Calories: 146; Fat: 8.9g; Carbs: 13.5g; Protein: 4g

Japanese Eggs

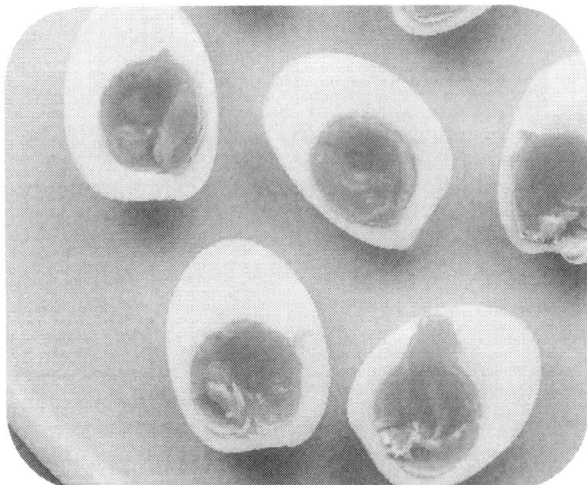

Prep Time: 30 minutes
Cook Time: 20 minutes
Servings: 4
Ingredients:
• 1 cup Chinese master stock
• 4 eggs
• 1 teaspoon salt
Directions:
1. Pour the Chinese master stock in the Ninja Foodi's insert and close the Ninja Foodi's pressure lid.
2. Cook the liquid on the "Pressure" mode for 10 minutes at Lo.
3. Remove the Chinese master stock from the Ninja Foodi's insert and chill it.
4. Meanwhile, place the eggs in the Ninja Foodi's insert.
5. Add water and boil the eggs on the "Pressure" mode for 10 minutes.
6. Once eggs are done, remove from the Ninja Foodi's insert and chill well.
7. Peel the eggs and place them in the Chinese master stock.
8. Leave the eggs in the liquid for 20 minutes.
9. Remove the eggs from the liquid. Cut the eggs into halves.
Nutritional Values Per Serving:
Calories: 134; Fat: 9.7g; Carbs: 2.01g; Protein: 9g

Cauliflower Gratin

Prep Time: 8 minutes
Cook Time: 8 minutes
Servings: 6
Ingredients:
• 3 tablespoons mustard
• 10 ounces cauliflower
• ½ cup dill, chopped
• 2 tablespoons butter
• 1 teaspoon salt
• 1 tablespoon garlic. minced
• 1 teaspoon paprika
• 1 teaspoon cilantro, chopped
• 1 tablespoon oregano
• 4 tablespoons water
Directions:
1. Wash the cauliflower and chop them into medium cubes with the skin on.
2. Sprinkle the cauliflower chunks with salt and oregano.
3. Stir the mixture and place it in the Ninja Foodi's insert. Add water and butter.
4. Close the Ninja Foodi's lid and cook the dish on the "Pressure" for 8 minutes.
5. Chop the dill. Combine the mustard, minced garlic, paprika, cilantro, and chopped dill together.
6. Stir the mixture well until smooth.
7. Once the cauliflower chunks are cooked, remove the dish from the Ninja Foodi's insert.
8. Transfer it to a serving bowl.
9. Add butter, sprinkle the dish with the mustard sauce and serve.
Nutritional Values Per Serving:
Calories: 75; Fat: 4.2g; Carbs: 8.7g; Protein: 1g

Cashew Cream

Prep Time: 8 minutes
Cook Time: 10 minutes
Servings: 10
Ingredients:
- 3 cups cashew
- 2 cups chicken stock
- 1 teaspoon salt
- 1 tablespoon butter
- 2 tablespoons ricotta cheese

Directions:
1. Combine the cashews with the chicken stock in the Ninja Foodi's insert.
2. Add salt and close the Ninja Foodi's lid.
3. Cook the dish in the "Pressure" mode for 10 minutes at HI.
4. Remove the cashews from the Ninja Foodi's insert and drain the nuts from the water.
5. Transfer the cashews to a blender, and add the ricotta cheese and butter.
6. Blend the mixture until it is smooth. When you get the texture you want, remove it from a blender.
7. Serve it immediately, or keep the cashew butter in the refrigerator.
Nutritional Values Per Serving:
Calories: 252; Fat: 20.6g; Carbs: 13.8g; Protein: 6.8 g

Chicken Pork Nuggets

Prep Time: 15 minutes
Cook Time: 20 minutes
Servings: 6
Ingredients:
- 2 cups ground chicken
- ½ cup dill, chopped
- 1 egg
- 2 tablespoons pork rinds
- 1 tablespoon heavy cream
- ½ cup almond flour
- 3 tablespoons butter
- 1 tablespoon canola oil
- 1 teaspoon black pepper

Directions:
1. Beat the egg in a suitable mixing bowl.
2. Add the chopped dill and ground chicken. Blend the mixture until it is smooth.
3. Sprinkle the dish with black pepper and cream.
4. Blend the nugget mixture again. Form the nuggets from the meat mixture and dip them in the almond flour and pork rinds.
5. Sprinkle the Ninja Foodi's insert with the canola oil and butter.
6. Set the Ninja Foodi's insert to "Pressure" mode. Once the butter mixture starts to melt, add the nuggets.
7. Close the Ninja Foodi's lid and cook the dish for 20 minutes at Hi.
8. Once done, check if the nuggets are cooked and remove them from the Ninja Foodi's insert.
9. Drain on a paper towel and serve.
Nutritional Values Per Serving:
Calories: 217; Fat: 15.4g; Carbs: 3.1g; Protein: 17.4 g

Jalapeno Salsa

Prep Time: 5 minutes
Cook Time: 7 minutes
Servings: 10
Ingredients:
10. 8 ounces jalapeno pepper
11. ¼ cup Erythritol
12. 5 tablespoons water
13. 2 tablespoons butter
14. 1 teaspoon paprika

Directions:
1. Wash the jalapeno pepper and remove the seeds.
2. Slice it into thin circles. Sprinkle the sliced jalapeno pepper with paprika and Erythritol.
3. Put the butter and jalaeno mixture into the Ninja Foodi's insert and add water.
4. Set the Ninja Foodi's insert to" Sauté" mode.
5. Once the butter melts, add the sliced jalapeno in the Ninja Foodi's insert.

6. Close the Ninja Foodi's lid and sauté the dish for 7 minutes.
7. Once done, remove the dish from the Ninja Foodi's insert.
8. Cool it and serve.
Nutritional Values Per Serving:
Calories: 28; Fat: 2.5g; Carbs: 7.5g; Protein: 0.4g

Cauliflower Nuggets

Prep Time: 10 minutes
Cook Time: 10 minutes
Servings: 8
Ingredients:
- 8 ounces cauliflower
- 1 big red onion, chopped
- 2 carrots
- ½ cup almond flour
- ¼ cup pork rinds
- 2 eggs
- 1 teaspoon salt
- ½ teaspoon red pepper
- ⅓ teaspoon ground white pepper
- 1 tablespoon olive oil
- 1 teaspoon dried dill

Directions:
1. Peel the red onion and carrots. Chop the vegetables roughly and transfer them to the food processor.
2. Wash the cauliflower and separate it into the florets.
3. Add the cauliflower florets to a food processor and puree until smooth.
4. Add the eggs and salt. Blend the mixture for 3 minutes, then transfer to a mixing bowl.
5. Add pork rinds, red pepper, ground white pepper, and dill.
6. Blend the mixture until smooth. Form the nuggets from the vegetable mixture and dip them in the almond flour.
7. Spray the Ninja Foodi's insert with olive oil inside.
8. Place the vegetable nuggets in the Ninja Foodi's insert and cook them on the" Sauté" mode for 10 minutes.
9. Once the nuggets are cooked, remove from the Ninja Foodi's insert and serve.

Nutritional Values Per Serving:
Calories: 85; Fat: 5.1g; Carbs: 5.9g; Protein: 5g

Dried Tomatoes

Prep Time: 5 minutes
Cook Time: 8 hours
Servings: 8
Ingredients:
- 5 medium tomatoes
- 1 tablespoon basil
- 1 teaspoon cilantro, chopped
- 1 tablespoon onion powder
- 5 tablespoon olive oil
- 1 teaspoon paprika

Directions:
1. Wash the tomatoes and slice them.
2. Combine the cilantro, basil, and paprika together and stir well.
3. Place the sliced tomatoes in the Ninja Foodi's insert and sprinkle them with the spice mixture.
4. Add olive oil and Close the Ninja Foodi's pressure lid. Cook the dish on the "Slow Cook" mode for 8 hours at LO.
5. Once done, the tomatoes should be semi-dry.
6. Remove them from the Ninja Foodi's insert.
7. Serve the dish warm or keep it in the refrigerator.
Nutritional Values Per Serving:
Calories: 92; Fat: 8.6g; Carbs: 3.84g; Protein: 1g

Nutmeg Peanuts

Prep Time: 5 minutes
Cook Time: 1.5 hour
Servings: 8
Ingredients:
- 3 cups peanuts in shells
- 1 tablespoon salt
- 4 cups of water
- ½ teaspoon nutmeg

Directions:
1. Combine the water, nutmeg, and salt together.
2. Stir the mixture well until salt is dissolved.
3. Transfer the water in the Ninja Foodi's insert.
4. Add peanuts in shells and Close the Ninja Foodi's lid.
5. Cook the dish on the "Pressure" mode for 90 minutes at Lo.
6. Once done, remove the peanuts from the Ninja Foodi's insert.
7. Let the peanuts cool before serving.
Nutritional Values Per Serving:
Calories: 562; Fat: 36.8g; Carbs: 8.57g; Protein: 28g

Pork Shank

Prep Time: 15 minutes
Cook Time: 45 minutes
Servings: 6
Ingredients:
- 1-pound pork shank
- ½ cup parsley, chopped
- 4 garlic cloves
- 1 teaspoon salt
- ½ teaspoon paprika
- 2 tablespoons olive oil
- 1 teaspoon cilantro, chopped
- 1 tablespoon celery
- 1 carrot, grated
- 1 cup of water
- 1 red onion, chopped
- ⅓ cup wine
- 2 tablespoons lemon juice

Directions:
1. Chop the parsley and slice the garlic cloves.
2. Combine the vegetables together and add salt, paprika, cilantro, wine, and lemon juice and stir the mixture.
3. Combine the pork shank and marinade together and leave the mixture.
4. Combine the sliced onion and grated carrot together.
5. Add celery and blend well. Add the vegetables to the pork shank mixture and stir using your hands.
6. Place the meat in the Ninja Foodi's insert and add water.
7. Close the Ninja Foodi's lid, and set the Ninja Foodi to" Pressure."
8. Cook for 45 minutes at HI. Once done, remove the meat from the Ninja Foodi's insert and chill the dish well.
9. Slice the pork shank and serve.
Nutritional Values Per Serving:
Calories: 242; Fat: 19.8g; Carbs: 5.38g; Protein: 11g

Zucchini Egg Tots

Prep Time: 15 minutes
Cook Time: 9 minutes
Servings: 8
Ingredients:
- 2 medium zucchinis
- 1 egg
- 1 teaspoon salt
- ½ teaspoon baking soda
- 1 teaspoon lemon juice
- 1 teaspoon basil
- 1 tablespoon oregano
- ⅓ cup oatmeal flour
- 1 tablespoon olive oil
- 1 teaspoon minced garlic
- 1 tablespoon butter
Directions:

1. Wash the zucchini and grate it. Beat the egg in a suitable mixing bowl and blend it using a whisk.
2. Add the baking soda, lemon juice, basil, oregano, and flour to the egg mixture.
3. Stir it carefully until smooth. Combine the grated zucchini and egg mixture together.
4. Knead the dough until smooth. Mix olive oil with minced garlic together.
5. Set the Ninja Foodi's insert to "Sauté" mode.
6. Add butter and transfer the mixture to the Ninja Foodi's insert. Melt the mixture.
7. Make the small tots from the zucchini dough and place them in the melted butter mixture.
8. Sauté the dish for 3 minutes on each side.
9. Once the zucchini tots are cooked, remove them from the Ninja Foodi's insert and serve.

Nutritional Values Per Serving:
Calories: 64; Fat: 4.4g; Carbs: 4.35g; Protein: 2g

Shallot Pepper Pancakes

Prep Time: 10 minutes
Cook Time: 15 minutes
Servings: 8
Ingredients:
- 8 ounces shallot, chopped
- 2 tablespoons chives, chopped
- 1 red onion, chopped
- 1 cup coconut flour
- 2 egg
- ¼ cup sour cream
- 1 teaspoon baking soda
- 1 tablespoon lemon juice
- 1 teaspoon salt
- 1 teaspoon cilantro, chopped
- ½ teaspoon basil
- 1 tablespoon olive oil
- 1 bell pepper, chopped

Directions:
1. Chop the shallot and chives and combine them into a mixing bowl.
2. Whisk the eggs in a another bowl and add baking soda and lemon juice.

3. Stir the mixture and add the cream, salt, cilantro, basil, and coconut flour.
4. Blend the mixture well until smooth.
5. Add the vegetables to the egg mixture.
6. Stir it to the batter that forms. Set the Ninja Foodi's insert to" Sauté" mode.
7. Pour the olive oil in the Ninja Foodi's insert and preheat it.
8. Ladle the batter and cook the pancakes for 2 minutes on each side.
9. Keep the pancakes under aluminium foil to keep them warm until all the pancakes are cooked.
10. Serve the pancakes while warm.

Nutritional Values Per Serving:
Calories: 138; Fat: 6g; Carbs: 7.6g; Protein: 4.7g

Crispy Chicken Skin

Prep Time: 10 minutes
Cook Time: 10 minutes
Servings: 7
Ingredients:
- 1 teaspoon red chili flakes
- 1 teaspoon black pepper
- 1 teaspoon salt
- 9 ounces of chicken skin
- 2 tablespoons butter
- 1 teaspoon olive oil
- 1 teaspoon paprika

Directions:
1. Combine the black pepper, chilli flakes, and paprika together.
2. Stir the mixture and combine it with the chicken skin.
3. Let the mixture rest for 5 minutes. Set the Ninja Foodi's insert to" Sauté" mode.
4. Add the butter to the Ninja Foodi's insert and melt it.
5. Add the chicken skin and sauté it for 10 minutes, stirring frequently.
6. Once the chicken skin gets crunchy, remove it from the Ninja Foodi's insert.
7. Place the chicken skin on the paper towel and drain.
8. Serve warm.

Nutritional Values Per Serving:
Calories: 134; Fat: 11.5g; Carbs: 0.98g; Protein: 7g

Cheesy Stuffed Mushroom

Prep Time: 5 minutes
Cook Time: 7 minutes
Servings: 7
Ingredients:
- 12 ounces Parmesan cheese
- 7 mushroom caps
- 2 teaspoons minced garlic
- ¼ sour cream
- 1 teaspoon butter
- 1 teaspoon ground white pepper
- 2 teaspoons oregano

Directions:
1. Mix the minced garlic, sour cream, ground white pepper, and oregano, and stir the mixture.
2. Add grated parmesan to the minced garlic mixture.
3. Blend the mixture until smooth.
4. Stuff the mushrooms with the cheese mixture and place the dish in the Ninja Foodi's insert.
5. Set the Ninja Foodi's insert to "Pressure" mode, add butter, and close the Ninja Foodi's lid.
6. Cook the dish for 7 minutes at Lo.
7. Once done, remove it from the Ninja Foodi's insert, let it rest briefly, and serve.

Nutritional Values Per Serving:
Calories: 203; Fat: 7.6g; Carbs: 8.35g; Protein: 8g

Parmesan Breadsticks

Prep Time: 25 minutes
Cook Time: 10 minutes
Servings: 8
Ingredients:
- 1 teaspoon baking powder
- ½ teaspoon Erythritol
- ½ teaspoon salt
- 1 cup of warm water
- 2 cups almond flour
- 5 ounces Parmesan
- 1 tablespoon olive oil
- 1 teaspoon onion powder
- 1 teaspoon basil

Directions:
1. Combine the baking powder, Erythritol, and warm water in a mixing bowl.
2. Stir the mixture well. Add the almond flour, onion powder, salt, and basil.
3. Knead the dough until smooth. Separate dough into 10 pieces and make the long logs.
4. Twist the logs in braids. Grate the Parmesan cheese.
5. Place the twisted logs in the Ninja Foodi's insert.
6. Sprinkle the grated Parmesan cheese and olive oil, and close the Ninja Foodi's lid.
7. Cook the breadsticks at the "Pressure" mode for 10 minutes at Lo.
8. Release the pressure and remove the lid.
9. Leave the breadsticks for 10 minutes to rest.
10. Serve the breadsticks immediately or keep them in a sealed container.

Nutritional Values Per Serving:
Calories: 242; Fat: 18.9g; Carbs: 2.7g; Protein: 11.7g

Ninja Foodi Cheddar Biscuits

Prep Time: 10 minutes
Cook Time: 15 minutes
Servings: 8
Ingredients:
- ¼ teaspoon baking powder
- ¼ cup butter
- ¼ teaspoon ginger powder
- ¼ teaspoon garlic powder
- 4 eggs
- ¼ cup coconut flour, sifted
- 1 cup cheddar cheese
- Salt, to taste

Directions:
1. Add flour, baking powder, garlic powder and salt in a large bowl. Mix well.
2. Now, add butter and eggs in another bowl. Whisk well.
3. Combine the two mixtures and mix properly. Set aside.
4. Place the batter in Ninja Foodi Deluxe XL Pressure Cooker and press the "Bake" button.
5. Close the Crisping Lid and press the "Start/Stop" button.
6. Bake for 15-minutes at 400 degrees F and open the lid.
7. Take out, serve and enjoy!
Nutritional Values Per Serving:
Calories: 155; Fat: 13g; Carbs: 3g; Protein: 6.9g

Ninja Foodi Spicy Peanuts

Prep Time: 5 minutes
Cook Time: 2 hours 40 minutes
Servings: 6
Ingredients:
- ¾ cups peanuts
- 1½ tablespoons chili seasoning mix
- ½ tablespoon butter

Directions:
1. Add peanuts, chili seasoning mix and butter in the pot of Ninja Foodi Deluxe XL Pressure Cooker. Mix well.
2. Select "Slow Cook" and close the pressure Lid.
3. Press the "Start/Stop" button and cook for about 2 hours and 30 minutes at Lo. Stir after every 30 minutes.
4. Open the lid and cook for 15 minutes.
5. Take out, serve and enjoy!
Nutritional Values Per Serving:
Calories: 134; Fat: 11.1g; Carbs: 6.7g; Protein: 5.6g

Ninja Foodi Cod Sticks

Prep Time: 10 minutes
Cook Time: 15 minutes
Servings: 8
Ingredients:
- 1 cup almond flour
- 2 eggs
- 1 cod fillet, thinly sliced
- 2 teaspoons dried parsley, crushed
- ½ teaspoon cayenne pepper
- Salt and black pepper, to taste

Directions:
1. Add eggs in one bowl and all the other ingredients except cod slices in another bowl. Mix well.
2. Dip cod slices first in egg mixture and then in the other mixture. Set aside.
3. Arrange cod slices in Ninja Foodi Deluxe XL Pressure Cooker and press the "Bake" button.
4. Close the Crisping Lid and press the "Start/Stop" button.
5. Bake for 6 minutes on each side at 350 degrees F and open the lid.
6. Take out, serve and enjoy!
Nutritional Values Per Serving:
Calories: 111; Fat: 7.9g; Carbs: 3.2g; Protein: 6.9g

Ninja Foodi Spicy Popcorns

Prep Time: 10 minutes
Cook Time: 5 minutes
Servings: 6

Ingredients:
- 1 cup popping corns
- 2 teaspoons ground turmeric
- ½ teaspoon garlic powder
- 6 tablespoons olive oil
- Salt, to taste

Directions:
1. Heat four tablespoons of olive-oil in a Ninja Foodi Deluxe XL Pressure Cooker and add popping corns in it.
2. Select "Pressure" and close the pressure Lid.
3. Press the "Start/Stop" button and cook for about 5 minutes at HIGH pressure.
4. Take out and set aside.
5. Meanwhile, add remaining olive oil, turmeric, garlic powder and salt in a bowl. Mix well.
6. Pour the mixture on popcorns and toss to coat well.
7. Serve and enjoy!

Nutritional Values Per Serving:
Calories: 143; Fat: 14.1g; Carbs: 5.3g; Protein: 0.3g

Ninja Foodi Spinach Chips

Prep Time: 12 minutes
Cook Time: 10 minutes
Servings: 4

Ingredients:
- ½ teaspoon paprika
- ¼ teaspoon ground cumin

- ¼ teaspoon olive oil
- 2 cups fresh spinach leaves
- Salt, to taste

Directions:
1. Add everything in a large-bowl and mix-well. Set aside.
2. Place spinach leaves in Ninja Foodi Deluxe XL Pressure Cooker and press the "Bake" button.
3. Close the Crisping Lid and press the "Start/Stop" button.
4. Bake for about 10 minutes at 325 degrees F and open the lid.
5. Take out, serve and enjoy!

Nutritional Values Per Serving:
Calories: 7; Fat: 0.4g; Carbs: 0.7g; Protein: 0.5g

Ninja Foodi Spiced Almonds

Prep Time: 10 minutes
Cook Time: 14 minutes
Servings: 6

Ingredients:
- 2 tablespoons unsweetened applesauce
- 1 cup almonds
- ¼ teaspoon cayenne pepper
- ¼ teaspoon ground cumin
- ½ teaspoon olive oil
- ½ tablespoon water
- ¼ teaspoon ground cinnamon
- ¼ teaspoon red chili powder
- Salt, to taste

Directions:
1. Arrange almonds in Ninja Foodi Deluxe XL Pressure Cooker and select "Bake".
2. Close the Crisping Lid and press the "Start/Stop" button.
3. Bake for about 10 minutes at 350 degrees F and open the lid.
4. Take out and set aside.
5. Meanwhile, add oil, water and applesauce in a bowl. Mix well.
6. Add in almonds and toss to coat well.
7. Add cinnamon, ground cumin, red chili powder, cayenne pepper and salt in another bowl. Mix well.
8. Arrange almonds again in the Ninja Foodi Deluxe XL Pressure Cooker and top them with cinnamon mixture.

9. Close the Crisping Lid and press the "Start/Stop" button.
10. Bake them for about 4 minutes at 350 degrees F and open the lid.
11. Take out, serve and enjoy!
Nutritional Values Per Serving:
Calories: 98; Fat: 8.4g; Carbs: 4.2g; Protein: 3.4g

Ninja Foodi Spicy Cashews

Prep Time: 10 minutes
Cook Time: 2 hours 45 minutes
Servings: 12
Ingredients:
- 2½ cups cashews
- 3 tablespoons chili seasoning mix
- 1½ tablespoons butter

Directions:
1. Add everything in the pot of Ninja Foodi Deluxe XL Pressure Cooker and mix well.
2. Close the pressure Lid and select "Slow Cook".
3. Press the "Start/Stop" button and cook for about 2 hours and 30 minutes on LOW TEMP.
4. Open the lid and cook for 15 more minutes.
5. Take out, serve and enjoy!
Serving Suggestions: Top with red chili powder before serving.
Variation Tip: You can add cayenne pepper for a stronger taste.
Nutritional Values Per Serving:
Calories: 741; Fat: 61.2g; Carbs: 40.2g; Protein: 18.6g

Ninja Foodi Popcorn

Prep Time: 5 Minutes
Cook Time: 10 Minutes
Servings: 14
Ingredients:
- 3 tablespoons oil, whatever kind you like
- ½ cup popcorn kernels
- ½ teaspoon salt
- 4 tablespoons butter, salted and room temp

Directions:
1. Measure out a piece of foil that is 4" larger than the diameter of the Ninja Foodi Deluxe XL Pressure Cooker Inner Pot and wide enough to be able to fold into a pouch. Tuck the ends under the lip of the inner pot and make multiple holes with a thin sharp object. I used the pointy end of my cake tester. You don't want the holes too big or the butter will just pour out in places.
2. Add the three tablespoons of oil to the inner pot and half cup of popped corn kernel. Turn the Ninja Foodi Deluxe XL Pressure Cooker on High Sear/Sauté and cover with Pressure Lid and turn Vent.
3. While you are waiting for the kernel to pop, cut or spread your butter on the foil.
4. When you hear the kernel pop, add in the remaining un popped kernels and the salt. Stir to combine.
5. Close the foil packet and secure by tucking under the lid of the inner pot. Cover with Pressure Lid. Leave the Sear/Sauté on high until to begin to hear the kernels rapidly popping (less than one second between pops), turn the heat down to Medium/Low. Insert a spatula or wooden spoon and stir the bottom to move the kernels around.
6. Once the popping has slowed down to about one pop every few seconds, turn the Ninja Foodi Deluxe XL Pressure Cooker off and stir again. If there is any butter left in the foil, shake it over the popcorn and stir.
7. Serve and enjoy!
Nutritional Values Per Serving:
Calories: 78; Fat: 7g; Carbs: 4g; Protein: 1g

Ninja Foodi Banana Cookies

Prep Time: 15 minutes
Cook Time: 20 minutes
Servings: 7
Ingredients:
- 1 banana, mashed
- ¼ cup soymilk
- ½ tablespoon canola oil
- ¼ tablespoon baking powder
- 1 cup white flour

Directions:
1. Add mashed bananas, oil and soymilk in a bowl. Mix well.
2. Add in flour and baking powder. Stir properly.
3. Knead the dough and roll it with the help of a rolling pin.
4. Cut the dough into circles and place them in Ninja Foodi Deluxe XL Pressure Cooker.
5. Select "Bake" and close the Crisping Lid.
6. Press the "Start/Stop" button and bake for about 20 minutes at 400 degrees F.
7. Open the lid and take out.
8. Serve and enjoy!

Nutritional Values Per Serving:
Calories: 94; Fat: 1.4g; Carbs: 18.3g; Protein: 2.3g

Ninja Foodi Chickpea Crackers

Prep Time: 15 minutes
Cook Time: 20 minutes
Servings: 5
Ingredients:
- ½ cup chickpea flour
- 1 tablespoon yeast
- ¼ cup water
- ¼ teaspoon sesame oil
- ¼ teaspoon baking powder
- 1 teaspoon toasted sesame seeds
- ¼ teaspoon turmeric
- Salt, to taste

Directions:
1. Add baking powder, chickpea flour, sesame seeds, yeast, salt and turmeric in a bowl. Mix well.
2. Add water and oil gradually in the mixture and mix until proper dough is formed.
3. Cover the dough and set aside till the dough rises.
4. Make square shapes out of the dough and place them in Ninja Foodi Deluxe XL Pressure Cooker.
5. Select "Bake" and close the Crisping Lid.
6. Press the "Start/Stop" button and bake for about 20 minutes at 350 degrees F.
7. Open the Crisping Lid and take out.
8. Serve and enjoy!

Nutritional Values Per Serving:
Calories: 86; Fat: 1.9g; Carbs: 13.4g; Protein: 4.9g

Ninja Foodi Lemon Scones

Prep Time: 10 minutes
Cook Time: 25 minutes
Servings: 3
Ingredients:
- ¾ cup all-purpose flour
- ¼ cup unsweetened soymilk
- 2 tablespoons sugar
- ½ teaspoon lemon extract
- ½ tablespoon sunflower oil
- ½ tablespoon baking powder
- Salt, to taste

Directions:
1. Add wet ingredients in one bowl and dry ingredients in another. Mix well.
2. Combine the two mixtures and mix until dough is formed.
3. Make spheres out of the mixture and press them with tortilla press.
4. Make triangular shapes out of the dough and place them in Ninja Foodi Deluxe XL Pressure Cooker.
5. Press the "Bake" button and close the Crisping Lid.
6. Press the "Start/Stop" button and bake for 15 minutes at 400 degrees F.
7. Open the Crisping Lid and take out.
8. Serve and enjoy!

Nutritional Values Per Serving:
Calories: 175; Fat: 3g; Carbs: 33.4g; Protein: 3.8g

Loaded Zucchini Chips

Prep Time: 9 Minutes
Cook Time: 23-25 Minutes
Servings: 6
Ingredients:
- 2 medium-sized zucchinis
- 1 cup toasted bread crumbs
- 1.2 cup grated parmesan
- ½ teaspoon kosher salt
- Chili powder ¼ teaspoon
- Black pepper to taste
- 1 beaten egg
- Oil spray

Directions:
1. Start by cutting the ends of the zucchini and then cut it into a round shape. Place a clean towel on a plate. Then place zucchini chips and sprinkle a little salt. Now place another towel on top and then a heavy pan on top.
2. Let it sit for about 12 to 15 minutes for the extra moisture to be drawn out.
3. On the other hand, mix crumbs, salt, pepper, and parmesan at the end. In a separate bowl beat the egg. Place the bowl with egg, crumb mix, and place side by side.
4. Dip the cut zucchini in the egg bowl with one of your hands, now with the other hand, coat it in the crumbs, and place it on a clean plate. At this step spray the zucchini rounds with a good amount of olive oil and let them sit for about 2 minutes.
5. Now you can either spray or brush the Ninja Foodi Deluxe XL Pressure Cooker Basket of the Air Crisp with olive oil.
6. Make sure you place the chips in a single layer.
7. Lastly, bake the zucchini chips for 6 minutes at 375° F.

Nutritional Values Per Serving:
Calories: 153; Fat: 6 g; Carbs: 11 g; Protein: 11.5 g

Roasted Chickpeas

Prep Time: 5 Minutes
Cook Time: 15 Minutes
Servings: 1
Ingredients:
- 50 grams chickpeas
- 1 teaspoon of olive oil
- 1 packet salad dressing
- 1 tablespoon of seasoning mix
- 1 tablespoon parmesan cheese

Directions:
1. Heat your Ninja Foodi Deluxe XL Pressure Cooker at 390° F. Rinse the chickpeas, and dry them.
2. Toss in with one tablespoon of extra virgin olive oil.
3. Now again toss with the parmesan cheese and the seasoning mix, make sure you get a nice coating.
4. Now put the chickpeas in the Ninja Foodi Deluxe XL Pressure Cooker Cook & Crisp Basket. Cook for about 15 minutes. Make sure you toss it a couple of times.
5. Remove them from the Cook & Crisp Basket and grab them for snacking. Store in an airtight container!

Nutritional Values Per Serving:
Calories: 205; Fat: 12.7g; Carbs: 12.2g; Protein: 6.2g

Buffalo Cauliflower Platter

Prep Time: 12 Minutes
Cook Time: 12-17 Minutes
Servings: 4
Ingredients:
- 1 medium-sized cauliflower head
- 1 cup of buffalo sauce
- 1 tablespoon of melted butter
- 1 cup of bread crumbs
- Salt to taste

For Sides
- Carrot sticks
- Celery sticks
- 2 tablespoons orange dressing

Directions:
1. Cut the cauliflower into florets and place them in a mixing bowl.
2. Mix the hot sauce and butter in a separate bowl.
3. Now on top of the cauliflower pieces, pour the hot sauce.
4. Let it marinate for 15 minutes, making sure you keep stirring it from time to time. Now in another shallow dish put the bread crumbs and season it with a bit of salt.
5. Now to coat the cauliflower, dip it in the crumb mixture.
6. Place the cauliflower pieces on the Cook & Crisp Basket and make sure to not overlap them.
7. It is recommended to cook this recipe in two batches so that the cauliflower does not get overcrowded.
8. Set the Air Crisp at 390° F and let it cook for about 12 to 15 minutes.
9. Serve these cauliflower buffalo bites with optional orange dressing, carrot, and celery sticks!

Nutritional Values Per Serving:
Calories: 201; Fat: 10.1g; Carbs: 18.5g; Protein: 5.8g

Air Crisped Chicken Nuggets

Prep Time: 10 Minutes
Cook Time: 8-10 Minutes
Servings: 6
Ingredients:
- 1 pound minced chicken
- Salt and pepper to taste
- 1 tablespoon olive oil
- 5 tablespoons of season bread crumbs
- 1 tablespoon of panko mix
- 1 tablespoon parmesan cheese (grated)

Directions:
1. At 320° F, preheat the Ninja Foodi Deluxe XL Pressure Cooker at Air Crisp Mode for 8 minutes.
2. In a bowl add bread crumbs, panko mix, parmesan cheese, and olive oil.
3. For the seasoning, dump in salt and pepper on the chicken.
4. To ensure the olive oil is evenly coated on all the chicken, put the olive oil well if needed.
5. Shape up the small pieces of chicken that pop out of the batter.
6. Don't add too many chicken chunks at a time into the breadcrumb mixture for the coating purpose. Then place it on the Cook & Crisp Basket and give a slight olive oil spray on the top.
7. Let it Air Crisp for 8 minutes, make sure to turn it halfway until the color is golden!

Nutrition Information per Serving:
Calories: 112; Fat: 3.9g; Carbs: 5.5g; Protein: 10.4g

Instant Cheesy Broccoli

Prep Time: 6 Minutes
Cook Time: 2-3 Minutes
Servings: 4
Ingredients:
- 1 broccoli head (florets)
- ½ cup chicken chunks
- 2 tablespoons melted butter
- 4 tablespoons parmesan cheese

Directions:
1. Into your Ninja Foodi Deluxe XL Pressure Cooker Pot pour in 1.5 cups of water and then place your vegetable in Cook & Crisp Basket inside it
2. Next, wash off your broccoli well then cut it into florets. Close the lid after putting it into the Ninja Foodi Deluxe XL Pressure Cooker Cook & Crisp Basket, then select the Steam valve and steam it for about 1 minute.
3. Lift your Ninja Foodi Deluxe XL Pressure Cooker Basket and do a quick release.
4. Dump those florets into a platter. Top up with chicken chunks.
5. Now put the melted butter and sprinkle the parmesan cheese on top and serve!
Nutritional Values Per Serving:
Calories: 122; Fat: 8.7g; Carbs: 5.7g; Protein: 5.7g

Garlic Pretzels with Ranch Dressing

Prep Time: 6 Minutes
Cook Time: 10 Minutes
Servings: 1
Ingredients:

- 120 grams regular pretzels
- 1 packet Ranch seasoning
- ⅓ teaspoon garlic powder
- 1 tablespoon olive oil
- ⅛ teaspoon cayenne pepper

Directions:
1. Align the Ninja Foodi Deluxe XL Pressure Cooker Cook & Crisp Basket with aluminum foil and give it an olive oil spray.
2. In the Ninja Foodi Deluxe XL Pressure Cooker Cook & Crisp Basket, place the pretzels and top up with the dry seasonings.
3. Now use an olive oil spray and spray a few coats of it and mix it up until they are fully coated at 390° F.
4. Cook in the Air Crisp Mode for 3 minutes at 390° F, then open the lid and remove the pretzels carefully. Spray a little bit of olive oil and mix up very well.
5. For another 3 minutes cook again then remove the pretzels carefully or open the lid, spray a bit of olive oil and mix well.
6. Cook it for two more minutes or you can wait until the pretzels are crispy enough!
Nutrition Information per Serving:
Calories: 159; Fat: 4.7g; Carbs: 17.3 g; Protein: 3.4g

Ninja Foodi Herb Crackers

Prep Time: 10 minutes
Cook Time: 20 minutes
Servings: 4
Ingredients:
- ½ cup almond flour
- ½ tablespoon water
- ½ tablespoon herbes de provence
- ¼ tablespoon olive oil
- Salt, to taste

Directions:
1. Add herbes de provence, salt and almond flour in a large bowl. Mix well.
2. Add in olive oil and water. Mix until a soft dough is formed.
3. Make small spheres out of the dough and press them with a tortilla press.
4. Arrange them in the Ninja Foodi Deluxe XL Pressure Cooker and press the "Bake" button.

5. Close the Crisping Lid and press the "Start/Stop" button.
6. Bake for about 20 minutes at 350 degrees F and open the Crisping Lid.
7. Take out, serve and enjoy!
Nutritional Values Per Serving:
Calories: 154; Fat: 12.6g; Carbs: 3.5g; Protein: 6.8g

Chicken Wings

Prep Time: 6 Minutes
Cook Time: 22 Minutes
Servings: 2
Ingredients:
- 8 chicken medium-sized wings
- 2 tablespoons flour
- 1 tablespoon brown sugar
- 1 tablespoon salt
- ½ tablespoon garlic paste
- 1 teaspoon pepper
- ½ tablespoon chili powder
- ½ tablespoon paprika
- 1 tablespoon olive oil
Directions:
1. Use paper towels to pat dry the wings. Add olive oil and spread it on all sides to coat them well.
2. Mix all dry ingredients and put them in the polythene bag. Then add the wings coated with olive oil into the bag and shake well. Now carefully place the wings inside the Ninja Foodi Deluxe XL Pressure Cooker Cook & Crisp Basket, making sure they don't overlap each other.
3. Air Crisp them for 8 minutes in Ninja Foodi Deluxe XL Pressure Cooker at Air Crisp Mode at 390° F and then flip to the other side and continue cooking for another 8 minutes until you get the desired crispiness.
Nutritional Values Per Serving:
Calories: 200; Fat: 13g; Carbs: 6g; Protein: 10.9g

Coated Onion Rings

Prep Time: 8 Minutes
Cook Time: 9 Minutes
Servings: 2
Ingredients:
- 1 large onion
- 2 tablespoon all-purpose flour
- ½ teaspoon baking powder
- ¼ teaspoon salt
- 1 egg
- ½ cup milk
- 1 teaspoon chili powder
- 4 tablespoons bread crumbs
Directions:
1. Start by slicing the onions into ¼ inch circular rings. The center of the onion needs to be removed.
2. Then divide the slices. Now take a large bowl and place the onion slices on it.
3. Add the flour and toss the slices making sure each piece of onion is coated well.
4. Take another bowl and whisk together the egg, milk, and baking powder.
5. Then add salt, bread crumbs, and chili powder into another bowl.
6. Now dip the coated rings into the egg mixture and then into the bread crumbs until coated well.
7. Spray the Ninja Foodi Deluxe XL Pressure Cooker Cook & Crisp Basket with a bit of olive oil or Air Crisp parchment paper can also be used. Place the coated rings into the Ninja Foodi Deluxe XL Pressure Cooker Basket until it's full.
8. At 390° F, Air Crisp it for 7 to 8 minutes or wait until the coating is crispy!
Nutritional Values Per Serving:
Calories: 142; Fat: 4.6g; Carbs: 17g; Protein: 7.9g

Sweet & Sour Scotched Eggs

Prep Time: 15 Minutes
Cook Time: 10 Minutes
Servings: 2
Ingredients:
- 2 eggs
- 178 grams sausage

For Bread Coating
- ¼ cup bread crumbs
- ¼ tablespoon maple sugar
- ¼ grounded pepper

For the egg mixture:
- 1 egg
- 1 teaspoon hot sauce
- 1 teaspoon of mustard

For the Dipping:
- 1 tablespoon sour cream
- 1 teaspoon maple syrup

Directions:
1. In Ninja Foodi Deluxe XL Pressure Cooker add one cup of cold water and put your eggs in the Basket.
2. Put on the pressure lid and turn the valve to seal and set the Ninja Foodi Deluxe XL Pressure Cooker Pressure Cook setting to High. And immediately release the pressure when the time is up, and place those eggs into a container filled with ice.
3. Meanwhile, mix up the bread mixture by combining the bread crumbs, sugar, and pepper in a bowl.
4. Dump the water and preheat on Broil for 10 minutes with the help of a Basket that's inside the Ninja Foodi Deluxe XL Pressure Cooker. After that turn on the Broil for another 10 minutes if wrapping in breaking your eggs is not done in 10 minutes. After being done with preparing your eggs, you can feel free to switch it up from Broil option to Air Crisp option.
5. Take the sausage and press them into an oval or round shape according to your liking but make sure that the thickness should be around ⅛ to ¼.
6. Wrap the sausage gently around the egg using parchment paper. Now take the sausage-encased eggs and dip them into the egg mixture and coat. Then again dip them into the breading mixture and coat completely. Now for the second coat repeat the step.
7. After the Ninja Foodi Deluxe XL Pressure Cooker has been preheated for 10 minutes for Broil options, give the Basket an oil spray and place the scorched eggs, and squirt a little oil. Now select the Ninja Foodi Deluxe XL Pressure Cooker function at 390° F for about seven minutes.
8. Take sour cream and combine it with maple sugar and it can be served as a drizzling or a dipping sauce. Serve the eggs after slicing them in half!

Nutrition Information per Serving:
Calories: 346; Fat: 25g; Carbs: 11g; Protein: 19.5g

Buttery Potatoes

Prep Time: 5 Minutes
Cook Time: 19 Minutes
Servings: 2
Ingredients:
- 2 large potatoes
- 1 cup water
- Salt to taste
- 1 tablespoon butter
- ½ teaspoon oregano

Directions:
1. Start by washing the potatoes well and add with the help of a fork, brick it five to six times.
2. Into Ninja Foodi Deluxe XL Pressure Cooker pour one cup of water, or enough water so that potatoes should not be sitting in the water, they should be raised enough. Place those

potatoes onto the Ninja Foodi Deluxe XL Pressure Cooker Cook & Crisp Basket. And place that Cook & Crisp Basket into Ninja Foodi Deluxe XL Pressure Cooker.

3. Now close the lid. Set Ninja Foodi Deluxe XL Pressure Cooker on High pressure setting, cook it on High for about 15 to 20 minutes keeping in mind the size of the potatoes.

4. Lastly, remove the lid and peel the potatoes. Mash the potatoes and add the melted butter, oregano, and salt and give it a good mix to get the butter flavor in every bite!

Nutritional Values Per Serving:
Calories: 80; Fat: 6.3g; Carbs: 5.2g; Protein: 0.6g

Tortilla Crackers

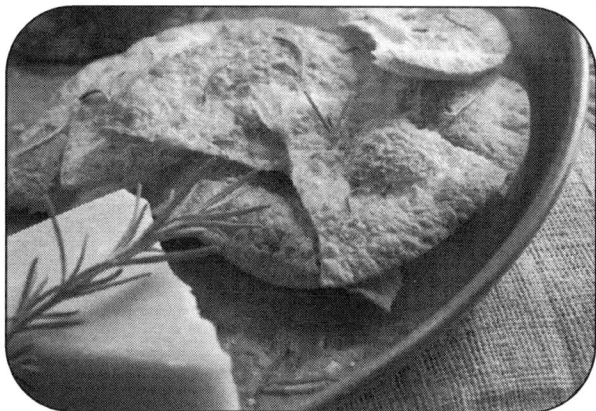

Prep Time: 6 Minutes
Cook Time: 6 Minutes
Servings: 4

Ingredients:
- 4 small tortillas
- Cooking spray
- Salt per taste
- 1 teaspoon Mexican Seasoning

Directions:
1. Start by preheating your Ninja Foodi Deluxe XL Pressure Cooker at Air Crisp Mode at 390° F.

2. Give the tortillas a cooking oil spray, and season them with salt to taste. Sprinkle the Mexican seasoning slightly.

3. Stack the tortillas and cut them in half. Then cut pieces once again into small triangles. Once the Air Crisp is ready, take out the Ninja Foodi Deluxe XL Pressure Cooker Basket now and scatter the tortilla pieces.

4. Now put the Ninja Foodi Deluxe XL Pressure Cooker Basket back.

5. After 2 to 3 minutes take the Ninja Foodi Deluxe XL Pressure Cooker Basket out and gently flip the chips.

6. Put the Ninja Foodi Deluxe XL Pressure Cooker Basket back into the Ninja Foodi Deluxe XL Pressure Cooker and Air Crisp for 2 more minutes, until you get the golden brown and crispy texture.

7. Cool them before serving, the reason being they will become crispier as they cool down!

Nutritional Values Per Serving:
Calories: 65; Fat: 10.5g; Carbs: 10.3g; Protein: 1g

Juicy Sesame and Garlic Chicken Wings

Prep Time: 10 minutes
Cook Time: 25 minutes
Serves: 4
Ingredients:
- 24 chicken wing segments
- 2 tbsp toasted sesame oil
- 2 tbsp Asian chili-garlic sauce
- 2 tbsp stevia
- 2 garlic cloves, minced
- 1 tbsp toasted sesame seeds

Preparation:
1. Add 1 cup of water to Foodi's inner pot. Put the reversible rack in the pot in the lower position, and place the chicken wings on the rack.
2. Put on the Pressure Lid and seal the valve.
3. Select PRESSURE mode on HI and cook for 10 minutes.
4. Meanwhile, make the glaze by taking a large bowl and whisking in the sesame oil, chili-garlic sauce, honey, and garlic.
5. Once the chicken is cooked, quick release the pressure and remove the lid.
6. Remove the rack from the pot and empty out the remaining water from the inner pot.
7. Return the inner pot to the Foodi's base.
8. Cover the Foodi with the Crisping Lid and select AIR CRISP mode. Adjust the temperature to 375°F and allow it to preheat for 3 minutes.
9. While the Foodi preheats, add the wings to the glaze and toss well to coat.
10. Transfer the wings to the Cook & Crisp Basket, leaving any excess sauce in the bowl.
11. Place the basket in the Foodi and close with the Crisping Lid. Select AIR CRISP mode and let the chicken cook for 8 minutes. Gently toss the wings and then let them cook for 8 minutes more.
12. Serve and enjoy!

Nutritional Information Per Serving:
Calories 440; Fat: 32g; Carbs: 12g; Protein: 28g

Lemon and Chicken Extravaganza

Prep Time: 5 minutes
Cook Time: 18 minutes
Serves: 4
Ingredients:
- 4 bone-in, skin-on chicken thighs
- Salt and pepper, to taste
- 2 tbsp butter, divided
- 2 tsp garlic, minced
- ½ cup herbed chicken stock
- ½ cup heavy whip cream
- ½ lemon, juiced

Preparation:
1. Season the chicken thighs generously with salt and pepper.
2. Set the Foodi to SEAR/SAUTÉ mode on MD:HI temperature setting, add the oil to the inner pot, and let it heat up.
3. Add the thighs. Sauté both sides for 6 minutes.
4. Remove the thighs, place them on a platter and keep it to one side.
5. Add the garlic to the inner pot and sauté for 2 minutes.
6. Whisk in the chicken stock, heavy cream, lemon juice, and gently stir.
7. Bring the mix to a simmer and reintroduce the chicken thighs.
8. Put on the Pressure Lid, select PRESSURE mode, and cook for 10 minutes on HI.
9. Release the pressure over 10 minutes.
10. Serve and enjoy!

Nutritional Information Per Serving:
Calories 294; Fat: 26g; Carbs: 4g; Protein: 12g

Stuffed Whole Chicken

Prep Time: 10 minutes
Cook Time: 8 hours
Servings: 6
Ingredients:
- 1 cup mozzarella cheese
- 4 whole garlic cloves, peeled
- 1 whole chicken 2 pounds, cleaned and pat dried
- Black pepper and salt, to taste
- 2 tablespoons fresh lemon juice

Directions:
1. Stuff the chicken cavity with garlic cloves and mozzarella cheese
2. Season chicken generously with black pepper and salt
3. Transfer chicken to your Ninja Foodi and drizzle lemon juice
4. Lock and secure the Ninja Foodi's lid and set to "Slow Cook" mode, let it cook on LOW for 8 hours
5. Once done, serve and enjoy.

Nutrition Values Per Serving
Calories: 309; Fat: 12g; Carbs: 1.6g; Protein: 45g

Lime Chicken Chili

Prep Time: 10 minutes
Cook Time: 23 minutes
Servings: 6
Ingredients:
- ¼ cup cooking wine Keto-Friendly
- ½ cup chicken broth
- 1 onion, diced
- 1 teaspoon salt
- ½ teaspoon paprika
- 5 garlic cloves, minced
- 1 tablespoon lime juice
- ¼ cup butter
- 2 pounds chicken thighs

- 1 teaspoon dried parsley
- 3 green chillies, chopped

Directions:
1. Set your Ninja-Foodi to Sauté mode and stir in onion and garlic.
2. Sauté for 3 minutes, add remaining ingredients.
3. Lock and secure the Ninja Foodi's lid and cook on "High" pressure for 20 minutes.
4. Release pressure naturally over 10 minutes.
5. Serve and enjoy.

Nutrition Values Per Serving
Calories: 282; Fat: 15g; Carbs: 6g; Protein: 27g

Hainanese Chicken

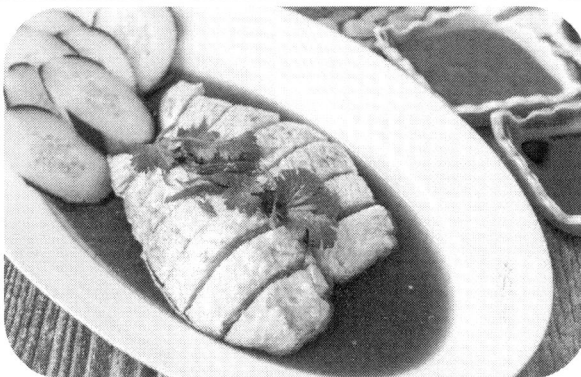

Prep Time: 20 minutes
Cook Time: 4 hours
Servings: 4
Ingredients:
- 1 ounce's ginger, peeled
- 6 garlic cloves, crushed
- 6 bundles cilantro/basil leaves
- 1 teaspoon salt
- 1 tablespoon sesame oil
- 3 1 and ½ pounds each chicken meat, ready to cook

For Dip
- 2 tablespoons ginger, minced
- 1 teaspoon garlic, minced
- 1 tablespoon chicken stock
- 1 teaspoon sesame oil
- ½ teaspoon erythritol
- Salt to taste

Directions:
1. Add chicken, garlic, ginger, leaves, and salt to your Ninja Food.
2. Add enough water to fully submerge chicken; Lock and secure the Ninja Foodi's lid cooks on SLOW COOK mode on LOW for 4 hours.
3. Release pressure naturally.
4. Take chicken out of the pot and chill for 10 minutes.
5. Take a suitable and add all the dipping ingredients and blend well in a food processor.
6. Take chicken out of ice bath and drain, chop into serving pieces.
7. Set onto a serving platter.
8. Brush chicken with sesame oil.
9. Serve with ginger dip.
10. Enjoy.

Nutrition Values Per Serving
Calories: 535; Fat: 45g; Carbs: 5g; Protein: 28g

Turkey Meatballs

Prep Time: 15 minutes
Cook Time: 4 minutes
Servings: 4
Ingredients:
- 1-pound ground turkey
- 1 cup onion, shredded
- ¼ cup heavy whip cream
- 2 teaspoon salt
- 1 cup carrots, shredded
- ½ teaspoon ground caraway seeds
- 1 and ½ teaspoons black pepper
- ¼ teaspoon ground allspice
- 1 cup almond meal
- ½ cup almond milk
- 2 tablespoons unsalted butter

Directions:
1. Transfer meat to a suitable
2. Add cream, almond meal, onion, carrot, 1 teaspoon of salt, caraway, ½ teaspoon of pepper, allspice, and mix well
3. Refrigerate the mixture for 30 minutes
4. Once the mixture is cooled, use your hands to scoop the mixture into meatballs
5. Place the turkey balls in your Ninja Foodi pot.
6. Add milk, pats of butter and sprinkle 1 teaspoon salt, 1 teaspoon black pepper
7. Lock and secure the Ninja Foodi's lid, then cook on "HIGH" pressure for 4 minutes
8. Quick-release pressure
9. UnLock and secure the Ninja Foodi's lid and serve
10. Enjoy.

Nutrition Values Per Serving
Calories: 338; Fat: 23g; Carbs: 7g; Protein: 23g

Braised Chicken Thigh

Prep Time: 10 minutes
Cook Time: 30 minutes
Servings: 4
Ingredients:
- 4 chicken thighs, bone-in
- 1 teaspoon salt
- 1 tablespoon olive oil
- ½ small onion, sliced
- ½ cup white wine vinegar
- ½ cup chicken stock
- 1 cup artichoke hearts
- 1 bay leaf
- Black pepper
- ¼ cup heavy cream

Directions:
1. Set your Ninja Foodi to Sauté mode and set it to Medium-HIGH, pre-heat for 5 minutes
2. Pour olive oil and wait until it shimmers
3. Add chicken thighs, skin side-side down, cook for 4-5 minutes per side, then transfer to a plate.
4. Add onion, sprinkle with remaining salt, cook for 2 minutes more until tender
5. Add wine and bring to a boil. Cook for 3 minutes, until reduced to half.
6. Add chicken stock, artichoke hearts, bay leaf, thyme, several grinds of pepper, stir well
7. Place chicken thigh back to the pot skin side up, lock pressure lid into place and seal the pressure valve
8. Select pressure mode to HIGH and cook for 5 minutes
9. Once done, quick release pressure
10. use tongs to transfer chicken to Reversible Rack in the upper position, add mushrooms to sauce and stir. Set rack in the pot
11. Close with crisping lid and select Bake/Roast, adjust the temperature to 375 degrees F, cook for 12 minutes
12. Once done, open the lid and transfer chicken to the platter, add heavy cream and stir into the sauce. stir in sauce, season with black pepper and salt
13. Pour sauce and vegetables around chicken, serve and enjoy.

Nutrition Values Per Serving
Calories: 268; Fat: 20g; Carbs: 7g; Protein: 19g

Sesame Chicken Wings

Prep Time: 10 minutes
Cook Time: 25 minutes
Servings: 4
Ingredients:
* 24 chicken wing segments
* 2 tablespoons toasted sesame oil
* 2 tablespoons Asian-Chile-Garlic sauce
* 2 tablespoons stevia
* 2 garlic cloves, minced
* 1 tablespoon toasted sesame seeds
Directions:
1. Add 1 cup of water to Foodi's inner pot, place reversible rack in the pot in lower portions, place chicken wings in the rack.
2. Place lid into place and seal the pressure valve.
3. Select pressure mode to HIGH and cook for 10 minutes.
4. Make the glaze by taking a large bowl and whisking in sesame oil, Chile-Garlic sauce, choc zero maple syrup and garlic.
5. Once the chicken is done, quick release the pressure and remove the pressure lid.
6. Remove rack from the pot and empty it.
7. Return inner pot to the base.
8. Cover with crisping lid and select Air Crisp mode, adjust the temperature to 375 degrees F, pre-heat for 3 minutes.
9. While the Foodi pre-heats, add wings to the sauce and toss well to coat it.
10. Transfer wings to the basket, leaving any excess sauce in the bowl.
11. Place the basket in Foodi and close with Crisping mode, select Air Crisp mode and let it cook for 8 minutes, gently toss the wings and let it cook for 8 minutes more.
12. Once done, drizzle any sauce and sprinkle sesame seeds.
13. Enjoy.
Nutrition Values Per Serving
Calories: 440; Fat: 32g; Carbs: 12g; Protein: 28g

Mexican Chicken Soup

Prep Time: 5 minutes
Cook Time: 20 minutes
Servings: 4
Ingredients:
* 2 cups chicken, shredded
* 4 tablespoons olive oil
* ½ cup cilantro, chopped
* 8 cups chicken broth
* ⅓ cup salsa
* 1 teaspoon onion powder
* ½ cup scallions, chopped
* 4 ounces green chillies, chopped
* ½ teaspoon habanero, minced
* 1 cup celery root, chopped
* 1 teaspoon cumin
* 1 teaspoon garlic powder
* Black pepper and salt to taste
Directions:
1. Add all ingredients to Ninja Foodi.
2. Stir and lock lid, cook on "HIGH" pressure for 10 minutes.
3. Release pressure naturally over 10 minutes.
4. Serve and enjoy.
Nutrition Values Per Serving
Calories: 204; Fat: 14g; Carbs: 4g; Protein: 14g

Taiwanese Chicken

Prep Time: 5 minutes
Cook Time: 10 minutes
Servings: 4
Ingredients:
- 6 dried red chilis
- ¼ cup sesame oil
- 2 tablespoons ginger
- ¼ cup garlic, minced
- ¼ cup red wine vinegar
- ¼ cup coconut aminos
- Salt, to taste
- 1.2 teaspoon xanthan gum for the finish
- ¼ cup Thai basil, chopped

Directions:
1. Select "Sauté" mode on your Ninja Foodi and add ginger, chilis, garlic and Sauté for 2 minutes.
2. Add remaining ingredients.
3. Lock and secure the Ninja Foodi's lid, then cook on "HIGH" pressure for 10 minutes.
4. Quick-release pressure.
5. Serve and enjoy.

Nutrition Values Per Serving
Calories: 307; Fat: 15g; Carbs: 7g; Protein: 31g

Lemon Chicken

Prep Time: 5 minutes
Cook Time: 18 minutes
Servings: 4
Ingredients:
- 4 bone-in, skin-on chicken thighs
- Black pepper and salt to taste
- 2 tablespoons butter

- 2 teaspoons garlic, minced
- ½ cup herbed chicken stock
- ½ cup heavy whip cream
- ½ a lemon, juiced

Directions:
1. Season the four chicken thighs generously with black pepper and salt.
2. Set your Ninja Foodi to sauté mode and add oil, let it heat up.
3. Add thigh, Sauté on both sides for 6 minutes.
4. Remove thigh to a platter and keep it on the side.
5. Add garlic, cook for 2 minutes.
6. Whisk in chicken stock, heavy cream, lemon juice and gently stir.
7. Bring the mix to a simmer and reintroduce chicken.
8. Lock and secure the Ninja Foodi's lid and cook for 10 minutes on "HIGH" pressure.
9. Release pressure over 10 minutes.
10. Serve and enjoy.

Nutrition Values Per Serving
Calories: 294; Fat: 26g; Carbs: 4g; Protein: 12g

Garlic Turkey Breasts

Prep Time: 10 minutes
Cook Time: 17 minutes
Servings: 4
Ingredients:
- ½ teaspoon garlic powder
- 4 tablespoons butter
- ¼ teaspoon dried oregano
- 1-pound turkey breasts, boneless
- 1 teaspoon pepper
- ½ teaspoon salt
- ¼ teaspoon dried basil

Directions:
1. Season turkey on both sides generously with garlic, dried oregano, dried basil, black pepper and salt
2. Select "Sauté" mode on your Ninja Foodi and stir in butter; let the butter melt
3. Add turkey breasts and sauté for 2 minutes on each side
4. Lock the lid and select the "Bake/Roast" setting; bake for 15 minutes at 355 degrees F
5. Serve and enjoy once done.

Nutrition Values Per Serving
Calories: 223; Fat: 13g; Carbs: 5g; Protein: 19g

Chicken and Broccoli

Prep Time: 10 minutes
Cook Time: 20 minutes
Servings: 4
Ingredients:
- 3 pounds boneless chicken, cut into thin strips
- 1 tablespoon olive oil
- 1 yellow onion, peeled and chopped
- ½ cup beef stock
- 1-pound broccoli florets
- 2 teaspoons toasted sesame oil
- 2 tablespoons arrowroot

For Marinade
- 1 cup coconut aminos
- 1 tablespoon sesame oil
- 2 tablespoons fish sauce
- 5 garlic cloves, peeled and minced
- 3 red peppers, dried and crushed
- ½ teaspoon Chinese five-spice powder
- Toasted sesame seeds, for serving

Directions:
1. Take a suitable and mix in coconut aminos, fish sauce, 1 tablespoon sesame oil, garlic, five-spice powder, crushed red pepper and stir
2. Stir in chicken strips to the bowl and toss to coat
3. Keep it on the side for 10 minutes
4. Select "Sauté" mode on your Ninja Foodi and stir in oil, let it heat up, add onion and stir cook for 4 minutes
5. Stir in chicken and marinade, stir cook for 2 minutes
6. Add stock and stir
7. Lock the pressure lid of Ninja Foodi and cook on "HIGH" pressure for 5 minutes
8. Release pressure naturally over 10 minutes
9. Mix arrowroot with ¼ cup liquid from the pot and gently pour the mixture back to the pot and stir
10. Place a steamer basket in the Ninja Foodi's pot and stir in broccoli to the steamer rack, Lock and secure the Ninja Foodi's lid.
11. Then cook on "HIGH" pressure mode for 3 minutes more, quick-release pressure
12. Divide the dish between plates and serve with broccoli, toasted sesame seeds and enjoy.

Nutritional Values Per Serving:
Calories: 433; Fat: 27g; Carbs: 8g; Protein: 20g

Ham-Stuffed Turkey Rolls

Prep Time: 10 minutes
Cook Time: 20 minutes
Servings: 8
Ingredients:
- 4 tablespoons fresh sage leaves
- 8 ham slices
- 8 6 ounces each turkey cutlets
- Black pepper and salt to taste
- 2 tablespoons butter, melted

Directions:
1. Season turkey cutlets with black pepper and salt
2. Roll turkey cutlets and wrap each of them with ham slices tightly
3. Coat each roll with butter and gently place sage leaves evenly over each cutlet
4. Transfer them to your Ninja Foodi
5. Lock and secure the Ninja Foodi's lid and select the "Bake/Roast" mode, bake for 10 minutes a 360 degrees F
6. Open the Ninja Foodi's lid and gently give it a flip, Lock and secure the Ninja Foodi's lid again and bake for 10 minutes more
7. Once done, serve and enjoy.

Nutrition Values Per Serving
Calories: 467; Fat: 24g; Carbs: 1.7g; Protein: 56g

Shredded Chicken Salsa

Prep Time: 5 minutes
Cook Time: 20 minutes
Servings: 4
Ingredients:
- 1-pound chicken breast, boneless
- ¾ teaspoon cumin
- ½ teaspoon salt
- Pinch of oregano
- Pepper to taste
- 1 cup chunky salsa

Directions:
1. Season chicken with spices and add to Ninja Foodi.
2. Cover with salsa and lock lid, cook on "HIGH" pressure for 20 minutes.
3. Quick-release pressure.
4. Add chicken to a platter and shred the chicken.
5. Serve and enjoy.

Nutrition Values Per Serving
Calories: 125; Fat: 3g; Carbs: 2g; Protein: 22g

Hassel Back Chicken

Prep Time: 5 minutes
Cook Time: 60 minutes
Servings: 4
Ingredients:
- 4 tablespoons butter
- Black pepper and salt to taste
- 2 cups fresh mozzarella cheese, sliced
- 8 large chicken breasts
- 4 large Roma tomatoes, sliced

Directions:
1. Make few deep slits in chicken breasts, season with black pepper and salt.
2. Stuff mozzarella cheese slices and tomatoes in chicken slits.
3. Grease Ninja Foodi pot with butter and set stuffed chicken breasts.
4. Lock and secure the Ninja Foodi's lid and "Bake/Roast" for 1 hour at 365 degrees F.
5. Serve and enjoy.

Nutrition Values Per Serving
Calories: 278; Fat: 15g; Carbs: 3.8g; Protein: 15g

Chicken Bruschetta

Prep Time: 5 minutes
Cook Time: 9 minutes
Servings: 4
Ingredients:
- 2 tablespoons balsamic vinegar
- ⅓ cup olive oil
- 2 teaspoons garlic cloves, minced
- 1 teaspoon black pepper
- ½ teaspoon salt
- ½ cup sun-dried tomatoes, in olive oil
- 2 pounds chicken breasts, quartered, boneless
- 2 tablespoons fresh basil, chopped

Directions:
1. Take a suitable and whisk in vinegar, oil, garlic, pepper, salt.
2. Fold in tomatoes, basil and add breast; mix well.
3. Transfer to fridge and let it sit for 30 minutes.
4. Add everything to Ninja Foodi and lock lid, cook on "HIGH" pressure for 9 minutes
5. Quick-release pressure.
6. Serve and enjoy.

Nutrition Values Per Serving
Calories: 480; Fat: 26g; Carbs: 4g; Protein: 52g

Chicken Tortilla

Prep Time: 15 minutes
Cook Time: 15 minutes
Servings: 4
Ingredients:
- 1 tablespoon avocado oil
- 1-pound pastured boneless chicken breasts
- ½ cup orange juice
- 2 teaspoons gluten-free Worcestershire sauce
- 1 teaspoon garlic powder
- 1 teaspoon salt
- ½ teaspoon chilli powder
- ½ teaspoon paprika

Directions:
1. Select "Sauté" mode on your Ninja Foodi and stir in oil; let the oil heat up
2. Add chicken on top, take a suitable and stir in remaining ingredients mix well
3. Pour the mixture over chicken
4. Lock and secure the Ninja Foodi's lid, then cook on "HIGH" pressure for 15 minutes
5. Release pressure naturally over 10 minutes
6. Shred the chicken and serve over salad green shells such as cabbage or lettuce
7. Enjoy.

Nutrition Values Per Serving
Calories: 338; Fat: 23g; Carbs: 10g; Protein: 23g

Paprika Chicken

Prep Time: 10 minutes
Cook Time: 5 minutes
Servings: 4
Ingredients:
- 4 chicken breasts, skin on
- Black pepper and salt, to taste
- 1 tablespoon olive oil

- ½ cup sweet onion, chopped
- ½ cup heavy whip cream
- 2 teaspoons smoked paprika
- ½ cup sour cream
- 2 tablespoons fresh parsley, chopped

Directions:
1. Season the four chicken breasts with black pepper and salt
2. Select "Sauté" mode on your Ninja Foodi and add oil; let the oil heat up
3. Add chicken and sear both sides until properly browned, should take about 15 minutes
4. Remove chicken and transfer them to a plate
5. Take a suitable skillet and place it over medium heat; stir in onion.
6. Sauté for 4 minutes until tender
7. Stir in cream, paprika and bring the liquid to a simmer.
8. Return chicken to the skillet and alongside any juices
9. Transfer the whole mixture to your Ninja Foodi and lock lid, cook on "HIGH" pressure for 5 minutes
10. Release pressure naturally over 10 minutes
11. Stir in sour cream, serve and enjoy.

Nutrition Values Per Serving
Calories: 389; Fat: 30g; Carbs: 4g; Protein: 25g

Turkey Cutlets

Prep Time: 10 minutes
Cook Time: 15 minutes
Servings: 4
Ingredients:
- 1 teaspoon Greek seasoning
- 1-pound turkey cutlets
- 2 tablespoons olive oil
- 1 teaspoon turmeric powder
- ½ cup almond flour

Directions:
1. Take a suitable and stir in turmeric powder, Greek seasoning, almond flour and mix well.

2. Dredge turkey cutlets in the bowl and let it sit for 30 minutes.
3. Select "Sauté" mode on your Ninja Foodi and stir in oil, heat up.
4. Add cutlets and Sauté for 2 minutes.
5. Lock and secure the Ninja Foodi's lid and cook on Low-Medium Pressure for 20 minutes.
6. Release pressure naturally over 10 minutes.
7. Take the dish out, serve and enjoy.
Nutrition Values Per Serving
Calories: 340; Fat: 19g; Carbs: 3.7g; Protein: 36g

Ninja Foodi Lime Chicken Soup

Prep Time: 10 minutes
Cook Time: 8 hours
Servings: 5
Ingredients:
- ¼ cup fresh lime juice
- 4 garlic cloves, minced
- ½ teaspoon oregano
- 1 onion, chopped
- 4 cups chicken broth
- 2 cups boneless chicken, cubed
- 1 tomato, chopped
- ½ teaspoon red chili powder
- ¾ cup chopped mushrooms
- ½ teaspoon ground cumin
- Salt and black pepper, to taste
Directions:
1. Add everything in the pot of Ninja Foodi Deluxe XL Pressure Cooker and select "Slow Cook".
2. Close the pressure Lid and press the "Start/Stop" button.
3. Cook for about 8 hours at LOW TEMP and open the lid.
4. Take out the chicken cubes and shred them properly.
5. Stir the shredded chicken in the Slow Cook and take out.
6. Serve and enjoy!
Nutritional Values Per Serving:
Calories: 157; Fat: 5.4g; Carbs: 4.9g; Protein: 21g

Ninja Foodi Turkey & Beans Wrap

Prep Time: 10 minutes
Cook Time: 13 minutes
Servings: 3
Ingredients:
- ¼ pound lean ground turkey
- ¼ teaspoon ground cumin
- 3 butternut lettuce leaves
- ¼ teaspoon garlic powder
- 1½ tablespoons tomato sauce
- ¼ cup cooked black beans
- ¼ cup chopped onion
- 1½ tablespoons extra-virgin olive oil
- Salt and black pepper, to taste
Directions:
1. Add turkey, onion, tomato sauce, garlic powder, cumin, salt and pepper in a large bowl. Mix well.
2. Meanwhile, heat oil in a Ninja Foodi Deluxe XL Pressure Cooker and add turkey mixture in it.
3. Select "Pressure" and press the "Start/Stop" button at LO.
4. Cook for 10 minutes and stir in tomato sauce and beans.
5. Cook for about 3 minutes and take out.
6. Divide the mixture evenly on lettuce leaves and serve.
Nutritional Values Per Serving:
Calories: 356; Fat: 28.7g; Carbs: 14.8g; Protein: 12.5g

Ninja Foodi Chicken & Carrot Stew

Prep Time: 10 minutes
Cook Time: 6 hours
Servings: 3
Ingredients:
- 2 (¼ pound) boneless chicken breasts, cubed
- ½ cup chopped onions
- ½ teaspoon dried thyme
- 1 garlic clove, minced
- 1½ cup cubed carrots
- ½ cup chopped tomatoes
- 1 cup chicken broth
- Salt and black pepper, to taste

Directions:
1. Add everything in the Ninja Foodi Deluxe XL Pressure Cooker and select "Slow Cook".
2. Close the pressure Lid and press the "Start/Stop" button.
3. Cook for about 6 hours at HIGH TEMP and take out.
4. Serve and enjoy!

Nutritional Values Per Serving:
Calories: 226; Fat: 6.4g; Carbs: 16.6g; Protein: 25g

Ninja Foodi Turkey Stew

Prep Time: 20 minutes
Cook Time: 48 minutes
Servings: 6
Ingredients:
- 1½ pounds cooked turkey, chopped

- 1 cup pumpkin puree
- 2 tablespoons olive oil
- 2 cups chopped tomatoes
- 4 scallions, chopped
- 1½ cups water
- 2 teaspoons grated ginger
- Salt and black pepper, to taste

Directions:
1. Heat 1 tablespoon olive oil in a Ninja Foodi Deluxe XL Pressure Cooker and select "Sear/Sauté".
2. Press the "Start/Stop" button and sauté scallions and ginger in it for about 3 minutes. Take out and set aside.
3. Now, add remaining oil in the pot of Ninja Foodi Deluxe XL Pressure Cooker and cook turkey in it for about 3 minutes.
4. Stir in scallion mixture and cook for about 2 minutes.
5. Add in remaining ingredients and simmer for about 40 minutes.
6. Dish out and serve hot.

Nutritional Values Per Serving:
Calories: 777; Fat: 25.8g; Carbs: 6.8g; Protein: 123g

Ninja Foodi Duck Stew

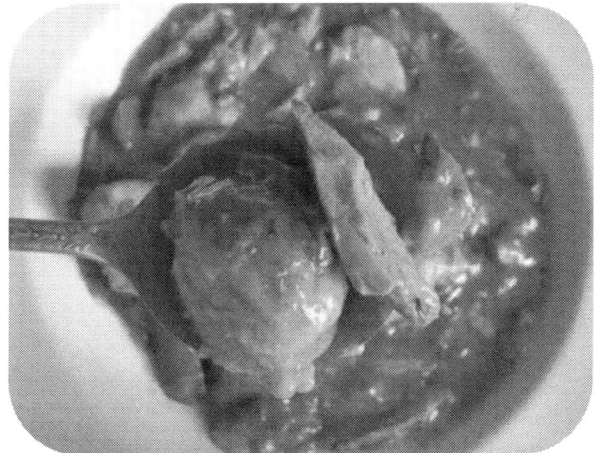

Prep Time: 10 minutes
Cook Time: 24 minutes
Servings: 3
Ingredients:
- 1 teaspoon canola oil
- ½ cup chopped carrot
- ¾ teaspoon minced garlic
- 1 cup beans, rinsed and drained
- ½ pound duck breasts, sliced
- ½ cup chopped celery
- ½ cup chopped onion
- ½ cup chicken broth
- 1 cup diced tomatoes
- Salt and pepper, to taste

Directions:
1. Heat oil inNinja Foodi Deluxe XL Pressure Cooker and select "Pressure".
2. Press the "Start/Stop" button and cook duck breasts in it for about 7 minutes.
3. Take out the duck and sauté celery, carrot, onion and garlic in the skillet for about 7 minutes.
4. Return duck in the pot of Ninja Foodi and stir in broth, beans and tomatoes.

5. Close the pressure Lid and cook for about 10 minutes.
6. Open the pressure Lid and take out.
7. Serve and enjoy!
Nutritional Values Per Serving:
Calories: 159; Fat: 5g; Carbs: 9.4g; Protein: 19.2g

Ninja Foodi Chicken & Salsa Chili

Prep Time: 10 minutes
Cook Time: 8 hours 5 minutes
Servings: 4
Ingredients:
- 1 cup salsa
- ¾ cup water
- ½ jalapeno pepper, minced
- ½ teaspoon ground cumin
- 1 teaspoon chili powder
- ½ pound boneless chicken breast
- 1 garlic clove, minced
- ½ onion, chopped
- ½ avocado, chopped
- 1½ green bell peppers, chopped
- Salt and black pepper, to taste
Directions:
1. Add chicken, garlic, cumin, salsa, and water in a Ninja Foodi Deluxe XL Pressure Cooker and select "Slow Cook".
2. Close the pressure Lid and press the "Start/Stop" button.
3. Cook for about 6 hours on HIGH TEMP and open the lid.
4. Meanwhile, heat the non-stick skillet and cook onions, jalapeno pepper and bell pepper in it for about 5 minutes.
5. Now, take the chicken out of the Ninja Foodi Deluxe XL Pressure Cooker and shred it properly.
6. Place it back in the Slow Cook along with onion mixture, chili powder, avocado, salt and pepper. Mix well.
7. Cook for about 2 hours and take out.
8. Serve and enjoy!
Nutritional Values Per Serving:
Calories: 239; Fat: 9.8g; Carbs: 20.7g; Protein: 19.9g

Ninja Foodi Cranberry Chicken

Prep Time: 20 minutes
Cook Time: 25 minutes
Servings: 6
Ingredients:
- 1½ pounds boneless chicken thighs
- 1 cup fresh cranberries
- ¼ cup chopped onion
- 2 tablespoons unsweetened applesauce
- 2 tablespoons fresh ginger, minced
- 2 tablespoons olive oil
- 1 cup chicken broth
- Salt and black pepper, to taste
Directions:
1. Heat oil in Ninja Foodi Deluxe XL Pressure Cooker and select "Pressure".
2. Press the "Start/Stop" button and add chicken, salt and pepper to it.
3. Cook for 5 minutes per side and take out the chicken. Set aside.
4. Sauté onions for about 3 minutes in the same pot and stir in broth.
5. Add cranberries after 5 minutes, followed by applesauce and cook for about 7 minutes.
6. Pour the cranberry mixture on the chicken and serve immediately.
Nutritional Values Per Serving:
Calories: 308; Fat: 22.1g; Carbs: 4.1g; Protein: 21.1g

Bagel Chicken Tenders

Prep Time: 8 Minutes
Cook Time: 15-20 Minutes
Servings: 2
Ingredients:
- 6-8 chicken tenders
- ½ cup bread crumbs/ pork rind crumbs
- 2 tablespoons bagel seasoning
- 1 egg

Directions:
1. Start by washing the chicken breasts and cut them into tenders. You can also buy chicken tenderloins.
2. Now take two bowls and add eggs to one and bread crumb mixture to the other. Add bagel seasoning to the bread crumbs and mix it well.
3. Prepare one tender at a time by first coating it with an egg then rolling it in the crumb mixture.
4. Air Crisp it in Ninja Foodi Deluxe XL Pressure Cooker by selecting Air Crisp Mode at 390° F for 20 minutes in a single layer.

Nutritional Values Per Serving:
Calories: 433; Fat: 6.3g; Carbs: 15.9g; Protein: 44.3g

Glazed Chicken & Vegetables

Prep Time: 8-10 Minutes
Cook Time: 20-25 Minutes
Servings: 2
Ingredients:
- ½ pound chicken thighs boneless
- 2 tablespoons soya sauce
- 2 teaspoons Worcestershire sauce
- 2 tablespoons brown sugar
- 4 crushed garlic cloves
- 1 pound bag of frozen mixed vegetables
- 1 tablespoon vinegar optional

- 1 tablespoon olive oil
- Black pepper to taste

Directions:
1. Start by adding soya sauce, Worcestershire sauce, brown sugar and ginger garlic in a closable container or zip lock bag. Now add chicken in it and seal to coat it well with the marinade. Let it rest in the fridge for two to three hours.
2. Oil spray the Ninja Foodi Deluxe XL Pressure Cooker Cook & Crisp Basket. Now put vegetables and chicken in the Ninja Foodi Deluxe XL Pressure Cooker Cook & Crisp Basket.
3. Give a spray of olive oil again and sprinkle just a pinch of salt if preferred.
4. Air Crisp it for about 25 minutes at 390° F.
5. When the chicken reaches 165 °F internally, serve it!

Nutritional Values Per Serving:
Calories: 397; Fat: 11.3g; Carbs: 25.5g; Protein: 27.4g

Ninja Foodi Spinach Chicken

Prep Time: 10 minutes
Cook Time: 10 minutes
Servings: 4
Ingredients:
- 1 pound chicken tenders
- 2 tablespoons sour cream
- 2 garlic cloves, minced
- 1¼ cups chopped spinach
- 2 tablespoons olive oil
- ¼ cup parmesan cheese, shredded
- Salt and black pepper, to taste

Directions:
1. Heat half of the oliveoil in a Ninja Foodi Deluxe XL Pressure Cooker and add chicken, salt and pepper in it.
2. Select "Pressure" and press the "Start/Stop" button.
3. Cook for about 2-minutes per side at Hi and take out the chicken. Set aside.
4. Add remaining oil in the pot of Ninja Foodi and sauté garlic in it for about 1 minute.

5. Add spinach, cream, and cheese in the skillet and cook for about 2 minutes.
6. Place chicken in the Ninja Foodi Deluxe XL Pressure Cooker's pot and simmer for about 5 minutes.
7. Take out and serve hot.
Serving Suggestions: Serve with onion rings on the top.
Variation Tip: Mozzarella cheese can also be used.
Nutritional Values Per Serving:
Calories: 301; Fat: 17.1g; Carbs: 1.6g; Protein: 34.3g

Ninja Foodi Ground Turkey

Prep Time: 10 minutes
Cook Time: 8 minutes
Servings: 6
Ingredients:
- 1 tablespoon sesame oil
- 2 pounds lean ground turkey
- 1 onion, chopped
- ½ cup soy sauce
- ½ cup chicken broth
- 2 teaspoons ground ginger
- 3 garlic cloves, minced
- Salt and black pepper, to taste
Directions:
1. Add oil in a Ninja Foodi Deluxe XL Pressure Cooker and press the "Sear" button.
2. Press the "Start/Stop" button and sauté onion in it for about 3 minutes.
3. Add in garlic and turkey and mash the mixture with a fork.
4. Stir in chicken broth, soy sauce, salt and pepper and cook for about 5 minutes.
5. Take out and serve hot.
Nutritional Values Per Serving:
Calories: 262; Fat: 13.3g; Carbs: 4.3g; Protein: 31.8g

Jalapeno Chicken Nachos

Prep Time: 8-9 Minutes
Cook Time: 8-9 Minutes
Servings: 2
Ingredients:
- 1 cup tortillas chips
- 1 pound minced chicken
- ¼ cup BBQ sauce
- Salt to taste
- ½ cup chicken broth
- ½ cup cheddar cheese
- ½ corn
- 2 tablespoons chopped olives
- ½ cup sliced jalapeno
- 1 coarsely cut onion
- Coriander to garnish
Directions:
1. Add the chicken, broth, and salt to a Ninja Foodi Deluxe XL Pressure Cooker. For 8 minutes, Pressure Cook it on High and releases the pressure when finished quickly.
2. Stir in BBQ sauce after draining the liquid.
3. At 390° F, preheat the Ninja Foodi Deluxe XL Pressure Cooker at Air Crisp Mode. Take Ninja Foodi Deluxe XL Pressure Cooker Cook & Crisp Basket and align the parchment paper.
4. Place tortilla chips on the base. Now give a layer of shredder BBQ chicken and corn and top it off with cheddar cheese evenly.
5. For about 5 to 10 minutes place it in the Ninja Foodi Deluxe XL Pressure Cooker and wait until cheese is melted. Then add olives, onions, jalapenos slice to the desired amount. Follow it by adding fresh coriander!
Nutritional Values Per Serving:
Calories: 550; Fat: 25.5g; Carbs: 29.7g; Protein: 55g

Ninja Foodi Basil Pesto Chicken

Prep Time: 20 minutes
Cook Time: 30 minutes
Servings: 4
Ingredients:
- 4 boneless chicken breasts
- 3 garlic cloves, minced
- ½ cup pine nuts
- 2 cups fresh basil leaves
- ½ teaspoon red pepper flakes
- ½ cup olive oil
- Salt and black pepper, to taste

Directions:
1. Add olive oil, garlic, pine nuts, basil and red pepper flakes in a food processor. Pulse well.
2. Now, arrange chicken breasts in the pot of Ninja Foodi Deluxe XL Pressure Cooker and pour basil mixture on it.
3. Select "Bake" and close the Crisping Lid.
4. Press the "Start/Stop" button and bake for about 30 minutes at 375 degrees F.
5. Open the Crisping Lid and take out.
6. Serve and enjoy!

Nutritional Values Per Serving:
Calories: 603; Fat: 47.3g; Carbs: 3.4g; Protein: 43.4g

Ninja Foodi Duck Fajita Platter

Prep Time: 10 minutes
Cook Time: 25 minutes
Servings: 4
Ingredients:
- 1 pound duck breasts, sliced
- ½ green bell pepper, chopped
- ½ red bell pepper, chopped
- 1 onion, sliced
- 2 tablespoons olive oil
- 1 teaspoon garlic powder
- 1 teaspoon ground cumin
- 2 teaspoons chili powder
- ½ teaspoon dried oregano
- Salt, to taste

Directions:
1. Add duck breasts, green bell pepper, red bell pepper and garlic powder in a large bowl. Mix well.
2. Add in chili powder, cumin, onion, olive oil, oregano and salt in the bowl. Toss to coat well.
3. Place the duck breasts in the pot of Ninja Foodi Deluxe XL Pressure Cooker and select "Bake".
4. Close the Crisping Lid and press the "Start/Stop" button.
5. Bake for about 25 minutes at 400 degrees F and open the lid.
6. Take out and serve hot.

Nutritional Values Per Serving:
Calories: 237; Fat: 12g; Carbs: 6.7g; Protein: 26.1g

Ninja Foodi Barbeque Chicken Drumsticks

Prep Time: 10 minutes
Cook Time: 8 hours
Servings: 4
Ingredients:
- 12 chicken drumsticks
- 2 tablespoons red chili powder
- 1 teaspoon onion powder
- 1 teaspoon garlic powder
- 4 tablespoons honey
- 2 tablespoons apple cider vinegar
- 1 cup barbeque sauce
- 1 tablespoon paprika
- ½ tablespoon ground cumin
- Salt and black pepper, to taste

Directions:
1. Add everything except honey in a Ninja Foodi Deluxe XL Pressure Cooker and select "Slow Cook".
2. Close the pressure Lid and press the "Start/Stop" button.

3. Cook for about 8 hours at HIGH TEMP and open the lid.
4. Take out the drumsticks and pour honey on them.
5. Serve and enjoy!
Nutritional Values Per Serving:
Calories: 416; Fat: 9.1g; Carbs: 44.4g; Protein: 39g

Chicken Pasta with Dried Tomatoes

Prep Time: 6 Minutes
Cook Time: 15-20 Minutes
Servings: 4
Ingredients:
- 1 pound chicken thigh
- 500 grams penne pasta
- 1 tablespoon butter
- 1 diced onion
- 1 teaspoon chopped garlic
- ½ cup dried tomatoes
- 1 tablespoon tomato paste
- 1 tablespoon Italian Seasoning
- Salt to taste
- 2 tablespoons parmesan cheese
- ¼ cup heavy cream
- 2 tablespoons cream cheese
- ¼ cup chicken broth
- 1 tablespoon extra-virgin olive oil

Directions:
1. When water comes to a boil, boil the pasta, don't forget to add salt to the pasta water. You can simply boil according to the given instructions on the package.
2. On the other hand, cut the chicken into strips. Preheat the Ninja Foodi Deluxe XL Pressure Cooker on Low Pressure setting.
3. Add half the oil and butter into a large skillet. Let it melt.
4. Add chicken and let it cook for three to 4 minutes.
5. Flip and cook it for another 2 minutes. Now take out the chicken from the pan.
6. Keep Ninja Foodi Deluxe XL Pressure Cooker to Low Pressure Mode. Now add the remaining olive oil and onion into the pan and cook the onions until they become translucent.

7. Add garlic and cook it for about 1 minute. Then add tomato paste and dried tomatoes.
8. Season it with salt and Italian seasoning and mix it well.
9. Now add chicken broth and let it simmer for 2 minutes.
10. Add parmesan cheese, cream cheese, and stir it well. After the cheese melts, add chicken into it, then pour it over the pasta and serve it hot!
Nutritional Values Per Serving:
Calories: 470; Fat: 14.5g; Carbs: 59g; Protein: 24.8g

Ninja Foodi Duck Broth

Prep Time: 10 minutes
Cook Time: 8 hours
Servings: 16
Ingredients:
- 1 roasted duck, meat removed
- 2 teaspoons apple cider vinegar
- 8 cups water
- 2 carrots, chopped
- 2 onions, chopped
- Salt, to taste

Directions:
1. Add duck bones in a Ninja Foodi Deluxe XL Pressure Cooker and sprinkle some salt on it.
2. Add in remaining ingredients and select "Slow Cook".
3. Cover the pressure Lid and press the "Start/Stop" button.
4. Cook for 8 hours at low TEMP and open the lid.
5. Take out the broth and serve.
Nutritional Values Per Serving:
Calories: 21; Fat: 0.7g; Carbs: 2g; Protein: 1.8g

Parmesan Chicken

Prep Time: 8-10 Minutes
Cook Time: 7 Minutes
Servings: 4

Ingredients:
- 1 medium-sized chicken breast
- ½ cup chicken broth
- 1 teaspoon garlic powder
- 1 teaspoon salt
- ⅛ teaspoon pepper

Italian seasoning:
- 1 teaspoon chili flakes
- ½ cup cream
- 1 tablespoon cornstarch
- ½ cup grated parmesan cheese
- Water as required to mix the cornstarch
- 1 tablespoon basil leaves paste

Directions:
1. Take a board and lay your chicken breast on it, pat dry it, and cut into halves. Take a half breast and cut it cross-sectionally to make two out of every half. Hammer the bread to flatten it with a pounder. A full breast yields four hammered fillets. Season it with salt, pepper, and garlic powder generously.
2. Leave it to marinate for 30 minutes in the bottom of the Ninja Foodi Deluxe XL Pressure Cooker Bowl. Turn on the Air Crisp Mode at 390° F and cook the fillet from both sides.
3. Now while the chicken is cooking, prepare seasoning. Start to melt the butter, add salt and pepper, lemon juice, crushed garlic, and some parmesan cheese and add other seasonings according to your taste.
4. Once cooked, take out the fillets. Pour the chicken broth along with the prepared sauce in the same Ninja Foodi Deluxe XL Pressure Cooker Bowl and cover it with a Ninja Foodi Deluxe XL Pressure Cooker Pressure Lid and then into the seal position, place the toggle switch.
5. Pressure Cook it for 5 minutes on High Pressure and do a pressure quick release. Remove it again.
6. Now at 390° F in Air Crisp Mode for 10 minutes. Let the chicken baste with your garlic parmesan sauce to infuse the flavors!

Nutritional Values Per Serving:
Calories: 338; Fat: 22.6g; Carbs: 25.9g; Protein: 7.1g

Chicken Marsala Pasta

Prep Time: 6-7 Minutes
Cook Time: 15-20 Minutes
Servings: 6

Ingredients:
- 2 pounds chicken boneless (2 inches cuts)
- 340 grams Bowties pasta
- 4 tablespoons all-purpose flour
- Salt and pepper to taste
- 1 tablespoon olive oil
- 1 tablespoon garlic powder
- 2 teaspoon butter
- 226 grams mushrooms
- ¾ cup Marsala wine
- 1 cup heavy cream
- 1 cup chicken broth

Directions:
1. Take a container and combine flour, salt pepper, and garlic in it and mix well. Coat the chicken with this flour mixture.
2. Preheat the Ninja Foodi Deluxe XL Pressure Cooker on Steam Mode. Add olive oil once Ninja Foodi Deluxe XL Pressure Cooker is hot.
3. Now add the coated chicken and let the chicken Sauté, until it's light brown.
4. Add the butter by moving the chicken over to a side and mushrooms to the other half of the pot. Stir the mushrooms a little bit to combine them with butter, then add garlic and stir it well.
5. Pour Marsala wine and stir it. Scrap the pan to get off any brown bits from the bottom of the pot.
6. Then add pasta but don't stir it. Instead, press it a little down into the liquid. Now add chicken broth and Pressure Cook on High Pressure for 3 minutes and close the lid.
7. Open the lid and add cream and place the lid back onto the Ninja Foodi Deluxe XL Pressure Cooker but don't turn it on. For 5 minutes let it set to allow the sauce to thicken up, remove the lid, stir it a little and enjoy!

Nutritional Values Per Serving:
Calories: 590; Fat: 22.7g; Carbs: 46.1g; Protein: 35.5g

Chicken Vegetable Soup

Prep Time: 8 Minutes
Cook Time: 3 Minutes
Servings: 2
Ingredients:
- ½ pound boneless chicken thigh (bite-size cuts)
- 1 diced carrot
- 1 chopped onion
- 1 teaspoon garlic
- ½ cup boiled pasta
- 4 cups broth
- 1 teaspoon salt
- ¾ teaspoon white pepper
- 1 tablespoon soy sauce
- 1 teaspoon oregano
- ¼ teaspoon red chili powder
- 2 bay leaves
- ¼ cup corn flour slurry

Directions:
1. In the Ninja Foodi Deluxe XL Pressure Cooker Pot, add carrots, onion, garlic, bay leaves then add the bite-size chicken cuts.
2. Now season it with salt, white pepper, oregano, red chili powder, and soy sauce and pour in the chicken broth.
3. Give it a good stir. Now set the valve to Seal and install the Ninja Foodi Deluxe XL Pressure Cooker Pressure Lid.
4. Select the Pressure function and set it to High. Press the start button and set the timer for 2 minutes. Usually, the pressure takes about 10 minutes to start building up.
5. Once it beeps, allow the pressure to naturally release for about 10 minutes after the completion of pressure cooking. And quickly release any remaining pressure by setting the valve to venting.
6. Now take out the bay leaves and discard them, select the option Steam and, let the soup simmer for another 3 to 5 minutes.
7. Pour in slurry and stir it well. Give it a boil until it's completely thickened. Serve instantly!
Nutritional Values Per Serving:
Calories: 389; Fat: 10.3g; Carbs: 16g; Protein: 31.9g

Pulled Barbecue Chicken

Prep Time: 6 Minutes
Cook Time: 9-10 Minutes
Servings: 2
Ingredients:
- 1 pound chicken breast
- 1 cup broth
- 4 tablespoons BBQ sauce
- ½ teaspoon liquid smoke
- Salt and pepper to taste

Directions:
1. Now inside the Ninja Foodi Deluxe XL Pressure Cooker Pot, place the chicken breast and sprinkle a little salt and pepper on both sides.
2. Then, add in broth over the chicken breasts, and install the Pressure Lid and switch the vent knob to Seal properly. Select the High option of the Ninja Foodi Deluxe XL Pressure Cooker Pressure setting function for about 8 minutes and then press the stop button.
3. Quickly release the pressure on food after the timer goes off and then remove the lid carefully.
4. Make sure that broth is reduced to half. Then add the barbecue sauce and let it cook on Air Crisp Mode at 390° F for 5 to 10 minutes. Make sure to shred it a bit with a spatula or fork.
5. Add the liquid smoke and it's good to go!
Nutritional Values Per Serving:
Calories: 311; Fat: 4g; Carbs: 6.1g; Protein: 34.7g

Chicken Potato Stew

Prep Time: 10-15 Minutes
Cook Time: 8-10 Minutes
Servings: 4-6
Ingredients:
- 2 pounds boneless chicken thighs
- 4 potatoes (coarsely sliced)
- Salt and pepper to taste
- 2-3 peppercorns
- 2 tablespoons olive oil
- 1 tablespoon thyme
- ½ tablespoon onion powder
- 1 teaspoon paprika powder
- 1 tablespoon chopped garlic
- 4 tablespoons chopped onion
- ½ cup chicken broth

Directions:
1. Start by combining thyme paprika, salt and pepper, and onion powder. Now take chicken thighs and season both sides with this spice mix.
2. Put olive oil in a Ninja Foodi Deluxe XL Pressure Cooker Pot and select the Air Crisp Mode at 390° F.
3. Air Crisp chicken thigh cuts in Ninja Foodi Deluxe XL Pressure Cooker Pot. Cook each side for about 2 to 3 minutes. Now take out the chicken and set it aside.
4. Add onions and chopped garlic to the Ninja Foodi Deluxe XL Pressure Cooker Pot. Add the peppercorns and steam for about 2 minutes. Now add chicken broth to it and continue to cook.
5. Now add potatoes and chicken, select Pressure, and cook on High Pressure Ninja Foodi Deluxe XL Pressure Cooker setting for 8 minutes. Then allow it to naturally release for about four to 5 minutes then quick release!
Nutritional Values Per Serving:
Calories: 385; Fat: 16.3g; Carbs: 7.7g; Protein: 35.5g

Chicken Saltimbocca

Prep Time: 6 Minutes
Cook Time: 10-15 Minutes
Servings: 2
Ingredients:
- 2 chicken cutlets
- 2 tablespoons all-purpose flour
- 2-3 slices of dry ham/prosciutto
- 2-3 sage leaves large
- Pepper as required
- 1 tablespoon extra-virgin olive oil
- 1 tablespoon butter

Directions:
1. Put the flour in a shallow dish. Fold each chicken cutlet in the flour and coat evenly. Make sure to shake off the excess flour. Now arrange the cutlets on a plate, place a slice of prosciutto on it and add a sage leaf over it and then secure it with a toothpick.
2. Take extra-virgin olive oil in Steam Mode in a Ninja Foodi Deluxe XL Pressure Cooker.
3. Align chicken cutlets in a single layer in the pot and make sure the prosciutto side is down.
4. Sear the chicken from one side until it's golden and crispy then flip the cutlets and season it with pepper. Until the chicken is cooked, continue to sear.
5. Take out the chicken from the pan, arrange it on the platter and cover it with foil to keep it warm. Now add the butter to the pan and cook it until it starts foaming.
6. Pour wine to it and gently stir it to combine. Now pour the sauce onto the chicken cutlets and it's ready to be served immediately!
Nutritional Values Per Serving:
Calories: 319; Fat: 18.1g; Carbs: 12g; Protein: 28g

Maroncaon Chicken

Prep Time: 10 Minutes
Cook Time: 28 Minutes
Servings: 4
Ingredients:
- 1 pound chicken
- 1 can chickpeas
- 1 teaspoon paprika powder
- ½ teaspoon turmeric
- Salt and pepper to taste
- 2 tablespoons olive oil (used in portions)
- 1 teaspoon garlic paste
- 2 tablespoons onion paste
- 1 tablespoon ginger paste
- ½ cup dried apricot
- 1 cup chicken broth

Directions:
1. Combine turmeric, cumin, salt, and pepper in a small bowl. Now coat the chicken with these spices evenly and on all sides. Set aside.
2. Add chicken and olive oil in the Multi-purpose pan and cook it for 3 minutes at High pressure setting. Flip chicken to the other side and cook for another 3 minutes until lightly browned. Remove it from the Ninja Foodi Deluxe XL Pressure Cooker and put it aside.
3. Then add one tablespoon olive oil in the same Ninja Foodi Deluxe XL Pressure Cooker. And Sauté garlic, ginger, and onion for 2 minutes and keep stirring slowly.
4. Now add chickpeas, broth, chicken, and dried apricot. Close the lid of the Ninja Foodi Deluxe XL Pressure Cooker Pot and Seal the valve. Now cook at Ninja Foodi Deluxe XL Pressure Cooker High Pressure setting for 10 minutes. Ninja Foodi Deluxe XL Pressure Cooker will create pressure. After that release the pressure and take it out.

Nutritional Values Per Serving:
Calories: 304; Fat: 10.2g; Carbs: 26.6g; Protein: 27.8g

Mexican Chicken with Rice

Prep Time: 12-15 Minutes
Cook Time: 10 Minutes
Servings: 4
Ingredients:
- 1 pound chicken breasts boneless
- 1 cup uncooked rice
- Salt to taste
- ½ teaspoon chili flakes
- 2-3 minced garlic cloves
- 1 can black beans
- ¼ cup corn
- ½ cup chicken broth
- ¼ cup cheese
- 2 diced onion
- 1 tablespoon olive oil

Directions:
1. Turn on the Ninja Foodi Deluxe XL Pressure Cooker Mode at 390° F and then add olive oil.
2. Add onions, garlic powder, chicken cubes, chili flakes, and salt once oil is hot and cook it until the protein changes its color.
3. Dump in black beans and corn alongside chicken broth after turning off the Ninja Foodi Deluxe XL Pressure Cooker Pot. Stir well together.
4. Now on top of that, sprinkle uncooked rice and by using the back of the spoon, submerge it into the liquid but don't stir it.
5. Put the lid back on and close the steam valve for nine minutes. After that let it naturally release pressure.
6. Lift the lid, fluff up the rice mixture and add cheese on top, mix it gently and set the top back again for about 3 minutes for the cheese to melt!

Nutritional Values Per Serving:
Calories: 31.5; Fat: 14.4g; Carbs: 31.5g; Protein: 61g

Honey Garlic Chicken

Prep Time: 12 Minutes
Cook Time: 15-20 Minutes
Servings: 2
Ingredients:
- 1 pound bone-in chicken pieces
- 1 tablespoon sesame oil
- ¼ cup broth
- 2 tablespoons honey
- 2 tablespoons soya sauce
- ½ tablespoon apple cider vinegar
- 1 teaspoon chopped garlic
- Salt to taste
- Pepper to taste
- 1 tablespoon cornstarch
- ¼ cup water

Directions:
1. Combine honey, broth, soy sauce, and apple cider vinegar in a bowl and whisk it well.
2. Meanwhile, add chicken and garlic to the Ninja Foodi Deluxe XL Pressure Cooker Pot. Steam for 2 to 3 minutes and pour the chicken broth mixture.
3. Now Seal the pressure lid and secure the valve and set Ninja Foodi Deluxe XL Pressure Cooker Pressure Cook at High and cook for 8 minutes.
4. Whisk cornstarch water together in a small bowl and prepare a slurry while the chicken is being cooked.
5. After 8 minutes, allow natural release of pressure for about ten min and then turn it to quick release manually. Carefully open the lid and take it out then set Ninja Foodi Deluxe XL Pressure Cooker Pressure Cook Low setting and mix the slurry into the sauce and keep stirring. Allow it to thicken for about 2 to 3 minutes. Coat all the chicken well.
6. Garnish it with some fresh green onion and a few sesame seeds!

Nutritional Values Per Serving:
Calories: 219; Fat: 13.4g; Carbs: 11.7g; Protein: 22.8g

Broccoli Chicken Shred

Prep Time: 7 Minutes
Cook Time: 20 Minutes
Servings: 2
Ingredients:
- ½ pound chicken fillets
- 4 tablespoons ranch seasoning
- ¼ cup cheese
- 2 bacon strips
- ¼ cup cream cheese
- 1 cup grated broccoli

Directions:
1. Start by turning Ninja Foodi Deluxe XL Pressure Cooker on Sauté High Mode. Now add the bacon slices to Ninja Foodi Deluxe XL Pressure Cooker, place the bacon on a paper towel to pat dry, and drain the grease out of the pan.
2. Take half of the ranch seasoning and spread it on the chicken generously. Sear the chicken in the Ninja Foodi Deluxe XL Pressure Cooker Pot until golden brown.
3. Now flip the chicken and add bacon and the remaining ranch spice into the pan, now add chicken broth, and now cook on High Pressure Ninja Foodi Deluxe XL Pressure Cooker setting for 20 minutes.
4. Now release the pressure and open the lid. And then shred the chicken.
5. Turn on the Sauté setting in Ninja Foodi Deluxe XL Pressure Cooker, mix in the cream and cheddar cheese once the broth starts to boil. Once the cheese is melted, mix in broccoli and shredded chicken, then simmer it for three to 4 minutes!

Nutritional Values Per Serving:
Calories: 520; Fat: 23.8g; Carbs: 5.9g; Protein: 36.9g

Ninja Foodi Chicken Broth

Prep Time: 10 minutes
Cook Time: 3 hours
Servings: 3
Ingredients:
- 1½ pounds chicken
- 1 bay leaf
- 1 celery stalk, chopped
- ¼ teaspoon dried rosemary, crushed
- 1 carrot, chopped
- ¼ teaspoon dried thyme
- 4 peppercorns
- 1 onion, quartered
- 4 cups cold water

Directions:
1. Add everything in a Ninja Foodi Deluxe XL Pressure Cooker and select "Slow Cook".
2. Close the pressure Lid and press the "Start/Stop" button at Hi.
3. Simmer for about 3 hours and open the lid.
4. Take out and set aside.
5. Strain the broth and serve hot.

Nutritional Values Per Serving:
Calories: 1281; Fat: 25.3g; Carbs: 5.9g; Protein: 241.6g

Pineapple Chicken

Prep Time: 2 hours
Cook Time: 9-10 Minutes
Servings: 2
Ingredients:
- 2 chicken steaks
- 1 tablespoons onion paste
- 4 tablespoons teriyaki sauce
- 2 tablespoons pineapple juice
- 1 tablespoon ginger garlic paste
- Salt and pepper to taste
- Coriander and cilantro to garnish

Directions:
1. Take a large bowl and combine all ingredients. Refrigerate it overnight.
2. Now remove it from the refrigerator and place the leftover marination in the bowl.
3. Place the chicken steak directly in the Ninja Foodi Deluxe XL Pressure Cooker Pot.
4. Now over Ninja Foodi Deluxe XL Pressure Cooker High Pressure Cook setting, cook the chicken for 3 minutes and use the reserved marinade to baste when meat is cooked halfway.
5. Now turn over the meat for five to seven minutes to cook and do this until the meat is cooked properly.
6. Turn off and plate the chicken, and garnish it with fresh coriander or cilantro!

Nutritional Values Per Serving:
Calories: 391; Fat: 18.1g; Carbs: 36.4g; Protein: 20.4g

Beef, Pork and Lamb Recipes

Mongolian Beef

Prep Time: 30 minutes
Cook Time: 11 minutes
Servings: 2
Ingredients:
- 1 lb. flank steak, sliced
- ¼ cup corn starch

Sauce:
- 2 teaspoon vegetable oil
- ½ teaspoon ginger, minced
- 1 tablespoon garlic, minced
- ½ cup soy sauce
- ½ cup water
- ¾ cup brown erythritol

Directions:
1. Coat the beef with corn starch. Put in the Ninja Foodi basket.
2. Seal the crisping lid. Set it to air crisp.
3. Cook at 390 degrees F for about 10 minutes per side.
4. Remove and set aside. Set the pot to sauté. Stir in the vegetable oil.
5. Sauté the ginger and garlic for 1 minute. Stir in the soy sauce, water and brown erythritol.
6. Pour the prepared sauce on top of the beef.

Nutritional Values Per Serving:
Calories: 399; Fat: 11.7g; Carbs: 39g; Protein: 33.7g

Pork Chops with Gravy

Prep Time: 40 minutes
Cook Time: 10 minutes
Servings: 5
Ingredients:
- 5 pork chops
- 1 tablespoon olive oil
- 1 teaspoon salt
- ½ teaspoon pepper
- ½ teaspoon garlic powder
- 2 cups beef broth
- 1 packet ranch dressing mix
- 10-½ oz. cream of chicken soup
- 1 packet brown gravy mix
- 2 tablespoons corn starch
- 2 tablespoons water

Directions:
1. Season both sides of the pat dried pork chops with salt, pepper and garlic powder.
2. Pour the olive oil into the Ninja Foodi. Set it to sauté.
3. Brown the pork chops on both sides. Remove and set aside.
4. Pour the beef broth to deglaze the pot.
5. Stir in the rest of the ingredients except the corn starch. Seal the pot.
6. Set it to pressure. Cook at "HIGH" pressure for 8 minutes. Release the pressure naturally.
7. Remove the pork chops. Turn the pot to sauté. Stir in the corn starch.
8. Simmer to thicken. Pour the gravy over the pork chops.

Nutritional Values Per Serving:
Calories: 357; Fat: 26.8g; Carbs: 6g; Protein: 21.6g

Garlicky Pork Chops

Prep Time: 1 hour and 30 minutes
Cook Time: 10 minutes
Servings: 2
Ingredients:
- 1 tablespoon coconut butter
- 1 tablespoon coconut oil
- 2 teaspoons cloves garlic, grated
- 2 teaspoons parsley, chopped
- Black pepper and salt to taste
- 4 pork chops, sliced into strips

Directions:
1. Combine all the ingredients except the pork strips. Mix well.
2. Marinate the pork in the mixture for 1 hour. Put the pork on the Ninja Foodi basket.
3. Set it inside the pot. Seal with the crisping lid. Choose air crisp function.
4. Cook at 400 degrees F for 10 minutes.
Nutritional Values Per Serving:
Calories: 388; Fat: 23.3g; Carbs: 0.5g; Protein: 18.1g

Beef Stew with Carrot

Prep Time: 50 minutes
Cook Time: 40 minutes
Servings: 4
Ingredients:
- 1 tablespoon olive oil

- 1½ lb. beef stew meat, sliced into cubes
- 1 teaspoon Italian seasoning
- Black pepper and salt to taste
- 2 tablespoons Worcestershire sauce
- 1 onion, chopped
- 3 cloves garlic, minced
- 1 lb. cauliflower, chopped
- 16 oz. baby carrots, sliced into cubes
- 10 oz. tomato sauce
- 2-½ cups beef broth
- 2 tablespoons corn starch
- 2 tablespoons water

Directions:
1. Set the Ninja Foodi to sauté. Pour in the oil. Add the beef.
2. Season with Italian seasoning, black pepper and salt. Cook until brown.
3. Stir in the rest of the ingredients. Cover the pot.
4. Set it to pressure. Cook at "HIGH" pressure for 35 minutes.
5. Release the pressure naturally. Mix cornstarch with water in a suitable bowl and pour into the pot.
6. Switch to sauté and simmer for 3 minutes or until the sauce has thickened.
Nutritional Values Per Serving:
Calories: 508; Fat: 15.6g; Carbs: 3.7g; Protein: 57.9g

Crusted Pork Chops

Prep Time: 30 minutes
Cook Time: 12 minutes
Servings: 6
Ingredients:
- Cooking spray
- 6 pork chops
- Black pepper and salt to taste
- ½ cup bread crumbs
- 2 tablespoons Parmesan cheese, grated
- ¼ cup cornflakes, crushed
- 1-¼ teaspoon sweet paprika
- ½ teaspoon onion powder
- ½ teaspoon garlic powder
- ¼ teaspoon chilli powder
- 1 egg, beaten

Directions:
1. Season the pork chops liberally with black pepper and salt.
2. In a suitable, mix the rest of the ingredients except the egg.

3. Beat the egg in a suitable. Dip the pork chops in the egg.
4. Coat the pork with the breading. Place the pork on the Ninja Foodi basket.
5. Set it to air crisp and close the crisping lid.
6. Cook at 400 degrees F for about 12 minutes, flipping halfway through.

Nutritional Values Per Serving:
Calories: 310; Fat: 21.3g; Carbs: 8.2g; rotein: 20.3g

Butter Pork Chops

Prep Time: 10 minutes
Cook Time: 10 minutes
Servings: 4

Ingredients:
- 4 pork chops
- Black pepper and salt, to taste
- 2 tablespoons butter
- 2 teaspoons garlic, minced
- ½ cup herbed chicken stock
- ½ cup heavy whip cream
- ½ a lemon, juiced

Directions:
1. Season the four pork chops with black pepper and salt.
2. Select "Sauté" mode on Ninja Foodi and add oil to heat up
3. Add pork chops and sauté both sides until the golden, total for 6 minutes
4. Remove thighs to a platter and keep it on the side
5. Add garlic and cook for 2 minutes
6. Whisk in chicken stock, heavy cream, lemon juice and bring the sauce to simmer and reintroduce the pork chops.
7. Lock and secure the Ninja Foodi's lid and cook for 10 minutes on "HIGH" pressure
8. Release pressure naturally over 10 minutes
9. Serve warm and enjoy.

Nutrition Values Per Serving
Calories: 294; Fat: 26g; Carbs: 4g; Protein: 12g

Pork Meatballs

Prep Time: 30 minutes
Cook Time: 6 minutes
Servings: 4

Ingredients:
- 1-pound ground pork
- ¼ cup heavy whip cream
- 2 teaspoons salt
- ½ teaspoon ground caraway seeds
- 1 and ½ teaspoons black pepper
- ¼ teaspoon ground allspice
- 2 zucchinis, shredded
- ½ cup almond milk
- 2 tablespoons unsalted butter

Directions:
1. Transfer meat to a suitable and add cream, 1 teaspoon salt, caraway, ½ teaspoon pepper, allspice and mix it well
2. Let the mixture chill for 30 minutes
3. Once the mixture is ready, use your hands to scoop the mixture into meatballs
4. Add half of your balls to the Ninja Foodi pot and cover with half of the cabbage
5. Add remaining balls and cover with rest of the cabbage
6. Add milk, pats of butter, season with black pepper and salt
7. Lock and secure the Ninja Foodi's lid, then cook on "HIGH" pressure for 4 minutes
8. Quick-release pressure
9. UnLock and secure the Ninja Foodi's lid and serve
10. Enjoy.

Nutrition Values Per Serving
Calories: 294; Fat: 26g; Carbs: 4g; Protein: 12g

Beef Jerky

Prep Time: 10 minutes
Cook Time: 20 minutes
Servings: 4
Ingredients:
* ½-pound beef, sliced into ⅛-inch-thick strips
* ½ cup of soy sauce
* 2 tablespoons Worcestershire sauce
* 2 teaspoons black pepper
* 1 teaspoon onion powder
* ½ teaspoon garlic powder
* 1 teaspoon salt

Directions:
1. Add listed ingredient to a large-sized Ziploc bag, seal it shut.
2. Shake well, seal and leave it in the fridge overnight.
3. Lay strips on dehydrator trays, making sure not to overlap them.
4. Lock Crisping Lid and set its cooking temperature to 135 degrees F, cook for 7 hours.
Nutritional Values Per Serving:
Calories: 62; Fat: 7g; Carbs: 2g; Protein: 9g

Maple Glazed Pork Chops

Prep Time: 45 minutes
Cook Time: 12 minutes
Servings: 4
Ingredients:
* 2 tablespoons choc zero maple syrup
* 4 tablespoons mustard
* 2 tablespoons garlic, minced
* Black pepper and salt to taste
* 4 pork chops
* Cooking spray

Directions:
1. Mix the choc zero maple syrup, mustard, garlic, black pepper and salt in a suitable.

2. Marinate the choc zero maple syruped pork chops in the mixture for 20 minutes.
3. Place the pork chops on the Ninja Foodi basket.
4. Put the basket inside the pot. Seal with the crisping lid.
5. Set it to air crisp. Cook at 350 degrees F for about 12 minutes, flipping halfway through.
Nutritional Values Per Serving:
Calories: 348; Fat: 23.3g; Carbs: 14g; Protein: 21.1g

Hawaiian Pork Meal

Prep Time: 45 minutes
Cook Time: 15 minutes
Servings: 8
Ingredients:
* 20 oz. pineapple chunks, undrained
* 2 tablespoons water
* 1 tablespoon corn starch
* 2 tablespoons soy sauce
* 3 tablespoons choc zero maple syrup
* 1 tablespoon ginger, grated
* 2 tablespoons brown erythritol
* 3 cloves garlic, minced
* 2 tablespoons olive oil
* 1 onion, chopped
* 2 lb. pork stew meat
* Black pepper and salt to taste
* 1 teaspoon oregano

Directions:
1. Mix the pineapple juice, soy sauce, choc zero maple syrup, ginger, erythritol and garlic in a suitable. Set aside. Set the Ninja Foodi to sauté. Stir in half of the oil. Saute onion for 1 minute.
2. Add the remaining oil. Brown the pork on both sides.
3. Stir in the pineapple chunks, oregano and pineapple juice mixture.
4. Cover the pot. Set it to pressure. Cook at "HIGH" pressure for 10 minutes.
5. Release the pressure naturally.
6. Serve warm.
Nutritional Values Per Serving:
Calories: 384; Fat: 27g; Carbs: 13g; Protein: 20g

Taco Meatballs

Prep Time: 8 minutes
Cook Time: 11 minutes
Servings: 4

Ingredients:
- 2 cups ground beef
- 1 egg, beaten
- 1 teaspoon taco seasoning
- 1 tablespoon sugar-free marinara sauce
- 1 teaspoon garlic, minced
- ½ teaspoon salt

Directions:
1. Take a suitable mixing bowl and place all the ingredients into the bowl.
2. Stir in all the ingredients into the bowl. Mix together all the ingredients by using a spoon or fingertips. Then make the small size meatballs and put them in a layer in the air fryer rack
3. Lower the crisping lid.
4. Cook the meatballs for 11 minutes at 350 degrees F.
5. Serve immediately and enjoy.

Nutritional Values Per Serving:
Calories: 205; Fat: 12.2g; Carbs: 2.2g; Protein: 19.4g

Beef Stir Fry

Prep Time: 45 minutes
Cook Time: 11 minutes
Servings: 4

Ingredients:
- 1 lb. beef sirloin, sliced into strips

- 1 tablespoon vegetable oil
- 1-½ lb. broccoli florets
- 1 red bell pepper, sliced into strips
- 1 yellow pepper, sliced into strips
- 1 green bell pepper, sliced into strips
- ½ cup onion, sliced into strips

Marinade:
- ¼ cup of hoisin sauce
- 1 teaspoon sesame oil
- 2 teaspoons garlic, minced
- 1 teaspoon of ground ginger
- 1 tablespoon soy sauce
- ¼ cup of water

Directions:
1. Put all the marinade ingredients in a suitable. Divide it in half.
2. Soak the beef in the marinade for 20 minutes. Toss the vegetables in the other half.
3. Place the vegetables in the Ninja Foodi basket. Seal the crisping lid.
4. Select air crisp. Cook at 200 degrees F for 5 minutes.
5. Remove the vegetables and set them aside. Put the meat on the basket.
6. Seal and cook at 360 degrees for 6 minutes.

Nutritional Values Per Serving:
Calories: 390; Fat: 13g; Carbs: 28.9g; Protein: 41.3g

Eastern Lamb Stew

Prep Time: 1 hour and 30 minutes
Cook Time: 60 minutes
Servings: 4

Ingredients:
- 2 tablespoons olive oil
- 1-½ lb. lamb stew meat, sliced into cubes
- 1 onion, diced
- 6 garlic cloves, chopped
- 1 teaspoon cumin
- 1 teaspoon coriander
- 1 teaspoon turmeric
- 1 teaspoon cinnamon
- Black pepper and salt to taste
- 2 tablespoons tomato paste
- ¼ cup red wine vinegar
- 2 tablespoons choc zero maple syrup
- 1-¼ cups chicken broth
- 15 oz. chickpeas, rinsed and drained

Directions:

1. Choose sauté function in the Ninja Foodi. Stir in the oil. Saute onion for 3 minutes.
2. Add the lamb and seasonings. Cook for 5 minutes, stirring frequently.
3. Stir in the rest of the ingredients. Cover the pot. Set it to pressure.
4. Cook at "HIGH" pressure for 50 minutes. Release the pressure naturally.
5. Serve with quinoa.
6. Freeze and serve the next day for a more intense flavor.

Nutritional Values Per Serving:
Calories: 867; Fat: 26.6g; Carbs: 87.4g; Protein: 71.2g

Rosemary Lamb Chops

Prep Time: 20 minutes
Cook Time: 10 minutes
Servings: 6
Ingredients:
- 3 lb. lamb chops
- 4 rosemary sprigs
- Salt to taste
- 1 tablespoon olive oil
- 2 tablespoons butter
- 1 tablespoon tomato paste
- 1 cup beef stock
- 1 green onion, sliced

Directions:
1. Season the lamb chops with rosemary, black pepper and salt.
2. Pour in the olive oil and stir in the butter to the Ninja Foodi. Set it to sauté.
3. Add the lamb chops and cook for one minute per side. Stir in the rest of the ingredients.
4. Stir well. Cover the pot. Set it to pressure. Cook at "HIGH" pressure for 5 minutes.
5. Release the pressure naturally.
6. Serve with pickled onions.

Nutritional Values Per Serving:
Calories: 484; Fat: 23g; Carbs: 1.2g; Protein: 64.4g

Mediterranean Lamb Roast

Prep Time: 40 minutes
Cook Time: 50 minutes
Servings: 4
Ingredients:
- 2 tablespoons olive oil
- 5 lb. leg of lamb
- Black pepper and salt to taste
- 1 teaspoon dried marjoram
- 3 cloves garlic, minced
- 1 teaspoon dried sage
- 1 teaspoon dried thyme
- 1 teaspoon ground ginger
- 1 bay leaf, crushed
- 2 cups broth
- 3 lb. cauliflower, diced
- 2 tablespoons arrowroot powder
- ⅓ cup water

Directions:
1. Set the Ninja Foodi to sauté. Pour in the olive oil. Stir in the lamb.
2. Coat with the oil. Season with the herbs and spices. Sear on both sides.
3. Pour in the broth. Stir in the cauliflower chunks. Close the pot. Set it to pressure.
4. Cook at "HIGH" pressure for 50 minutes. Release the pressure naturally.
5. Dissolve the arrowroot powder in water.
6. Stir in the diluted arrowroot powder into the cooking liquid.
7. Leave for a few minutes before serving.
8. Serve with cauliflower rice.

Nutritional Values Per Serving:
Calories: 688; Fat: 24.8g; Carbs: 27.7g; Protein: 83.8g

Bacon Strips

Prep Time: 5 minutes
Cook Time: 7 minutes
Servings: 2
Ingredients:
- 10 bacon strips
- ¼ teaspoon chilli flakes
- ⅓ teaspoon salt
- ¼ teaspoon basil, dried

Directions:
1. Rub the bacon strips with chilli flakes, dried basil, and salt
2. Turn on your air fryer and place the bacon on the rack
3. Lower the crisping lid. Cook the bacon at 400 degrees F for 5 minutes
4. Cook for 3 minutes more if the bacon is not fully cooked. Serve and enjoy.

Nutritional Values Per Serving:
Calories: 500; Fat: 46g; Carbs: 0g; Protein: 21g

Corned Cabbage Beef

Prep Time: 10 minutes
Cook Time: 100 minutes
Servings: 4
Ingredients:
- 1 corned beef brisket
- 4 cups of water
- 1 small onion, peeled and quartered
- 3 garlic cloves, smashed and peeled
- 2 bay leaves
- 3 whole black peppercorns
- ½ teaspoon allspice berries
- 1 teaspoon dried thyme
- 5 medium carrots

- 1 cabbage, cut into wedges

Directions:
1. Stir in corned beef, onion, garlic cloves, water, allspice, peppercorn, thymes to the Ninja Foodi.
2. Lock up the lid and cook for about 90 minutes at "HIGH" pressure.
3. Allow the pressure to release naturally once done.
4. Open up and transfer the meat to your serving plate.
5. Cover it with tin foil and allow it to cool for 15 minutes.
6. Stir in carrots and cabbage to the lid and let them cook for 10 minutes at "HIGH" pressure.
7. Once done, do a quick release. Take out the prepped veggies and serve with your corned beef.

Nutritional Values Per Serving:
Calories: 297; Fats: 17g; Carbs:1g; Protein: 14g

Adobo Steak

Prep Time: 5 minutes
Cook Time: 25 minutes
Servings: 4
Ingredients:
- 2 cups of water
- 8 steaks, cubed, 28 ounces pack
- Pepper to taste
- 1 and ¾ teaspoons adobo seasoning
- 1 can (8-ounce) tomato sauce
- ⅓ cup green pitted olives
- 2 tablespoons brine
- 1 small red pepper
- ½ a medium onion, sliced

Directions:
1. Chop peppers, onions into ¼ inch strips.
2. Prepare beef by seasoning with adobo and pepper.
3. Add into Ninja Foodi.
4. Stir in remaining ingredients and Lock lid, cook on "HIGH" pressure for 25 minutes.
5. Release pressure naturally.
6. Serve and enjoy.

Nutritional Values Per Serving:
Calories: 154; Fat: 5g; Carbs: 3g; Protein: 23g

Corned Beef

Prep Time: 10 minutes
Cook Time: 60 minutes
Servings: 4

Ingredients:
- 4 pounds beef brisket
- 2 garlic cloves, peeled and minced
- 2 yellow onions, peeled and sliced
- 11 ounces celery, sliced
- 1 tablespoon dried dill
- 3 bay leaves
- 4 cinnamon sticks, cut into halves
- Black pepper and salt to taste
- 17 ounces of water

Directions:
1. Take a suitable and stir in beef, add water and cover, let it soak for 2-3 hours
2. Drain and transfer to the Ninja Foodi
3. Stir in celery, onions, garlic, bay leaves, dill, cinnamon, dill, salt, pepper and the rest of the water to the Ninja Foodi
4. Stir and combine it well
5. Lock and secure the Ninja Foodi's lid, then cook on "HIGH" pressure for 50 minutes
6. Release pressure naturally over 10 minutes
7. Transfer meat to cutting board and slice, divide amongst plates and pour the cooking liquid alongside veggies over the servings
8. Enjoy.

Nutritional Values Per Serving:
Calories: 289; Fat: 21g; Carbs: 14g; Protein: 9g

Asian Beef

Prep Time: 30 minutes
Cook Time: 15 minutes
Servings: 6

Ingredients:
- ¼ cup soy sauce
- ½ cup beef broth
- 1 tablespoon sesame oil
- ¼ cup brown erythritol, packed
- 4 cloves garlic, minced
- 1 teaspoon hot sauce
- 1 tablespoon rice wine vinegar
- 1 tablespoon ginger, grated
- ½ teaspoon onion powder
- ½ teaspoon pepper
- 3 lb. boneless beef chuck roast, cubed
- 3 tablespoons corn starch dissolved in 1 teaspoon water

Directions:
1. Mix all the seasonings in a suitable bowl except the chuck roast and corn starch.
2. Pour the mixture into the Ninja Foodi. Stir in the beef. Seal the pot.
3. Select pressure. Cook at "HIGH" pressure for 15 minutes.
4. Do a quick pressure release. Stir in the corn starch.
5. Select sauté setting to thicken the sauce.

Nutritional Values Per Serving:
Calories: 482; Fat: 16.6g; Carbs: 8.4g; Protein: 70.1g

Lamb Curry

Prep Time: 1 hour and 30 minutes
Cook Time: 20 minutes
Servings: 6

Ingredients:
- 1-½ lb. lamb stew meat, cubed
- 1 tablespoon lime juice
- 4 cloves garlic, minced
- ½ cup coconut milk
- 1-inch piece fresh ginger, grated
- Black pepper and salt to taste
- 1 tablespoon coconut oil
- 14 oz. diced tomatoes
- ¾ teaspoon turmeric
- 1 tablespoon curry powder
- 1 onion, diced
- 3 carrots, sliced

Directions:
1. In a suitable, toss the lamb meat in lime juice, garlic, coconut milk, ginger, black pepper and salt. Marinate for 30 minutes.
2. Put the meat with its marinade and the rest of the ingredients in the Ninja Foodi.
3. Mix well. Seal the pot. Set it to pressure.
4. Cook at "HIGH" pressure for 20 minutes.
5. Release the pressure naturally.
6. Garnish with chopped cilantro.
7. Use freshly squeezed lime juice.

Nutritional Values Per Serving:
Calories: 631; Fat: 31.4g; Carbs: 19.7g; Protein: 67.2g

Beef Broccoli

Prep Time: 40 minutes
Cook Time: 16 minutes
Servings: 6
Ingredients:
• 1-½ lb. beef chuck roast boneless, trimmed and sliced
• Black pepper and salt to taste
• 2 teaspoons olive oil
• 1 onion, chopped
• 4 cloves garlic, minced
• ¾ cup beef broth
• ½ cup soy sauce
• ⅓ cup erythritol
• 2 tablespoons sesame oil
• 1 lb. broccoli florets
• 3 tablespoons water
• 3 tablespoons corn starch
Directions:
1. Season the beef strips with black pepper and salt.
2. Stir in the olive oil to the Ninja Foodi. Switch it to sauté.
3. Add the onion and saute for 1 minute. Stir in the garlic and cook for 30 seconds.
4. Stir in the beef and cook in batches until brown on both sides.
5. Deglaze the pot with broth and soy sauce.
6. Stir in the erythritol and sesame oil. Cover the pot.
7. Set it to pressure. Cook at "HIGH" pressure for 12 minutes.
8. Release the pressure naturally. Stir in the broccoli. Seal the pot.
9. Cook at "HIGH" pressure for 3 minutes. Release the pressure quickly.
10. Mix corn starch with water and add to the pot.
11. Simmer until the sauce has thickened.
12. Serve warm.
Nutritional Values Per Serving:
Calories: 563; Fat: 38.1g; Carbs: 10.7g; Protein: 34.1g

Philly Willy Steak

Prep Time: 10 minutes
Cook Time: 40 minutes
Servings: 4
Ingredients:
• 2 tablespoons olive oil
• 2 large onion, sliced
• 8 ounces mushrooms, sliced
• 1-2 teaspoons steak seasoning
• 1 tablespoon butter
• 2 pounds beef chuck roast
• 12 cup beef stock
Directions:
1. Select "Sauté" mode on your Ninja Foodi and stir in oil, let it heat up.
2. Rub seasoning over roast and Sauté for 1-2 minutes per side.
3. Remove and add butter, onion.
4. Stir in mushrooms, pepper, stock, and roast.
5. Lock and secure the Ninja Foodi's lid, then cook on "HIGH" pressure for 35 minutes.
6. Naturally, release the pressure over 10 minutes.
7. Shred meat and sprinkle cheese if using. Enjoy.
Nutritional Values Per Serving:
Calories: 425; Fats: 25g; Carbs: 3g; Protein: 46g

Korean Ribs

Prep Time: 10 minutes
Cook Time: 45 minutes
Servings: 6
Ingredients:
- 1 teaspoon olive oil
- 2 green onions, cut into 1-inch length
- 3 garlic cloves, smashed
- 3 quarter-sized ginger slices
- 4 pounds beef short ribs, 3 inches thick, cut into 3 rib portions
- ½ cup of water
- ½ cup coconut aminos
- ¼ cup dry white wine
- 2 teaspoons sesame oil
- Mince green onions for serving

Directions:
1. Set your Ninja Foodi to "Sauté" mode and stir in oil, let it shimmer
2. Add green onions, garlic, ginger, Sauté for 1 minute
3. Stir in short ribs, water, amines, wine, sesame oil, and stir until the ribs are coated well
4. Lock and secure the Ninja Foodi's lid, then cook on "HIGH" pressure for 45 minutes
5. Release pressure naturally over 10 minutes
6. Remove short ribs from pot and serve with the cooking liquid
7. Enjoy.

Nutritional Values Per Serving:
Calories: 423; Fat: 35g; Carbs: 4g; Protein: 22g

Beef Bourguignon

Prep Time: 10 minutes
Cook Time: 30 minutes
Servings: 4
Ingredients:
- 1-pound stewing steak

- ½-pound bacon
- 5 medium carrots, diced
- 1 large red onion, peeled and sliced
- 2 garlic cloves, minced
- 2 teaspoons salt
- 2 tablespoons fresh thyme
- 2 tablespoons fresh parsley, chopped
- 2 teaspoons ground pepper
- ½ cup beef broth
- 1 tablespoon olive oil
- 1 tablespoon sugar-free maple syrup

Directions:
1. Select "Sauté" mode on your Ninja Foodi and stir in 1 tablespoon of oil, allow the oil to heat up.
2. Pat your beef dry and season it well.
3. Stir in beef into the Ninja Foodi in batches and Sauté them until nicely browned up.
4. Slice up the cooked bacon into strips and add the strips to the pot.
5. Add onions as well and brown them.
6. Stir in the rest of the listed ingredients and lock up the lid.
7. Cook for 30 minutes on "HIGH" pressure.
8. Allow the pressure to release naturally over 10 minutes. Enjoy.

Nutritional Values Per Serving:
Calories: 416; Fats: 18g; Carbs: 12g; Protein:27g

Veggies & Beef Stew

Prep Time: 10 minutes
Cook Time: 10 minutes
Servings: 4
Ingredients:
- 1-pound beef roast
- 4 cups beef broth
- 3 garlic cloves, chopped
- 1 carrot, chopped
- 2 celery stalks, chopped
- 2 tomatoes, chopped
- ½ white onion, chopped
- ¼ teaspoon salt
- ⅛ teaspoon black pepper

Directions:
1. Stir in listed ingredients to your Ninja Foodi and lock lid, cook on "HIGH" pressure for 10 minutes
2. Quick-release pressure.
3. Open the Ninja Foodi's lid and shred the bee using forks
4. Serve and enjoy.

Nutritional Values Per Serving:
Calories: 211; Fat: 7g; Carbs: 2g; Protein: 10g

Picadillo Dish

Prep Time: 10 minutes
Cook Time: 15-20 minutes
Servings: 4
Ingredients:
- ½-pound lean ground beef
- 2 garlic cloves, minced
- ½ large onion, chopped
- 1 teaspoon salt
- 1 tomato, chopped
- ½ red bell pepper, chopped
- 1 tablespoon cilantro, chopped
- ½ can 4 ounces tomato sauce
- 1 teaspoon ground cumin
- 1-2 bay leaves
- 2 tablespoons green olives, capers
- 2 tablespoons brine
- 3 tablespoons water

Directions:
1. Select "Sauté" mode on your Ninja Foodi and stir in meat, salt, and pepper, slightly brown
2. Add garlic, tomato, onion, cilantro and Sauté for 1 minute.
3. Add olives, brine, leaf, cumin, and mix
4. Pour in sauce, water, and stir. Lock and secure the Ninja Foodi's lid, then cook on "HIGH" pressure for 15 minutes
5. Quick-release pressure

Nutritional Values Per Serving:
Calories: 207; Fats: 8g; Carbs: 4g; Protein: 25g

Beef Sirloin Steak

Prep Time: 5 minutes
Cook Time: 17 minutes
Servings: 4

Ingredients:
- 3 tablespoons butter
- ½ teaspoon garlic powder
- 1-2 pounds beef sirloin steaks
- Black pepper and salt to taste
- 1 garlic clove, minced

Directions:
1. Select "Sauté" mode on your Ninja Foodi and add butter; let the butter melt
2. Stir in beef sirloin steaks
3. Sauté for 2 minutes on each side
4. Add garlic powder, garlic clove, salt, and pepper
5. Lock and secure the Ninja Foodi's lid and cook on "High" pressure for 15 minutes
6. Release pressure naturally over 10 minutes
7. Transfer prepare Steaks to a serving platter, enjoy.

Nutritional Values Per Serving:
Calories: 246; Fat: 13g; Carbs: 2g; Protein: 31g

Carne Guisada

Prep Time: 10 minutes
Cook Time: 45 minutes
Servings: 4
Ingredients:
- 3 pounds beef stew
- 3 tablespoon seasoned salt
- 1 tablespoon oregano chilli powder
- 1 tablespoon cumin
- 1 pinch crushed red pepper
- 2 tablespoons olive oil
- ½ medium lime, juiced
- 1 cup beef bone broth
- 3 ounces tomato paste
- 1 large onion, sliced

Directions:
1. Trim the beef stew to taste into small bite-sized portions
2. Toss the beef stew pieces with dry seasoning
3. Select "Sauté" mode on your Ninja Foodi and stir in oil; allow the oil to heat up
4. Add seasoned beef pieces and brown them
5. Combine the browned beef pieces with the rest of the ingredients
6. Lock the Ninja foodi's lid and cook on "HIGH" pressure for 3 minutes
7. Release the pressure naturally
8. Enjoy.

Nutritional Values Per Serving:
Calories: 274; Fats: 12g; Carbs: 11g;Protein: 33g

Braised Lamb Shanks

Prep Time: 20 minutes
Cook Time: 46 minutes
Servings: 4
Ingredients:
* 2 tablespoons olive oil
* 4 lamb shanks
* Black pepper and salt to taste
* 4 cloves garlic, minced
* ¾ cup dry red wine
* 1 teaspoon dried basil
* ¾ teaspoons dried oregano
* 28 oz. crushed tomatoes

Directions:
1. Turn the Ninja Foodi to sauté. Stir in the oil. Season the lamb with Black pepper and salt.
2. Cook until brown. Remove and set aside. Add the garlic and cook for 15 seconds.
3. Pour in the wine. Simmer for 2 minutes. Stir in the basil, oregano and tomatoes.
4. Put the lamb back to the pot. Seal the pot. Set it to pressure.
5. Cook at "HIGH" pressure for 45 minutes. Release the pressure naturally.
6. Serve over polenta.

Nutritional Values Per Serving:
Calories: 790; Fat: 31g; Carbs: 18.3g; Protein: 96.8g

Beef Enchiladas

Prep Time: 15 Minutes
Cook Time: 10-12 Minutes
Servings: 4
Ingredients:
* 1 pound ground beef
* 1 packet taco seasoning
* 4 tortillas
* 2 diced tomatoes
* 2 sliced green chilies
* 1 can of black beans
* 1 tablespoon olive oil
For Sauce:
* 1 tablespoon red chili sauce
* 1 cup Mexican cheese
* ½ cup fresh coriander
* ¼ cup sour cream

Directions:
1. In a medium-size skillet, take a start by browning the ground beef in olive oil.
2. Then add the taco seasoning to it. Give it a good mix.
3. Once mixed well, put in tomatoes, beans, and chilies. Give it a good mix and set aside.
4. Stir in all the sauce ingredients in a pan and heat the sauce until the cheese melts. Keep stirring until well-thickened. Stuff in the beef batter in the tortillas and wrap them.
5. Place the tortilla wraps in a foil-lined Ninja Foodi Deluxe XL Pressure Cooker Cook & Crisp Basket. Pour the prepared sauce on it.
6. Top up with cheese evenly. Air Crisp it for 5 to 8 minutes at 390° F, until the cheese melts. Enchiladas are ready to be served.

Nutritional Values Per Serving:
Calories: 255; Fat: 14.8g; Carbs: 23.1g; Protein: 9.2g

Shepherd's Pie

Prep Time: 10 minutes
Cook Time: 10-15 minutes
Servings: 4
Ingredients:
- 2 cups of water
- 4 tablespoons butter
- 4 ounces cream cheese
- 1 cup mozzarella
- 1 whole egg
- Black pepper and salt to taste
- 1 tablespoon garlic powder
- 2-3 pounds ground beef
- 1 cup frozen carrots
- 8 ounces mushrooms, sliced
- 1 cup beef broth
Directions:
1. Add water to Ninja Foodi, set cauliflower on top, Lock and secure the Ninja Foodi's lid and cook for 5 minutes on "HIGH" pressure.
2. Quick-release and transfer to a blender, stir in cream cheese, butter, mozzarella cheese, egg, pepper, and salt.
3. Blend well. Drain water from Ninja Foodi and add beef
4. Stir in carrots, garlic powder, broth and pepper, and salt
5. Add in cauliflower mix and lock lid, cook for 10 minutes on "HIGH" pressure
6. Release pressure naturally over 10 minutes. Serve and enjoy.
Nutritional Values Per Serving:
Calories: 303; Fats: 21g; Carbs: 4g; Protein: 21g

Beef Lasagna

Prep Time: 10 minutes
Cook Time: 10-15 minutes
Servings: 4
Ingredients:
- 2 small onions

- 2 garlic cloves, minced
- 1-pound ground beef
- 1 large egg
- 1 and ½ cups ricotta cheese
- ½ cup parmesan cheese
- 1 jar 25 ounces0 marinara sauce
- 8 ounces mozzarella cheese, sliced
Directions:
1. Select "Sauté" mode on your Ninja Foodi and stir in beef, brown the beef
2. Add onion and garlic
3. Add parmesan, ricotta, egg in a small dish and keep it on the side
4. Stir in sauce to browned meat, reserve half for later
5. Sprinkle mozzarella and half of ricotta cheese into the browned meat
6. Top with remaining meat sauce
7. For the final layer, add more mozzarella cheese and the remaining ricotta
8. Stir well
9. Cover with a foil transfer to Ninja Foodi
10. Lock and secure the Ninja Foodi's lid, then cook on "HIGH" pressure for 8-10 minutes
11. Quick-release pressure
12. Drizzle parmesan cheese on top
13. Enjoy.
Nutritional Values Per Serving:
Calories: 365; Fats: 25g; Carbs: 6g; Protein: 25g

Beef Prime Roast

Prep Time: 10 minutes
Cook Time: 45 minutes
Servings: 4
Ingredients:
- 2 pounds chuck roast
- 1 tablespoon olive oil
- 1 teaspoon salt
- 1 teaspoon black pepper
- 1 teaspoon onion powder
- 1 teaspoon garlic powder
- 4 cups beef stock
Directions:
1. Place roast in Ninja Food pot and season it well with black pepper and salt

2. Stir in oil and set the pot to Sauté mode, sear each side of the roast for 3 minutes until slightly browned
3. Add beef broth, onion powder, garlic powder, and stir
4. Lock and secure the Ninja Foodi's lid, then cook on "HIGH" pressure for 40 minutes.
5. Once done, naturally release the pressure over 10 minutes
6. Open the Ninja Foodi's lid and serve hot. Enjoy.
Nutritional Values Per Serving:
Calories: 308; Fat: 22g; Carbs: 2g; Protein: 24g

Beef Spaghetti Squash

Prep Time: 5 minutes
Cook Time: 15 minutes
Servings: 4
Ingredients:
- 2 pounds ground beef
- 1 medium spaghetti squash
- 32 ounces marinara sauce
- 3 tablespoons olive oil
Directions:
1. Slice squash in half lengthwise and dispose of seeds
2. Add trivet to your Ninja Foodi
3. Stir in 1 cup water
4. Set squash on the rack and lock lid, cook on "HIGH" pressure for 8 minutes
5. Quick-release pressure
6. Remove from pot
7. Clean pot and Select "Sauté" mode on your Ninja Foodi
8. Add ground beef and add olive oil, let it heat up
9. Stir in ground beef and cook until slightly browned and cooked
10. Separate strands from cooked squash and transfer to a suitable
11. Stir in cooked beef, and mix with marinara sauce.
12. Serve and enjoy.
Nutritional Values Per Serving:
Calories: 174; Fat: 6g; Carbs: 5g; Protein: 19g

Instant Lamb Steaks

Prep Time: 3 Minutes
Cook Time: 7-8 Minutes
Servings: 1
Ingredients:
- 1 pound lamb steaks
- Olive oil
Dry Ingredients:
- Salt to taste
- Black pepper to taste
- 1 teaspoon paprika powder
- 1 tablespoon garlic powder
- 1 tablespoon ginger powder
- ¼ teaspoon red chili flakes
- 1 teaspoon five-spice powder
- 1 teaspoon oregano
Directions:
1. Take out the steaks from the refrigerator and allow them to defrost.
2. Preheat the Ninja Foodi Deluxe XL Pressure Cooker at Air Crisp Mode at 390° F. Pat dry the lamb steaks and rub them with olive oil.
3. Combine all dry ingredients in a bowl. Press each side of the steaks into the dry mixture then place it in the Ninja Foodi Deluxe XL Pressure Cooker Cook & Crisp Basket.
4. Air Crisp the lamb sticks at Medium-rare for 7 to 8 minutes. Instant bread meat treatment can be used to check the internal temperature at 145° F. Dish out the steaks and serve!
Nutritional Values Per Serving:
Calories: 647; Fat: 43.4g; Carbs: 8.2g; Protein: 1.9g

Ninja Foodi Pork Shoulder Roast

Prep Time: 10 minutes
Cook Time: 10 hours
Servings: 14
Ingredients:
- 4 pounds pork shoulder roast
- 4 carrots, peeled and sliced
- 4 onions, sliced
- 4 tablespoons Italian seasonings
- Salt and black pepper, to taste

Directions:
1. Add pork shoulder, Italian seasonings, salt and pepper in a large bowl. Mix-well and set aside for about 4 hours.
2. Now, place carrots and onions in the bottom of Ninja Foodi Deluxe XL Pressure Cooker and add marinated pork shoulder in it.
3. Select "Slow Cook" and close the pressure Lid.
4. Press the "Start/Stop" button and cook for about 10 hours on low TEMP.
5. Open the pressure Lid and take out.
6. Serve and enjoy!

Nutritional Values Per Serving:
Calories: 365; Fat: 27.6g; Carbs: 5.1g; Protein: 22.3g

Ninja Foodi Carrot & Pork Stew

Prep Time: 10 minutes
Cook Time: 8 hours
Servings: 4
Ingredients:
- 1 pound pork meat, trimmed

- 1½ onions, sliced thinly
- 3 carrots, sliced thinly
- ¾ cup vegetable broth
- Salt and black pepper, to taste

Directions:
1. Add everything in a Ninja Foodi Deluxe XL Pressure Cooker and mix well.
2. Select "Slow Cook" and press the "Start/Stop" button.
3. Close the pressure Lid and cook for about 8 hours.
4. Open the lid and take out.
5. Serve and enjoy!

Nutritional Values Per Serving:
Calories: 465; Fat: 34.8g; Carbs: 21.2g; Protein: 17.1g

Ninja Foodi Mushroom & Beef Stew

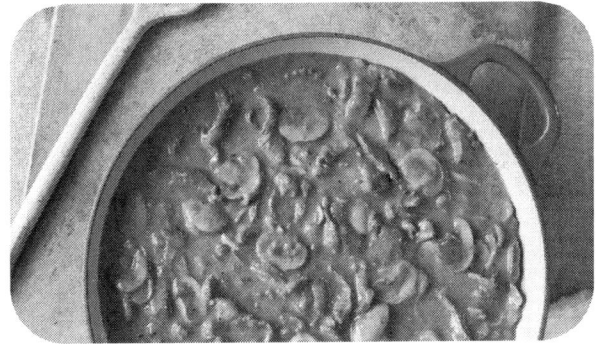

Prep Time: 10 minutes
Cook Time: 8 hours
Servings: 5
Ingredients:
- 1 pound beef, chopped
- 1½ onions, chopped
- 1 cup mushrooms, sliced
- ½ cup vegetable broth
- Salt and black pepper, to taste

Directions:
1. Add everything in a Ninja Foodi Deluxe XL Pressure Cooker and select "Slow Cook".
2. Close the pressure Lid and press the "Start/Stop" button.
3. Cook for about 8-hours on LOW TEMP and open the lid.
4. Take out, serve and enjoy!

Nutritional Values Per Serving:
Calories: 224; Fat: 6g; Carbs: 11.9g; Protein: 29.8g

Ninja Foodi Beef Casserole

Prep Time: 10 minutes
Cook Time: 8 hours
Servings: 3
Ingredients:
- ½ pound beef steak, chopped
- ½ cup chopped tomatoes
- ½ onion, chopped
- ¼ cup beef broth
- Salt and black pepper, to taste

Directions:
1. Add everything in a Ninja Foodi Deluxe XL Pressure Cooker and select "Slow Cook".
2. Cover the lid and press the "Start/Stop" button.
3. Cook for about 8-hours on LOW TEMP and open the lid.
4. Take out, serve and enjoy!
Nutritional Values Per Serving:
Calories: 156; Fat: 4.9g; Carbs: 3g; Protein: 23.8g

Ninja Foodi Minced Beef with Tomatoes

Prep Time: 10 minutes
Cook Time: 10 hours
Servings: 4
Ingredients:
- ¾ cup chopped tomatoes
- ½ cup water
- ½ pound minced beef
- 1½ tablespoons mixed herbs
- Salt and black pepper, to taste

Directions:

1. Mix all the ingredients in a Ninja Foodi Deluxe XL Pressure Cooker and select "Slow Cook".
2. Close the pressure Lid and press the "Start/Stop" button.
3. Cook for about 8-hours on LOW TEMP and open the lid.
4. Take out, serve and enjoy!
Nutritional Values Per Serving:
Calories: 116; Fat: 3.7g; Carbs: 2.3g; Protein: 17.7g

Ninja Foodi Steak Fajitas

Prep Time: 10 minutes
Cook Time: 8 hours
Servings: 3
Ingredients:
- 1 pound beef, trimmed and sliced
- 1¼ cups salsa
- 1 tablespoon fajita seasoning
- ½ bell pepper, sliced
- ½ onion, sliced
- Salt and black pepper, to taste

Directions:
1. Place salsa in the bottom of Ninja Foodi Deluxe XL Pressure Cooker and top it with fajita seasoning, onion, beef, bell pepper, salt and pepper.
2. Stir well and select "Slow Cook".
3. Close the pressure Lid and cook for about 8 hours.
4. Open the lid and take out.
5. Serve and enjoy!
Nutritional Values Per Serving:
Calories: 369; Fat: 9.9g; Carbs: 20.3g; Protein: 49.9g

Ninja Foodi Lamb & Kale Stew

Prep Time: 10 minutes
Cook Time: 6 hours 5 minutes
Servings: 10
Ingredients:
- 3 pounds lamb meat, cubed
- 1 teaspoon dried thyme
- 1 celery stalk, chopped
- 2 tablespoons olive oil
- 1 teaspoon dried basil
- 1 cup chopped tomatoes
- 2 onions, chopped
- ½ cup chopped carrots
- 2 cups water
- 2 garlic cloves, minced
- 10 cups fresh kale, chopped
- Salt and black pepper, to taste

Directions:
1. Heat oil in the pot of Ninja Foodi Deluxe XL Pressure Cooker and add lamb, salt and pepper in it.
2. Select "Slow Cook" and press the "Start/Stop" button.
3. Cook for about 5 minutes and take out. Set aside.
4. Now, add lamb with all the other ingredients in a Ninja Foodi Slow Cook and close the pressure Lid.
5. Cook for about 6 hours at HIGH TEMP and open the lid.
6. Take out, serve and enjoy!
Nutritional Values Per Serving:
Calories: 350; Fat: 20.9g; Carbs: 10.6g; Protein: 27.8g

Ninja Foodi Beef Chili

Prep Time: 10 minutes
Cook Time: 6 hours
Servings: 3
Ingredients:
- ¾ pound lean ground beef

- ¼ tablespoon garlic, minced
- ½ tablespoon dried basil
- ¼ onion, chopped
- 1 tablespoon tomato paste
- ½ tablespoon chili powder
- ¼ cup chicken broth
- ½ tablespoon balsamic vinegar
- 2 tablespoons water
- ¾ tablespoon capers
- ½ tablespoon dried thyme
- ¼ tablespoon cayenne pepper
- Salt, to taste

Directions:
1. Add everything in a Ninja Foodi Deluxe XL Pressure Cooker and select "Slow Cook".
2. Press the "Start/Stop" button and close the pressure Lid.
3. Cook for about 6 hours on low TEMP and open the lid.
4. Take out and serve hot.
Nutritional Values Per Serving:
Calories: 231; Fat: 7.6g; Carbs: 3.5g; Protein: 35.5g

Ninja Foodi Lamb & Carrot Stew

Prep Time: 10 minutes
Cook Time: 9 hours
Servings: 3
Ingredients:
- ¾ pound lamb chops, trimmed
- ½ cup vegetable broth
- 2½ carrots, chopped
- 1 onion, chopped
- Salt and black pepper, to taste

Directions:
1. Add all the ingredients in Ninja Foodi Deluxe XL Pressure Cooker and mix well. Select "Slow Cook".
2. Cover the pressure Lid and press the "Start/Stop" button.
3. Cook for about 9 hours on LOW TEMP and open the lid.
4. Serve and enjoy!
Nutritional Values Per Serving:
Calories: 320; Fat: 8.6g; Carbs: 24.6g; Protein: 34.8g

Ninja Foodi Lamb Chops with Tomatoes

Prep Time: 10 minutes
Cook Time: 8 hours
Servings: 4
Ingredients:
- 1 pound lamb chops
- 3 tablespoons mixed herbs
- 1 cup water
- 1½ cups chopped tomatoes
- Salt and black pepper, to taste
Directions:
1. Mix everything in Ninja Foodi Deluxe XL Pressure Cooker and cover the lid.
2. Select "Slow Cook" and press the "Start/Stop" button.
3. Cook for about 8 hours at low TEMP and open the lid.
4. Take out, serve and enjoy!
Nutritional Values Per Serving:
Calories: 258; Fat: 8.9g; Carbs: 10.2g; Protein: 34.2g

Ninja Foodi Plum & Beef Salad

Prep Time: 20 minutes
Cook Time: 10 minutes
Servings: 6
Ingredients:
- 2 pounds beef, trimmed
- 2 teaspoons unsweetened applesauce
- 8 plums, thinly sliced
- 4 tablespoons olive oil
- Salt and black pepper, to taste
Directions:
1. Add 1 tablespoon salt, olive oil and pepper in a large bowl. Mix well.
2. Add in beef and toss to coat well.
3. Place beef in Ninja Foodi Deluxe XL Pressure Cooker and select "Pressure".
4. Close the pressure Lid and press the "Start/Stop" button.
5. Cook for about 5 minutes at LO per side and open the lid.
6. Take out the beef in a bowl and add in remaining ingredients. Mix properly.
7. Serve and enjoy!
Nutritional Values Per Serving:
Calories: 402; Fat: 19g; Carbs: 10.9g; Protein: 46.5g

Ninja Foodi Filling Beef Dish

Prep Time: 10 minutes
Cook Time: 10 minutes
Servings: 4
Ingredients:
- 2 tablespoons olive oil
- 4 garlic cloves, minced
- 1 pound beef sirloin steak, chopped
- 3 tablespoons low-sodium soy sauce
- 2 cups fresh kale, chopped
- 2 cups carrots, chopped
- Salt and pepper, to taste
Directions:
1. Heat olive oil in Ninja Foodi Deluxe XL Pressure Cooker and select "Pressure".
2. Sauté garlic in it for about 1 minute and press the "Start/Stop" button.
3. Add in black pepper and beef. Stir well and cook for about 4 minutes at LO.
4. Stir in kale, soy sauce, salt and carrots and cook for about 5 minutes.
5. Take out and serve hot.
Nutritional Values Per Serving:
Calories: 318; Fat: 14.1g; Carbs: 10.7g; Protein: 36.8g

Ninja Foodi Ground Beef Soup

Prep Time: 20 minutes
Cook Time: 21 minutes
Servings: 6
Ingredients:
- 1 pound lean ground beef
- 1 ginger, minced
- ½ pound fresh mushrooms, sliced
- 1 onion, chopped
- 2 tablespoons soy sauce
- 1 garlic clove, minced
- 4 cups chicken broth
- Salt and black pepper, to taste

Directions:
1. Add beef in a large Ninja Foodi Deluxe XL Pressure Cooker, press the "Broil" button and cook for about 2 minutes.
2. Press the "Start/Stop" button and stir in mushrooms, garlic and onion and cook for about 4 minutes.
3. Add in remaining ingredients and cook for 15 minutes on low heat.
4. Take out, serve and enjoy!

Nutritional Values Per Serving:
Calories: 186; Fat: 5.8g; Carbs: 4.4g; Protein: 27.9g

Ninja Foodi Spinach Beef Soup

Prep Time: 10 minutes
Cook Time: 30 minutes
Servings: 4
Ingredients:
- 1 tablespoon olive oil
- 4 cups spinach, chopped
- 1 onion, chopped
- 4 cups chicken broth
- 1 pound ground beef
- 1 teaspoon ground ginger
- 1 cup chopped carrots
- Salt and black pepper, to taste

Directions:
1. Add oil and beef in Ninja Foodi Deluxe XL Pressure Cooker and select "Pressure".
2. Press the "Start/Stop" button and cook for about 5-minutes.
3. Add in broth, spinach, carrots, onions, ginger, salt and pepper. Mix well.
4. Cook for about 25 minutes at LO and take out.
5. Serve and enjoy!

Nutritional Values Per Serving:
Calories: 310; Fat: 12.1g; Carbs: 7.6g; Protein: 40.7g

Tomahawk Rib-Eye Steak

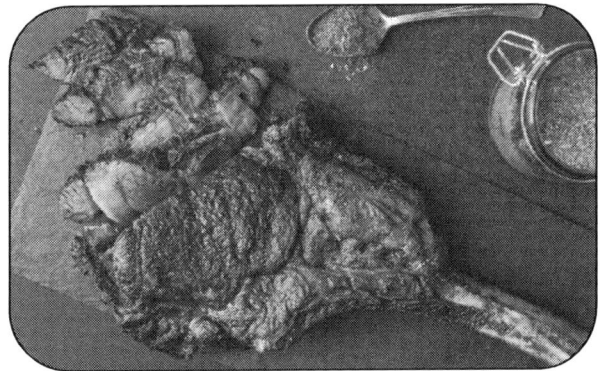

Prep Time: 10 Minutes
Cook Time: 52 Minutes
Servings: 1-2
Ingredients:
- 1 tomahawk rib-eye steak, about 1 ¾ inches thick
- Kosher salt, to taste
- Freshly ground pepper, to taste
- 1 small head garlic
- 2 tablespoons oil, plus more for drizzling (canola or grapeseed)
- 4 tablespoons (½ stick) unsalted butter
- 4 large sprigs fresh thyme

Directions:
1. Pat dry the tomahawk steak with paper towels.
2. Season steak very liberally with kosher salt and freshly ground pepper. Let the steak come to room temperature.
3. Meanwhile, prepare the garlic. Trim off the top ¼inch of the garlic bulb. Drizzle with the oil and add a pinch of salt, then wrap in a foil tent, and cook in Ninja Foodi Deluxe XL Pressure Cooker on Pressure Cook low Setting the garlic for 30 minutes, until the cloves are soft. Remove from the Ninja Foodi Deluxe XL Pressure Cooker and allow to cool.
4. Moisten a paper towel and wrap it around the steak's rib bone, then wrap aluminum foil around the paper towel.
5. In Ninja Foodi Deluxe XL Pressure Cooker, lay the tomahawk steak into the Ninja Foodi

Multi-Cooker and Sear for 3 minutes in 2 tablespoon oil without touching it, on selecting Sear Setting at Medium.
6. Using tongs and the bone as a handle, turn the steak over and cook for another 3 minutes without touching it on Sear setting on Medium Setting. Using tongs and the bone as a handle, sear the short side of the steak opposite the bone, about 3 minute.
7. Sear tomahawk rib-eye steak on both sides.
8. Transfer the steak to a rimmed baking sheet and place again in the Ninja Foodi Deluxe XL Pressure Cooker, and set it at Roast Setting at 400°F and roast for 10 minutes, or until the desired doneness is reached.
9. Use an instant-read thermometer to measure the steak's internal temperature—125° F for rare, 135° F for Medium-rare, or 145° F for Medium.
10. Make paste of butter and garlic.
11. When the steak is ready, take it out of the Ninja Foodi Deluxe XL Pressure Cooker, and use a spoon to paste the butter and garlic over the steak. Turn the steak, and paste again, about 1 minute total. Transfer the steak to a cutting board, tent it with foil, and let it rest 10 minutes.
12. Then add this cutted steaks into Ninja Foodi Multi-Cooker and Cook tomahawk rib-eye steak again in Ninja Foodi Deluxe XL Pressure Cooker on High Pressure Mode for 5 minutes.
13. Then take out steaks and top with butter and garlic. You can, simply spoon the butter and garlic over the steak. Serve and enjoy.
Nutritional Values Per Serving:
Calories: 1990; Fat: 145g; Carbs: 7g; Protein: 160g

Beef Onion Pattie Burgers

Prep Time: 6 Minutes
Cook Time: 12-15 Minutes
Servings: 4
Ingredients:
- 1 pound ground beef
- 8 tablespoons onion soup mix
For Assembling:
- Cheese slices
- Onion rings
- Lettuce leaves
- Ketchup
- 4 burger buns
Directions:

1. Combine the ground beef and onion soup mix in a large bowl to make four patties.
2. Oil spray the parchment paper-lined Ninja Foodi Deluxe XL Pressure Cooker Cook & Crisp Basket evenly.
3. Place the patties in Ninja Foodi Deluxe XL Pressure Cooker and turn on the Air Crisp function at 390° F for 5 minutes. Once done, assemble the burgers as per your likings.
4. Again, place the burgers in the Ninja Foodi Deluxe XL Pressure Cooker. Turn the burgers carefully and for an additional 6 to 7 minutes Air Crisp it, until the internal temperature reaches 165° F.
Nutritional Values Per Serving:
Calories: 329; Fat: 13.7g; Carbs: 23.9g; Protein: 27.3g

Roasted Lamb

Prep Time: 7 Minutes
Cook Time: 25 Minutes
Servings: 4
Ingredients
- 283 grams lamb leg
- 1 tablespoon ginger garlic paste
- 1 teaspoon black pepper
- 1 tablespoon rosemary
- 1 tablespoon olive oil
- 1 tablespoon dried thyme
Directions:
1. Preheat the Ninja Foodi Deluxe XL Pressure Cooker at Air Crisp Mode at 390° F.
2. Mix olive oil with rosemary, black pepper, ginger garlic paste, and thyme in a bowl. Pat dry the lamb roast leg and then rub the herb oil mixture until it is well-coated. Let it rest to infuse the flavors.
3. Place it carefully in the Ninja Foodi Deluxe XL Pressure Cooker Cook & Crisp Basket and Air Crisp it for 15 minutes.
4. It's recommended to check the temperature with a meat thermometer to ensure that it's cooked according to your preference.
5. Cook it for another 8 to 10 minutes and then wrap it with kitchen foil for 5 minutes and leave it to rest before serving!
Nutritional Values Per Serving:
Calories: 321; Fat: 11.2g; Carbs: 49.3g; Protein: 21.8g

Beef Stew

Prep Time: 9-10 hours
Cook Time: 25-30 Minutes
Servings: 2-3

Ingredients
- 1 pound beef cuts
- 2 carrots (coarsely sliced)
- 2 potatoes (coarsely sliced)
- 4 tablespoons gram flour
- Salt 1 teaspoon
- 1 teaspoon dried thyme
- 1 teaspoon pepper
- 1 diced onions
- 1 cup red wine
- 2 tablespoons Worcestershire sauce
- 4-5 minced garlic cloves
- 1 cup sliced mushrooms
- 1 tablespoon olive oil

Directions:
1. Into a container add flour, thyme, pepper, and salt. Take the beef cuts and add them into the flour mixture to coat them well.
2. In the inner pot of Ninja Foodi Deluxe XL Pressure Cooker, add olive oil and turn the Pressure Cook on High. Add floured beef when the oil is very hot. Sear it from all sides for about 10 minutes.
3. Then add chopped garlic and onion into the Ninja Foodi Deluxe XL Pressure Cooker Pot.
4. Now with the help of wine, deglaze the Ninja Foodi Deluxe XL Pressure Cooker Pot and remove the brown bits from the bottom with a non-stick spatula.
5. Once the wine thickens, add beef broth and Worcestershire sauce to the inner pot of Ninja Foodi Deluxe XL Pressure Cooker. Put on the pressure lid and turn the valve to Seal and cook in Ninja Foodi Deluxe XL Pressure Cooker High Pressure Setting for 20 minutes. Release the pressure when time is up.
6. Cut carrots, mushrooms, potatoes, and onions into slices while beef is being Pressure Cooked. After the pressure has been released, add in vegetables, put on the Pressure Lid and Seal the valve.
7. Pressure Cook it for 2 minutes and serve. Enjoy!

Nutritional Values Per Serving:
Calories: 390; Fat: 7.8g; Carbs: 25.2g; Protein: 38.4g

Roasted Beef

Prep Time: 9-10 Minutes
Cook Time: 25-30 Minutes
Servings: 2

Ingredients:
- 1 pound beef round steaks
- Salt to taste
- Pepper to taste
- 2 tablespoons onion powder
- 1 tablespoon garlic powder
- ½ teaspoon red pepper
- ½ teaspoon paprika
- 1 teaspoon cumin powder
- 1 tablespoon coriander powder
- 1 tablespoon butter

Directions:
1. Combine the dry ingredients with butter and apply them generously to the meat.
2. Select the option Broil and let the beef be broiled for 25 minutes on the Ninja Foodi Deluxe XL Pressure Cooker reversable rack in a Low position. Turn off the Ninja Foodi Deluxe XL Pressure Cooker and keep the lid closed for about 20 to 25 minutes.
3. Remove it and let it rest for 10 minutes, slice it finely and serve!

Nutritional Values Per Serving:
Calories: 327; Fat: 15.4g; Carbs: 16.5g; Protein: 27.7g

Cheesy Beef Casserole

Prep Time: 7 Minutes
Cook Time: 15-20 Minutes
Servings: 6
Ingredients
- 1 pound ground beef
- 2 cups frozen vegetable
- 1 teaspoon pea salt
- 1 cup rice
- 4 minced garlic cloves
- Black pepper to taste
- 1 cup beef stalk
- ¼ cup cheddar cheese
- ¼ cup whipping cream
- 2 tablespoons melted butter
- ½ cup bread crumbs

Directions:
1. Turn the Ninja Foodi Deluxe XL Pressure Cooker on High Pressure setting and add the ground beef, salt, pepper, onion. Cook a bit and then add rice.
2. When cooking, shred the beef and stir occasionally. Add in chopped garlic after the beef is partially cooked and cook it for two to three more minutes.
3. Pour in beef stalk. Put on a pressure lid and Seal the valve. Cook for 2 minutes on Ninja Foodi Deluxe XL Pressure Cooker High Pressure, then let it naturally release pressure for 5 minutes when time is up, and release the remaining pressure manually.
4. Add vegetables and cream. Stir it and mix well.
5. Put back the Ninja Foodi Deluxe XL Pressure Cooker Pressure Lid and check the valve to Vent. While you get the topping mixed up, let it sit for 3 to 5 minutes, and keep a check on the vegetables to make sure they are cooked properly.
6. Once cooked, put a layer of cheese on it.
7. Combine melted butter, bread crumbs and mix it well. Top up the casserole with this layer.
8. On top of the casserole cut the topping in an even layer, select the Ninja Foodi Deluxe XL Pressure Cooker function at 390° F for 8 to 10 minutes and put down the Cook & Crisp lid. And keep checking from time to time until the cheese is melted. Serve and enjoy!

Nutritional Values Per Serving:
Calories: 505; Fat: 26.8g; Carbs: 24.8g; Protein: 32.5g

Sweet and Sour Pork

Prep Time: 15-20 Minutes
Cook Time: 15 Minutes
Servings: 4
Ingredients:
- 2 pound boneless pork
- 3 teaspoons paprika powder
- 1 can pineapple chunks
- 1 chopped onion
- 1 teaspoon chopped green chili
- 2 tablespoons apple cider vinegar
- 2 tablespoons brown sugar
- 2 tablespoons Worcestershire sauce
- Salt to taste
- 2 tablespoons of cornstarch
- ½ cup sliced green onion

Directions:
1. Add pork to a large shallow dish, and sprinkle paprika all over it. Turn on the Sauté setting and adjust for Medium heat. Pour in oil and sear the pork cuts.
2. Now invert the pork to the Ninja Foodi Deluxe XL Pressure Cooker and set it on high Pressure Cook setting. Now add onion, green pepper, soya sauce, vinegar, salt, brown sugar, and pineapple juice to the Ninja Foodi Deluxe XL Pressure Cooker. Lock the lid and block the pressure Release valve.
3. Cook in your Ninja Foodi Deluxe XL Pressure Cooker Pressure Cook on High For 10 minutes. Then release the pressure quickly and click on Slow Cook setting and adjust on High and let it simmer. Now take a small bowl and make a slurry with cornstarch and water.
4. Stir it slowly into the pork gravy, then add pineapple and cook until the sauce thickens up for about one to 2 minutes and sprinkle refreshing green onion on it!

Nutritional Values Per Serving:
Calories: 403; Fat: 12.7g; Carbs: 31.8g; Protein: 42.8g

Lamb Shanks

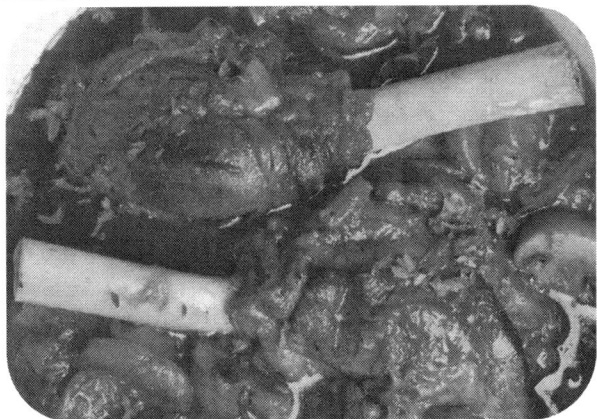

Prep Time: 35-40 Minutes
Cook Time: 1 hour and 20 Minutes
Servings: 1
Ingredients:
- 2 skinless lamb shanks
- 1 teaspoon ginger garlic paste
- 1 teaspoon oregano
- ¾ teaspoon paprika
- ¾ teaspoon salt
- ½ teaspoon black pepper
- ½ teaspoon ground cumin powder
- 1 tablespoon brown sugar
- 1 onion
- 2 small carrots
- 2 bay leaves
- ½ cup red wine
- 2 cups beef stock
- 2 tablespoons cornstarch
- ¼ cup water
- ¼ cup olive oil
- 1 tablespoon olive oil (for cooking)

Directions:
1. Combine lamb, salt, pepper, oregano, ginger garlic paste, paprika, cumin powder, brown sugar, and in a large bowl, and then add oil to it. Coat it well and let it marinate for 30 minutes, or over a night.
2. Click on Pressure Cook on Low setting and heat the Ninja Foodi Deluxe XL Pressure Cooker Pot. Now pour in olive oil and place shanks side by side. Cook for 15 minutes and then remove lamb shanks once they are brown and put them aside.
3. Now add bay leaves, carrots, onions, and the remaining leftover marinade to the Ninja Foodi Deluxe XL Pressure Cooker Pot and cook it until onions become translucent. Cook for about 5 minutes.
4. To deglaze the pot, add red wine and make sure to scrape out all the bits that are stuck on the bottom. Now return the shanks to the pot for 10 minutes, simmer it to reduce by half.
5. Pour in the stock, and cook for 30 minutes at High Pressure on Ninja Foodi Deluxe XL Pressure Cooker and lock pressure lid.
6. And then naturally release the pressure once it's cooked. Now remove shanks and put them aside.
7. Make a slurry of cornstarch with water in a bowl and add it to the pot.

8. Switchback the Ninja Foodi Deluxe XL Pressure Cooker Instant Pot to Low Pressure setting until sauce reaches the desired thickness. Now return lamb to the Ninja Foodi Deluxe XL Pressure Cooker Pot and let it sit in the sauce until it's ready to be served!
Nutritional Values Per Serving:
Calories: 995; Fat: 69.3g; Carbs: 56g; Protein: 12.2g

Maple Lamb Chops

Prep Time: 6-8 Minutes
Cook Time: 12-15 Minutes
Servings: 2
Ingredients:
- 4 lamb chops
- 2 tablespoons maple syrup
- 1 tablespoon rosemary
- 2 tablespoons extra-virgin olive oil
- 1 teaspoon garlic paste
- Salt and pepper to taste
- 8-10 fresh mint leaves

Directions:
1. Add oil, maple syrup, rosemary, and garlic to a bowl to mix the ingredients well. Now add pepper and salt to it. Dump in lamb chops and coat it well, leave it to marinate in the refrigerator for 2 to 4 hours.
2. Preheat Ninja Foodi Deluxe XL Pressure Cooker at 375° F at Bake option for 10 minutes.
3. Place the marinated lamb and close the lids. Let the chops cook for 6 minutes on the Bake. Then flip the chops by opening the top lid and then cook them for six more minutes with a closed lid.
4. Once cooked, its internal temperature should reach 145° F. Now plate it out and add chopped mint and maple syrup on top of it!
Nutritional Values Per Serving:
Calories: 508; Fat: 24.9g; Carbs: 19.6g; Protein: 29.4g

Pork Tenderloin

Prep Time: 5 Minutes
Cook Time: 15-20 Minutes
Servings: 1
Ingredients:
- 1 pound pork tenderloin
- Salt to taste
- 1 teaspoon Schezwan pepper
- 1 tablespoon soy sauce
- 1 tablespoon vinegar
- 1 teaspoon hot sauce
- 1 tablespoon oyster sauce
- ¼ teaspoon chili flakes

Directions:
1. Preheat the Ninja Foodi Deluxe XL Pressure Cooker at Air Crisp Mode at 390° F for 5 minutes. Use the Ninja Foodi Deluxe XL Pressure Cooker function.
2. Combine all the sauces, chili flakes, salt, and pepper in a bowl. Put in the tenderloin and let it rest for 15-20 minutes.
3. Place the tenderloin in the Ninja Foodi Deluxe XL Pressure Cooker Basket. Give it an olive oil spray and let it cook at 390° F for 20 minutes. Once the internal temperature reaches 145° F, it's done.
4. Serve pork with cooked brown gravy!

Nutritional Values Per Serving:
Calories: 367; Fat: 9.1g; Carbs: 5.1g ; Protein: 59.9g

Lamb Balls

Prep Time: 10 Minutes
Cook Time: 10-12 Minutes
Servings: 2
Ingredients:
- 300 grams lamb mince
- 1 tsp ginger garlic paste
- 1 small onion
- 1 tablespoon soy sauce
- ½ cup bread crumbs

Spice Mix Ingredients:
- 1 teaspoon cumin powder
- 1 teaspoon coriander powder
- ½ teaspoon turmeric powder
- Salt to taste
- Black pepper to taste

Directions:
1. Grate the onion and put it in a bowl. Now add the remaining ingredients and with the help of your hand mix all the ingredients. Mix it until the batter is well-combined.
2. Shape the balls in a round shape and set them aside on a plate.
3. Now at 390° F, preheat the Ninja Foodi Deluxe XL Pressure Cooker at Air Crisp Mode and align balls in the Cook & Crisp Basket for 10 to 12 minutes.

Nutritional Values Per Serving:
Calories: 506; Fat: 31.5g; Carbs: 19g; Protein: 36.6g

Pork Chili Verde

Prep Time: 25 Minutes
Cook Time: 30-35 Minutes
Servings: 6
Ingredients:
- 2 pounds pork sirloin (1-inch cuts)
- 4 tablespoons Enchilada sauce
- 1 teaspoon garlic paste
- 2 tablespoons canola oil
- ½ cup sliced carrot
- 1 diced onion
- ½ cup cold water
- 2-3 sliced jalapenos
- ¼ cup fresh cilantro

Directions:
1. In Ninja Foodi Deluxe XL Pressure Cooker select Pressure Cook High setting.
2. Pour in oil and pork and cook the pork in it until it changes its color.
3. Then add carrots, onion, and garlic in it until garlic becomes fragrant and onion becomes translucent.

4. Now add enchilada sauce, water, cilantro, and jalapenos to the Ninja Foodi Deluxe XL Pressure Cooker Pot at High Pressure Cook setting. Stir it and seal the pressure lid and close the valve. Cook for 30 minutes then allow the pressure to release naturally for 10 minutes.

5. Dish it out and serve it with tortillas!

Nutritional Values Per Serving:
Calories: 464; Fat: 20.7g; Carbs: 13g; Protein: 49.6g

Char Siu Pork

Prep Time: 25 Minutes
Cook Time: 1.5 hours
Servings: 2

Ingredients:
- 1 pound pork fillet
- ½ cup chicken broth
- 2 tablespoons soy sauce
- ¼ cup ketchup
- 2 tablespoons honey
- 3 tablespoons bean paste
- 1 teaspoon garlic paste
- 1 teaspoon ginger paste
- 1 teaspoon five-spice powder
- ¼ cup fresh coriander leaves

Directions:
1. Start by combining honey, bean paste, soya sauce, ketchup, ginger garlic, and the five-spice powder into a large shallow dish. Now add pork to the dish and turn to coat evenly in the dry mix.

2. Transfer pork in a Ninja Foodi Deluxe XL Pressure Cooker Pot. Take Ninja Foodi Deluxe XL Pressure Cooker Pressure Cook and add chicken broth to it. Seal the pressure lid and close the valve for 75 minutes, adjust your Ninja Foodi Deluxe XL Pressure Cooker Pressure Cook setting on High, and then after time allow for 10 minutes to pressure to release naturally. Then quickly release the remaining pressure manually.

3. When pork is done, cut the pork coarsely.

4. Then turn on Sauté setting and let it cook for 2 to 3 minutes at Low heat. Press cancel and top up with fresh coriander!

Nutritional Values Per Serving:
Calories: 521; Fat: 15g; Carbs: 34.6g; Protein: 59.7g

Fish and Seafood Recipes

Glazed Coho Salmon

Prep Time: 10 minutes
Cook Time: 25 minutes
Serves: 4

Ingredients:
- 1–2 coho salmon fillets
- 1 cup water
- ¼ cup soy sauce
- ¼ cup brown sugar
- 1 tbsp honey
- 1½ tbsp ginger root, minced
- ½ tsp white pepper
- 2 tbsp corn starch
- ¼ cup cold water

Preparation:
1. Preheat the Ninja Foodi on AIR CRISP mode at 350°F for 15 minutes.
2. Put a medium saucepan over medium heat. Add in all the ingredients (except the salmon, corn starch, and cold water) and bring to a gentle boil.
3. Combine the corn starch and water in another bowl. Then, slowly whisk the corn starch mixture into the sauce in the saucepan until it thickens.
4. Brush the sauce over the salmon fillets (reserving some of the sauce for serving).
5. Place the salmon in the Cook & Crisp Basket and close the Crisping Lid.
6. Cook on AIR CRISP for 15 minutes at 350°F.
7. When done, brush the salmon with another coat of sauce and serve.

Nutritional Information Per Serving:
Calories 163; Fat: 2g; Carbs: 15g; Protein: 18g

Spicy Crispy Shrimp

Prep Time: 5–10 minutes (plus 60 minutes for marinating)
Cook Time: 6 minutes
Serves: 4

Ingredients:
- 1 tsp garlic salt
- ½ tsp black pepper
- 1 tbsp paprika
- 1 tbsp garlic powder
- 2 tbsp olive oil
- 1 lb. jumbo shrimps, peeled and deveined
- 2 tbsp brown sugar

Preparation:
1. Mix together all the ingredients in a large mixing bowl until well combined.
2. Let the mixture chill and marinate for 30–60 minutes.
3. Preheat the Ninja Foodi on BAKE/ROAST mode at 360°F for 6 minutes.
4. Let it preheat until you hear the beep.
5. Arrange the prepared shrimp over the reversible rack in the Ninja Foodi. Lock the lid and cook for 3 minutes. Open the lid, flip the shrimp, close the lid, and cook for 3 minutes more.
6. Serve and enjoy!

Nutritional Information Per Serving:
Calories 370; Fat: 27.9g; Carbs: 23g; Protein: 6g

Low-Carb Crab Soup

Prep Time: 5 minutes
Cook Time: 15 minutes
Serves: 6

Ingredients:
Soup
- 12 oz lump crab meat
- 24 oz marinara sauce
- 4 cups chicken broth
- 3 ribs celery, chopped
- 2 bell peppers, chopped
- 2 tbsp Old Bay Seasoning
- ½ cup butter
- Salt and pepper, to taste
- 1 cup heavy cream

Onion and cream cheese topping
- 8 oz cream cheese, softened for 30 seconds in the microwave
- 3 green onions, chopped
- ½ tsp Old Bay Seasoning

Preparation:
1. Place all the soup ingredients except the heavy cream into the Ninja Foodi cooking pot and stir well.
2. Select PRESSURE mode. Close the Pressure Lid and cook on HI for 15 minutes.
3. When done, naturally release the pressure for 15 minutes before venting the rest of the steam.
4. Meanwhile, combine the cream cheese topping ingredients. Put the mixture in an airtight container and refrigerate.
5. Once the soup is done cooking, stir in the heavy cream.

Nutritional Information Per Serving:
Calories 391; Fat: 36.6g; Carbs: 8.3g; Protein: 9.32g

Salmon and Dill Sauce

Prep Time: 10 minutes
Cook Time: 20–25 minutes
Serves: 4

Ingredients:
- 4 salmon fillets (6 oz each)
- 2 tsp olive oil, divided
- 1 pinch salt

Dill sauce
- ½ cup non-fat Greek yogurt
- ½ cup sour cream
- Pinch of salt
- 2 tbsp fresh dill, chopped

Preparation:
1. Preheat the Ninja Foodi on AIR CRISP mode at 270°F for 25 minutes.
2. Drizzle the salmon fillets with 1 teaspoon of the olive oil and season with salt.
3. Once the Foodi has preheated, place the salmon in the Cook & Crisp Basket, put it in the Ninja Foodi, and cook for 20–23 minutes.
4. Meanwhile, take a bowl and add the sour cream, salt, chopped dill, yogurt, and mix well to prepare the dill sauce.

Nutritional Information Per Serving:
Calories 600; Fat: 45g; Carbs: 5g; Protein: 60g

Coconut Curry Salmon with Zucchini Noodles

Prep Time: 10 minutes
Cook Time: 15 minutes
Serves: 2
Ingredients:
- 2 tbsp yellow curry paste
- 1 small sweet onion, halved and sliced
- 1 red bell pepper seeded, halved, and sliced
- 2 garlic cloves, pressed
- 1 (14½ oz) can coconut milk
- 1 dash fish sauce
- ¾-lb salmon, skinned, deboned, and cut into 2 fillets
- 1 zucchini, spiralized

Preparation:
1. Set the Ninja Foodi to SEAR/SAUTÉ mode on HI. Allow it to preheat for 3 minutes.
2. When the Foodi has preheated, add the yellow curry paste and onions. Stir the onions around with a wooden spoon to coat them with the curry. Allow them to cook for 5 minutes.
3. Add the bell pepper and garlic once the onions are tender, cooking for an additional 2 minutes.
4. Pour in the coconut milk and add a dash of fish sauce. Stir to combine.
5. Place the salmon fillets on top of the curry mixture.
6. Place the Pressure Lid on. Select PRESSURE mode and cook for 3 minutes on HI.
7. After the cooking time is up, open the Foodi and place the zucchini delicately on top of the fish. Replace the lid and steam for an additional minute.
8. Turn off the Foodi, and remove the lid. Use tongs to transfer the zucchini noodles to wide bowls. Place a salmon fillet on top of each mound of zucchini, then ladle on the sauce with the onions and bell peppers.

Nutritional Information Per Serving:
Calories 251.8; Fat: 12.3g ; Carbs: 33.7g ; Protein: 2.6g

Fish Stew

Prep Time: 5 minutes
Cook Time: 20 minutes
Serves: 4
Ingredients:
- 1 lb. white fish fillets, chopped
- 1 cup broccoli, chopped
- 3 cups fish stock
- 1 onion, diced
- 2 cups celery stalks, chopped
- 1 cup heavy cream
- 1 bay leaf
- 1½ cups cauliflower, diced
- 1 carrot, sliced
- 2 tbsp butter
- ¼ tsp garlic powder
- ½ tsp salt
- ¼ tsp pepper

Preparation:
1. Set your Ninja Foodi to SEAR/SAUTÉ mode on HI temperature setting.
2. Add the butter, and let it melt.
3. Add the onion and carrots, cook for 3 minutes.
4. Stir in the remaining ingredients.
5. Close the Pressure Lid.
6. Cook for 4 minutes on HI on PRESSURE mode.
7. Release the pressure naturally over 10 minutes.
8. Remove the bay leaf once cooked.

Nutritional Information Per Serving:
Calories 298; Fat: 18g; Carbs: 6g; Protein: 24g

Spicy Indian Shrimp Curry

Prep Time: 10 minutes
Cook Time: 20 minutes
Serves: 4
Ingredients:
- 1 tbsp olive oil
- 1 onion, chopped
- 1 tbsp garlic, minced
- 2 lbs. shrimp, peeled and cleaned
- 1 (48 oz) can crushed tomatoes
- 1 tsp cayenne pepper
- 1 tsp curry powder
- 1 tsp ground ginger
- 2 tsp parsley flakes
- 1 tsp garlic powder
- 2 tsp salt
- 1 tbsp sugar
- ½–1 cup sour cream
- 3 tbsp corn starch and ½ cup cold water, combined

Preparation:
1. Turn the Foodi to SEAR/SAUTÉ mode on HI.
2. Add the olive oil and sauté the onion and garlic. Add the shrimp. Try to leave the shrimp a little undercooked. Remove from the pot.
3. Add the crushed tomatoes, cayenne pepper, curry, ginger, parsley flakes, garlic powder, salt, and sugar. Cook until bubbling hot.
4. Return the shrimp to the pot and stir in your preferred amount of sour cream, depending on how creamy you want it.
5. Turn to BAKE/ROAST mode at 425°F for about 10 minutes. Adjust any seasonings you prefer.
6. Take the corn starch slurry and add it to the curry. Stir well. Cook for another 3 minutes until thickened to the desired consistency.

Nutritional Information Per Serving:
Calories 197.3; Fat: 11.6g; Carbs: 21.5g ; Protein: 2.5g

Sweet and Sour Fish

Prep Time: 10 minutes
Cook Time: 6 minutes
Serves: 4
Ingredients:
- 1 lb. fish chunks
- 1 tbsp vinegar
- 2 drops liquid stevia
- ¼ cup butter
- Salt and pepper, to taste

Preparation:
1. Set your Ninja Foodi to SEAR/SAUTÉ mode on MD:HI temperature setting.
2. Add the butter to the Foodi's pot and melt it.
3. Add the fish chunks, sauté for 3 minutes.
4. Add the stevia, salt, and pepper, and stir.
5. Close the Foodi with the Crisping Lid. Select AIR CRISP mode.
6. Cook for 3 minutes at 360°F.
7. Serve and enjoy!

Nutritional Information Per Serving:
Calories 274; Fat: 15g; Carbs: 2g; Protein: 33g

Mahi-Mahi with Citrus Sauce

Prep Time: 5 minutes
Cook Time: 10 minutes
Serves: 4
Ingredients:
- 1 cup water
- 1 tbsp olive oil
- 1 cup white wine
- ½ cup orange juice
- 2 tbsp soy sauce
- 1 tbsp lime juice
- 4 (4 oz each) mahi-mahi fillets
- Salt and pepper, to taste
- 4 tsp Chinese five-spice powder
- 1 tsp sesame seeds
- 2 tsp butter

Preparation:
1. Add the water, olive oil, white wine, orange juice, soy sauce, and lime juice to the Ninja Foodi pot. Set to STEAM mode and set the timer to 10 minutes.
2. Meanwhile, season each fillet with salt and pepper, five-spice, and sesame seeds.
3. When the beep sounds, carefully place the reversible rack into the pot topped with the fish fillets. Cover and steam for 8–10 minutes for the desired doneness.
4. Remove the rack with the fish. Whisk butter into the sauce at the bottom of the pot.

Nutritional Information Per Serving:
Calories 215.3; Fat: 14.7g; Carbs: 19.4g ; Protein: 3.7g

Lobster with Fried Rice

Prep Time: 5 minutes
Cook Time: 15 minutes
Serves: 3
Ingredients:
- 1 cup cooked lobster flesh
- 2–3 cups cooked rice
- 2 tbsp sesame oil
- 1 small white onion, chopped
- 1 cup peas
- 7 mini carrots, chopped
- 2-3 tbsp soy sauce
- 2 eggs, lightly beaten
- 2 tbsp green onions, chopped

Preparation:
1. Preheat the Ninja Foodi on SEAR/SAUTÉ mode on HI for 5 minutes.
2. When the Foodi has preheated, pour the sesame oil into the Foodi's pot. Add the white onion and carrots and fry until tender. Add the peas and cook for 5 minutes.
3. Place the onion, peas, and carrots to one side of the pot, and pour the beaten eggs onto the other side.
4. Using a spatula, scramble the eggs. Once cooked, mix the eggs with the vegetable mix.
5. Add the rice to the veggie and egg mixture. Pour the soy sauce on top. Stir and fry the rice and veggie mixture until heated through and combined.
6. Add the lobster meat and stir. Switch the Foodi to KEEP WARM mode for about 2 minutes.
7. Add the chopped green onions on top.

Nutritional Information Per Serving:
Calories 190; Fat: 9g; Carbs: 26g ; Protein: 4g

Fish Broccoli Stew

Prep Time: 5 minutes
Cook Time: 20 minutes
Servings: 4
Ingredients:
- 1-pound white fish fillets, chopped
- 1 cup broccoli, chopped
- 3 cups fish stock
- 1 onion, diced
- 2 cups celery stalks, chopped
- 1 cup heavy cream
- 1 bay leaf
- 1 and ½ cups cauliflower, diced
- 1 carrot, sliced
- 2 tablespoons butter
- ¼ teaspoon garlic powder
- ½ teaspoon salt
- ¼ teaspoon black pepper

Directions:
1. Select "Sauté" mode on your Ninja Foodi
2. Add butter, and let it melt
3. Stir in onion and carrots, cook for 3 minutes.
4. Stir in remaining ingredients
5. Close the Ninja Foodi's lid.
6. Cook for 4 minutes on High.
7. Release the pressure naturally over 10 minutes.
8. Remove the bay leave once cooked.
9. Serve and enjoy.

Nutritional Values Per Serving:
Calories: 298g; Fat: 18g; Carbs: 6g; Protein: 24g

Buttered Fish

Prep Time: 10 minutes
Cook Time: 6 minutes
Servings: 4
Ingredients:
- 1-pound fish chunks
- 1 tablespoon vinegar
- 2 drops liquid stevia
- ¼ cup butter
- Black pepper and salt to taste

Directions:
1. Select "Sauté" mode on your Ninja Foodi
2. Stir in butter and melt it
3. Add fish chunks, Sauté for 3 minutes
4. Stir in stevia, salt, pepper, stir it
5. Close the crisping lid
6. Cook on "Air Crisp" mode for 3 minutes to 360 degrees F
7. Serve and enjoy.

Nutritional Values Per Serving:
Calories: 274g; Fat: 15g; Carbs: 2g; Protein: 33g

Awesome Shrimp Roast

Prep Time: 5-10 minutes
Cook Time: 7 minutes
Servings: 2
Ingredients:
- 3 tablespoons chipotle in adobo sauce, minced
- ¼ teaspoon salt
- ¼ cup BBQ sauce
- ½ orange, juiced
- ½ pound large shrimps

Directions:
1. Preheat Ninja Foodi by pressing the "Bake/Roast" mode and setting it to "400 Degrees F" and timer to 7 minutes.
2. Let it preheat until you hear a beep.
3. Set shrimps over Grill Grate and lock lid, cook until the timer runs out.
4. Serve and enjoy.
Nutritional Values Per Serving:
Calories: 173; Fat: 2g; Carbs: 21g; Protein: 17g

Salmon with Dill Sauce

Prep Time: 10 minutes
Cook Time: 20-25 minutes
Servings: 4
Ingredients:
- 4 salmon, each of 6 ounces
- 2 teaspoons olive oil
- 1 pinch salt
- Dill Sauce
- ½ cup non-Fat: Greek Yogurt
- ½ cup sour cream
- Pinch of salt
- 2 tablespoons dill, chopped
Directions:

1. Preheat Ninja Foodi by pressing the "AIR CRISP" option and setting it to "270 Degrees F" and timer to 25 minutes
2. Wait until the appliance beeps
3. Drizzle cut pieces of salmon with 1 teaspoon olive oil
4. Season with salt
5. Take the cooking basket out and transfer salmon to basket, cook for 20-23 minutes
6. Take a suitable and stir in sour cream, salt, chopped dill, yogurt and mix well to prepare the dill sauce
7. Serve cooked salmon by pouring the sauce all over
8. Garnish with chopped dill and enjoy.
Nutritional Values Per Serving:
Calories: 600; Fat: 45g; Carbs: 5g; Protein: 60g

Roasted BBQ Shrimp

Prep Time: 5-10 minutes
Cook Time: 7 minutes
Servings: 2
Ingredients:
- 3 tablespoons chipotle in adobo sauce, minced
- ¼ teaspoon salt
- ¼ cup BBQ sauce
- ½ orange, juiced
- ½-pound large shrimps
Directions:
1. Toss shrimp wth chipotles and rest of the ingredients in a suitable bowl.
2. Preheat Ninja Foodi by pressing the "Bake/Roast" mode and setting it to "400 Degrees F" and timer to 7 minutes
3. Let it preheat until you hear a beep
4. Set shrimps over the pot and lock lid, cook until the timer runs out
5. Serve and enjoy.
Nutritional Values Per Serving:
Calories: 173; Fat: 2g; Carbs: 21g; Protein: 17g

Sweet Sour Fish

Prep Time: 10 minutes
Cook Time: 6 minutes
Servings: 4
Ingredients:
- 1-pound fish chunks
- 1 tablespoon vinegar
- 2 drops liquid stevia
- ¼ cup butter
- Black pepper and salt to taste

Directions:
1. Select "Sauté" mode on your Ninja Foodi
2. Stir in butter and melt it
3. Add fish chunks, sauté for 3 minutes
4. Stir in stevia, salt, pepper, stir it
5. Close the crisping lid
6. Cook on "Air Crisp" mode for 3 minutes to 360-degrees F
7. Serve and enjoy.

Nutritional Values Per Serving:
Calories: 274g; Fat: 15g; Carbs: 2g; Protein: 33g

Air Fried Scallops

Prep Time: 5 minutes
Cook Time: 5 minutes
Servings: 4
Ingredients:
- 12 scallops
- 3 tablespoons olive oil
- Black pepper and salt, to taste

Directions:
1. Rub the scallops with salt, pepper and olive oil
2. Transfer it to Ninja foodi

3. Place the insert in your Ninja foodi
4. Close the air crisping lid
5. Air crisp for 4 minutes to 390 degrees F
6. Flip them after 2 minutes
7. Serve and enjoy.

Nutritional Values Per Serving:
Calories: 372g; Fat: 11g; Carbs: 0.9g; Protein: 63g

Cajun Shrimp

Prep Time: 10 minutes
Cook Time: 7 minutes
Servings: 4
Ingredients:
- 1 ¼ pound shrimp
- ¼ teaspoon cayenne pepper
- ½ teaspoon old bay seasoning
- ¼ teaspoon smoked paprika
- 1 pinch of salt
- 1 tablespoon olive oil

Directions:
1. Preheat Ninja Foodi by pressing the "AIR CRISP" option and setting it to "390 Degrees F" and timer to 10 minutes
2. Dip the shrimp into a spice mixture and oil
3. Transfer the prepared shrimp to your Ninja Foodi Grill cooking basket and cook for 5 minutes
4. Serve and enjoy.

Nutritional Values Per Serving:
Calories: 170; Fat: 2g; Carbs: 5g; Protein: 23g

Panko Crusted Cod

Prep Time: 10 minutes
Cook Time: 15 minutes
Servings: 4
Ingredients:
- 2 uncooked cod fillets
- 3 teaspoons kosher salt
- ¾ cup panko bread crumbs
- 2 tablespoons butter, melted
- ¼ cup fresh parsley, minced
- 1 lemon. Zested and juiced

Directions:
1. Pre-heat your Ninja Foodi at 390 degrees F and place the Air Crisper basket inside
2. Season cod and salt
3. Take a suitable and stir in bread crumbs, parsley, lemon juice, zest, butter, and mix well
4. Coat fillets with the bread crumbs mixture and place fillets in your Air Crisping basket
5. Lock Crisping lid and cook on Air Crisp mode for 15 minutes at 360 degrees F
6. Serve and enjoy.
Nutritional Values Per Serving:
Calories: 554; Fat: 24g; Carbs: 5g; Protein: 37g

Buttery Scallops

Prep Time: 18 minutes
Cook Time: 6 minutes
Servings: 4
Ingredients:
- 2 pounds sea scallops
- 12 cup butter
- 4 garlic cloves, minced
- 4 tablespoons rosemary, chopped

- Black pepper and salt to taste
Directions:
1. Select "Sauté" mode on your Ninja Foodi on Medium-High heat.
2. Add rosemary, garlic and butter, Sauté for 1 minute
3. Stir in scallops, Black pepper and salt, Sauté for 2 minutes.
4. Close the crisping lid.
5. Cook for 3 minutes.
6. Serve and enjoy.
Nutritional Values Per Serving:
Calories: 278g; Fat: 15g; Carbs: 5g; Protein: 25g

Shrimp Zoodles

Prep Time: 10 minutes
Cook Time: 3 minutes
Servings: 4
Ingredients:
- 4 cups zoodles
- 1 tablespoon basil, chopped
- 2 tablespoons Ghee
- 1 cup vegetable stock
- 2 garlic cloves, minced
- 2 tablespoons olive oil
- ½ lemon
- ½ teaspoon paprika

Directions:
1. Select "Sauté" mode on your Ninja Foodi and add ghee, let it heat up
2. Stir in olive oil as well
3. Add garlic and cook for 1 minute
4. Stir in lemon juice, shrimp and cook for 1 minute approximately.
5. Stir in the rest of the ingredients then lock lid, cook on LOW pressure for 5 minutes
6. Quick-release pressure and serve
7. Enjoy.
Nutritional Values Per Serving:
Calories: 277; Fat: 6g; Carbs: 5g; Protein: 27g

Ninja Foodi Salmon Soup

Prep Time: 15 minutes
Cook Time: 24 minutes
Servings: 10
Ingredients:
- 2 pounds boneless salmon, cubed
- 2 tablespoons olive oil
- 8 cups chicken broth
- 2 tablespoons tamari
- Salt and black pepper, to taste

Directions:
1. Add oil and salmon in a large Ninja Foodi Deluxe XL Pressure Cooker, sauté for about 5 minutes and press the "Broil" button.
2. Stir in broth and close the Crisping Lid.
3. Press the "Start/Stop" button and boil the mixture for about 15 minutes.
4. Open the lid and add in salt, pepper and tamari.
5. Cook for 4 minutes and take out.
6. Serve and enjoy!

Nutritional Values Per Serving:
Calories: 88; Fat: 5.3g; Carbs: 0.9g; Protein: 8.9g

Salmon Kale Meal

Prep Time: 16 minutes
Cook Time: 4 minutes
Servings: 4
Ingredients:
- 1 lemon, juiced
- 2 salmon fillets
- ¼ cup extra virgin olive oil
- 1 teaspoon Dijon mustard
- 4 cups kale, sliced, ribs removed

- 1 teaspoon salt
- 1 avocado, diced
- 1 cup pomegranate seeds
- 1 cup walnuts, toasted
- 1 cup goat parmesan cheese, shredded

Directions:
1. Season salmon with salt and keep it on the side
2. Place a rack in your Ninja Foodi
3. Place salmon over the rack.
4. Release pressure naturally over 10 minutes
5. Transfer salmon to a serving platter
6. Take a suitable and stir in kale, season with salt
7. Season kale with dressing and add diced avocado, pomegranate seeds, walnuts and cheese
8. Toss and serve with the fish
9. Enjoy.

Nutritional Values Per Serving:
Calories: 234; Fat: 14g; Carbs: 12g; Protein: 16g

Ninja Foodi Squid Rings

Prep Time: 10 minutes
Cook Time: 13 minutes
Servings: 6
Ingredients:
- ½ onion, sliced
- 2 pounds squid, cut into rings
- 2 teaspoons extra-virgin olive oil
- 2 eggs, beaten
- Salt and black pepper, to taste

Directions:
1. Add oil and onion in a Ninja Foodi Deluxe XL Pressure Cooker and select "Pressure".
2. Press the "Start/Stop" button and sauté for about 5 minutes.
3. Add in squid rings, salt and pepper. Toss to coat well.
4. Simmer for about 5-minutes and stir in eggs.
5. Close the pressure Lid and cook for about 3 minutes at HIGH pressure.
6. Take out, serve and enjoy!

Nutritional Values Per Serving:
Calories: 177; Fat: 5.1g; Carbs: 5.6g; Protein: 25.5g

Ninja Foodi Stir-Fried Shrimp

Prep Time: 5 minutes
Cook Time: 6 minutes
Servings: 6
Ingredients:
* 2 pounds shrimp, peeled and deveined
* 8 tablespoons tamari
* 8 garlic cloves, minced
* 2 tablespoons olive oil
* Salt and black pepper, to taste
Directions:
1. Add oil in Ninja Foodi Deluxe XL Pressure Cooker and sauté garlic in it for about 1 minute.
2. Stir in shrimp, salt, tamari and black pepper and close the pressure Lid.
3. Select "Pressure" and press the "Start/Stop" button.
4. Cook for about 5 minutes at HIGH pressure and open the lid.
5. Take out, serve and enjoy!
Nutritional Values Per Serving:
Calories: 240; Fat: 7.3g; Carbs: 5g; Protein: 37.2g

Ninja Foodi Rosemary Scallops

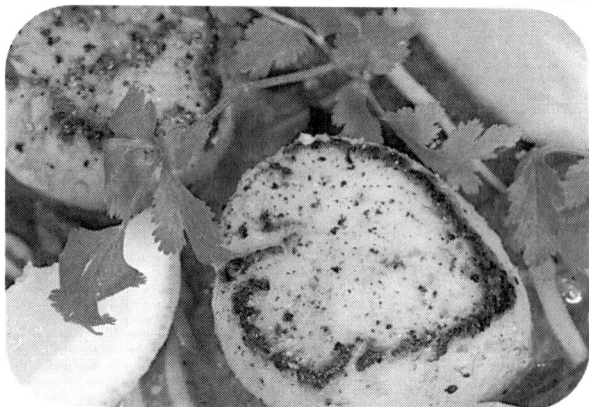

Prep Time: 10 minutes
Cook Time: 8 minutes
Servings: 6
Ingredients:
* 2 pounds sea scallops
* 4 tablespoons fresh rosemary, chopped
* 4 tablespoons extra-virgin olive oil

* 4 garlic cloves, minced
* Salt and black pepper, to taste
Directions:
1. Add olive oil, rosemary and garlic in the pot of Ninja Foodi Deluxe XL Pressure Cooker, sauté for about 2 minutes and select "Sear".
2. Stir in scallops, salt and pepper and close the pressure Lid.
3. Press the "Start/Stop" button and cook for about 3 minutes on each side.
4. Open the lid and take out.
5. Serve and enjoy!
Nutritional Values Per Serving:
Calories: 223; Fat: 10.8g; Carbs: 5.7g; Protein: 25.6g

Ninja Foodi Parsley Baked Salmon

Prep Time: 10 minutes
Cook Time: 20 minutes
Servings: 3
Ingredients:
* 1 pound salmon fillets
* ¾ tablespoon olive oil
* 1½ tablespoons fresh parsley, minced
* ¼ teaspoon ginger powder
* Salt and black pepper, to taste
Directions:
1. Place salmon fillets in Ninja Foodi Deluxe XL Pressure Cooker and top them with olive oil, parsley, ginger powder, salt and pepper.
2. Press the "Bake" button and close the Crisping Lid.
3. Press the "Start/Stop" button and bake for 20 minutes at 400 degrees F.
4. Open the lid and take out.
5. Serve and enjoy!
Nutritional Values Per Serving:
Calories: 233; Fat: 12.9g; Carbs: 0.6g; Protein: 29.6g

Ninja Foodi Broiled Mahi-Mahi

Prep Time: 10 minutes
Cook Time: 10 minutes
Servings: 2
Ingredients:
- ½ pound mahi-mahi fillets
- ½ tablespoon olive oil
- 2 tablespoon fresh orange juice
- ½ teaspoon dried thyme
- ½ teaspoon cayenne pepper
- Salt and black pepper, to taste

Directions:
1. Add everything except mahi-mahi fillets in a large bowl and mix well.
2. Stir in mahi-mahi and toss to coat well.
3. Set aside the mixture for about half an hour and remove the fillets from the bowl.
4. Place them in Ninja Foodi Deluxe XL Pressure Cooker and press the "Broil" button.
5. Close the Crisping Lid and press the "Start/Stop" button.
6. Broil for about 10 minutes and open the lid.
7. Dish out and serve hot.

Nutritional Values Per Serving:
Calories: 130; Fat: 3.6g; Carbs: 2.1g; Protein: 21.3g

Ninja Foodi Roasted Tilapia

Prep Time: 10 minutes
Cook Time: 6 minutes
Servings: 2
Ingredients:
- ½ pound tilapia
- ½ tablespoon fresh lime juice
- ¼ tablespoon red pepper flakes
- ½ tablespoon olive oil
- ½ teaspoon black pepper
- Salt, to taste

Directions:
1. Add everything except tilapia fillets in a large bowl. Mix well.
2. Add in tilapia, toss to coat well and set aside for about half an hour.
3. Place marinated tilapia fillets the pot of Ninja Foodi Deluxe XL Pressure Cooker and select "Roast".
4. Close the Crisping Lid and press the "Start/Stop" button.
5. Roast for about 3-minutes per side and open the lid.
6. Take out, serve and enjoy!

Nutritional Values Per Serving:
Calories: 130; Fat: 4.7g; Carbs: 1.6g; Protein: 21.3g

Ninja Foodi Ginger Cod

Prep Time: 10 minutes
Cook Time: 20 minutes
Servings: 2
Ingredients:
- ½ pound cod fillets
- 1 tablespoon fresh lime juice
- ½ tablespoon fresh ginger, minced
- 1 tablespoon coconut aminos
- Salt and black pepper, to taste

Directions:
1. Add lime juice, fresh ginger, coconut aminos, salt and pepper in a bowl. Mix well.
2. Add cod fillets in the mixture and toss to coat well.
3. Place them in the pot of Ninja Foodi Deluxe XL Pressure Cooker and press the "Bake" button.
4. Close the Crisping Lid and press the "Start/Stop" button.
5. Bake for about 20-minutes at 325 degrees F and open the lid.
6. Take out, serve and enjoy!

Nutritional Values Per Serving:
Calories: 109; Fat: 1.1g; Carbs: 4.3g; Protein: 20.5g

Shrimp Scampi Linguini

Prep Time: 5 Minutes
Cook Time: 3 Minutes
Servings: 8
Ingredients:
- 1 pound linguini
- 1 pound (31 to 40) shrimp
- Salt and pepper (to taste)
- 3 tablespoons olive oil
- 3 tablespoons butter (salted)
- 2 tablespoons garlic (minced)
- 1 cup dry white wine
- 1 cup chicken broth
- ¼ teaspoon red pepper flakes
- 1 lemon (juice of the lemon)
- ¼ cup parmesan cheese (shredded)

Directions:
1. Turn Ninja Foodi Deluxe XL Pressure Cooker on Sauté on High.
2. Pour in olive oil.
3. Add butter and stir.
4. Add shrimp, season with salt and pepper and then stir.
5. Add garlic and juice of one lemon. Be careful not to get the lemon seeds in the pot.
6. Pour in white wine and chicken broth.
7. Add red pepper flakes and stir.
8. Break linguine in half and add in layers, criss crossing each layer so the pasta does not stick to itself.
9. Once all pasta has been added to the Ninja Foodi Deluxe XL Pressure Cooker Pot, press pasta into liquid as much as possible, without stirring. **Do not stir** once you have added the pasta. If you do, your pasta may burn to the bottom of the pan.
10. Put Pressure Lid on Ninja Foodi Deluxe XL Pressure Cooker and move valve to Seal position.
11. Change Ninja Foodi Deluxe XL Pressure Cooker to Pressure Cook setting on High for 3 minutes and push start.
12. When timer beeps, quick release pressure by moving valve to Vent position. Turn Ninja Foodi Deluxe XL Pressure Cooker off.
13. Open Ninja Foodi Deluxe XL Pressure Cooker Pressure Lid and stir shrimp and pasta until its well-combined. Don't panic if your pasta is not 100% cooked. It will continue to cook after you add in the parmesan cheese.
14. Add parmesan cheese and stir.
15. Close the Ninja Foodi Deluxe XL Pressure Cooker Lid (**do not turn on**) and let the pasta and sauce continue to combine for about 5 minutes. Stir and Enjoy!!!

Nutritional Values Per Serving:
Calories: 396; Fat: 12g; Carbs:s 45g; Protein: 21g

Ninja Foodi Salmon with Sweet Potatoes

Prep Time: 10 minutes
Cook Time: 9 hours
Servings: 3
Ingredients:
- ½ pound salmon fillets, cubed
- ¾ cup chicken broth
- ¼ teaspoon ground nutmeg
- 2 sweet potatoes, sliced thinly
- ½ onion, chopped
- Salt and black pepper, to taste

Directions:
1. Place half of the sweetpotatoes in the bottom of the Ninja Foodi Deluxe XL Pressure Cooker and season them with salt and pepper.
2. Place salmon fillets and onion on the top and sprinkle ground nutmeg on it.
3. Then, top with remaining sweet potato slices and close the pressure Lid.
4. Select "Slow Cook" and press the "Start/Stop" button.
5. Cook for about 9 hours at LOW TEMP and open the lid.
6. Take out, serve and enjoy!

Nutritional Values Per Serving:
Calories: 236; Fat: 5.3g; Carbs: 29.9g; Protein: 17.6g

Lobster Tail

Prep Time: 4 Minutes
Cook Time: 6 Minutes
Servings: 2
Ingredients:
- 4 lobster tails
- 4 tablespoons butter (unsalted)
- 2 crushed garlic cloves
- 1 tablespoon mixed dried herbs
- 1 teaspoon Slash parsley
- Salt and pepper to taste

Directions:
1. Preheat the Ninja Foodi Deluxe XL Pressure Cooker at 375° F for the Bake function by setting the Bake Mode for 5 minutes.
2. Meanwhile, cut the lobster using kitchen scissors then cut the center of the tail until you reach the fins. Do not cut them. Use your fingers to bring the meat up to the top by pulling apart the tail and closing the shell.
3. It should create a butterfly with the meat when you're cutting it so that it can easily be moved to the top of the shell.
4. Melt the butter, add garlic and parsley and mix well in a small bowl. Now drench the lobster tails in a butter mixture.
5. Now place the lobster tail in the Ninja Foodi Deluxe XL Pressure Cooker Cook & Crisp Basket very carefully, and spray olive oil generously.
6. For 5 minutes cook the lobsters, or until the internal temperature of the meat reaches at least 145° F. Lift the lid of the Ninja Foodi Deluxe XL Pressure Cooker once it's done.
7. Take out the golden lobsters and serve!

Nutritional Values Per Serving:
Calories: 565; Fat: 36g; Carbs: 0.2g; Protein: 46.3g

Ninja Foodi Salmon

Prep Time: 5-6 Minutes
Cook Time: 4-5 Minutes
Servings: 4
Ingredients:
- 2 salmon fillets
- 1 cup water
- Juice from 1 lemon, about ½ cup
- Lemon slices
- 4-5 sprigs of fresh dill (or rosemary)
- Salt and pepper to taste

Directions:
1. Pour water and lemon juice into the Ninja Foodi Deluxe XL Pressure Cooker.
2. Add lemon slices and dill.
3. Add the fillets.
4. Add the lemon slices on top of the salmon.
5. Sprinkle with salt and pepper.
6. Secure the Ninja Foodi Deluxe XL Pressure Cooker Pressure Lid.
7. Make sure the valve is set to Seal, use the manual settings and cook on High Pressure for 4 minutes. Add an additional minute if the fillet is frozen.
8. Once done, release the valve to Vent (quick release) and then open the lid.
9. Serve the salmon immediately or store in fridge.

Nutritional Values Per Serving:
Calories: 273; Fat: 14g; Carbs: 10g; Protein: 25g

Butter Lime Salmon

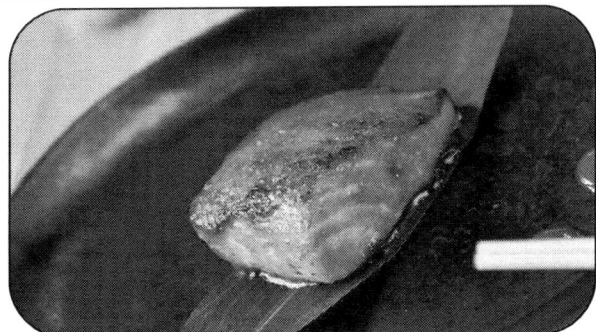

Prep Time: 5-6 Minutes
Cook Time: 4-5 Minutes
Servings: 1
Ingredients
- 2 salmon fillets
- 4 tablespoons lemon juice
- ½ teaspoon lemon zest
- 1 teaspoon rosemary

- 2 fresh dill stalks
- Salt and pepper to taste

Directions:
1. Into the instant pot of Ninja Foodi Deluxe XL Pressure Cooker, pour water and lemon juice.
2. Then add lemon zest and dill into it.
3. Into the Ninja Foodi Deluxe XL Pressure Cooker Pot, add a wire rack at the lowest setting.
4. Now place salmon fillets on the rack, it is suggested to cut them if they don't fit well in it.
5. Season it by sprinkling salt and pepper on it. Sprinkle rosemary on both sides.
6. Secure the Ninja Foodi Deluxe XL Pressure Cooker Pressure Lid.
7. Make sure to set the valve on the Seal. Cook on High Pressure for 4 minutes. For the frozen fillet add another minute to the Cook Time:. Release the valve on the Vent and then open its lid once done fully. And it's ready to be served instantly or it can also be stored in the freezer!

Nutritional Values Per Serving:
Calories: 405; Fat: 15.1g; Carbs: 26g; Protein: 41.7g

Ninja Foodi Asparagus Scallops

Prep Time: 10 minutes

Cook Time: 10 minutes

Servings: 8

Ingredients:
- 1½ pounds scallops
- 2 tablespoons coconut oil
- 2 teaspoons lemon zest, finely grated
- ¼ cup shallots, chopped
- 1½ pounds asparagus, chopped
- 2 garlic cloves, minced
- 2 tablespoons fresh lemon juice
- 2 tablespoons fresh rosemary, chopped
- Salt and black pepper, to taste

Directions:
1. Add oil in Ninja Foodi Deluxe XL Pressure Cooker and sauté shallots in it for about 2 minutes.
2. Select "Sear" and press the "Start/Stop" button.

3. Add in garlic and rosemary and Sauté for about 1 minute.
4. Stir in asparagus and lemon zest and cook for about 2 minutes.
5. Add in scallops, lemon juice, salt and pepper and cook for about 5 minutes.
6. Take out and serve hot.

Nutritional Values Per Serving:
Calories: 375; Fat: 6.3g; Carbs: 21.3g; Protein: 59.5g

Ninja Foodi Ginger Salmon

Prep Time: 10 minutes

Cook Time: 18 minutes

Servings: 3

Ingredients:
- ¼ pound salmon fillets
- ½ teaspoon fresh ginger, minced
- ½ tablespoon sesame seeds
- ½ tablespoon coconut aminos
- ½ tablespoon fresh lime juice
- Salt and black pepper, to taste

Directions:
1. Add all the ingredients to a large bowl and mix well.
2. Dredge salmon fillets in the mixture and transfer them to the pot of Ninja Foodi Deluxe XL Pressure Cooker.
3. Press the "Bake" button and close the Crisping Lid.
4. Press the "Start/Stop" button and bake for about 18 minutes at 325 degrees F.
5. Open the Crisping Lid and take out.
6. Serve and enjoy!

Nutritional Values Per Serving:
Calories: 64; Fat: 3.1g; Carbs: 1.7g; Protein: 7.7g

Instant Catfish Fillet

Prep Time: 4-5 Minutes
Cook Time: 15-20 Minutes
Servings: 1
Ingredients:
- 3-4 Catfish fillets
- ½ cup fish fry
- Olive oil spray

Directions:
1. Now evenly coat each catfish fillet with fish fry.
2. Place it in at Air Crisp Mode of Ninja Foodi Deluxe XL Pressure Cooker and give it an oil spray. Let it cook for 10 minutes at 390° F.
3. Flip the catfish, give another oil spray and cook for another 10 minutes and serve it!

Nutritional Values Per Serving:
Calories: 266; Fat: 3.4g; Carbs: 28g; Protein: 27g

Ninja Foodi Air Crisp Herbed Salmon

Prep Time: 1 Minutes
Cook Time: 4-5 Minutes
Servings: 6
Ingredients:
- 8 ounces sizzle fish salmon fillets, I used two, 4 ounces sizzle fish sockeye salmon fillets
- 1 teaspoon Herbes de Provence
- ¼ teaspoon natural ancient sea salt
- ¼ teaspoon black pepper
- ¼ teaspoon smoked paprika

- 2 tablespoon olive oil
- 1 tablespoon Medlee Seasoned Butter

Directions:
1. Dry your filets with a paper towel and run the surface gently to ensure that there are no bones
2. Drizzle the olive oil on the fish and rub it in on both sides of the fish.
3. Mix the seasonings and sprinkle them on both sides of the fish.
4. Turn your Air Crisp on 390° F and set Timer for five to 8 minutes and cook. I recommend starting with 5 minutes, checking the fish, and increasing the time by one additional minute until it flakes easily with a fork.
5. Melt the seasoned butter for 30 seconds in the microwave and pour it over the fish before eating.

Nutritional Values Per Serving:
Calories: 338; Fat: 27g; Carbs:s 1g; Protein: 23g

Spicy Shrimps

Prep Time: 8-10 Minutes
Cook Time: 12-15 Minutes
Servings: 2
Ingredients:
- 1 pound shrimps
- Salt to taste
- Pepper to taste
- ½ teaspoon cumin powder
- 1 teaspoon coriander powder
- ½ teaspoon red chili powder
- 1 tablespoon lemon juice
- 1 cup mixed vegetables
- Foil (3 to 4 sheets)
- Cooking oil spray (olive or coconut)

Directions:
1. Spray the foil sheets with olive oil. Do this on about a maximum of four sheets.
2. Season it up with salt, pepper, red chili padder, cumin, and coriander powder. Pour in some lemon juice and coat all the shrimps well.
3. Again, spray another coat of olive oil on foil sheets and put the shrimps on the foil.
4. Using the Bake function, preheat the Ninja Foodi Deluxe XL Pressure Cooker at 375° F.
5. Cook it using a Bake function at 375° F for 13 to 15 minutes. Do this by placing foil sheets in it.

Nutritional Values Per Serving:
Calories: 188; Fat: 10g; Carbs: 10.1g; Protein: 37.3g

Beer Battered Fish

Prep Time: 8-10 Minutes
Cook Time: 12-15 Minutes
Servings: 4
Ingredients:
- 1 pound codfish cuts
- 1 cup flour
- ½ teaspoon baking soda
- 2 tablespoons Cornstarch
- 4 ounces beer
- 1 beaten egg
- Salt as required
- ¼ teaspoon Cayenne pepper
- 1 tablespoon olive oil

For Flour Mix
- ¾ cup of flour
- 1 teaspoon paprika powder
- ½ teaspoon black pepper

Directions:
1. Combine flour, cornstarch, salt, cayenne pepper, and baking soda in a large bowl. Then add egg and beer, and stir it until it becomes a smooth batter. Let it refrigerate for 20 minutes.
2. Take ¾ cup of flour, paprika, black pepper in a shallow pan.
3. The fish should be at least one half-inch thick so that it does not dry out in the Ninja Foodi Deluxe XL Pressure Cooker Cook & Crisp Basket. Take a paper towel and pat dry the codfish cuts.
4. Now coat all sides while dipping the fish into the batter.
5. Allow the eggs batter to dip off and again coat it with seasoned flour mix. Any leftover flour can be sprinkled on the fish fillet.

6. Now preheat the Ninja Foodi Deluxe XL Pressure Cooker at Air Crisp Mode at 390° F for 5 minutes. Spray both sides of the coated fish fillet with vegetable oil and then place them in the Ninja Foodi Deluxe XL Pressure Cooker Cook & Crisp Basket for 12 minutes.
7. During the cooking process, add a little more oil if there is any dryness in the coating!
Nutritional Values Per Serving:
Calories: 407; Fat: 6g; Carbs: 26.6g; Protein: 7.3g

Gluten-free fish tacos

Prep Time: 8 Minutes
Cook Time: 15-17 Minutes
Servings: 6
Ingredients:
- 4 fish fillets
- 1 teaspoon paprika powder
- ½ teaspoon salt and pepper
- 1 teaspoon mixed herbs
- 6-8 tortillas wrap

For Corn Salsa:
- 1 cup soft-cooked corn
- 1 cup tomatoes
- ½ cup onion
- ½ cup chopped coriander
- 1 tablespoon lemon juice

Directions:
1. Take the thawed fish and place it into the Cook & Crisp Basket, then add paprika, salt, and pepper.
2. Spray the Cook & Crisp Basket with olive oil and put it in the Ninja Foodi Deluxe XL Pressure Cooker.
3. Preheat Ninja Foodi Deluxe XL Pressure Cooker at Air Crisp Mode at 390° F for 12 minutes.
4. Meanwhile, combine the ingredients in a bowl for corn salsa. Squeeze a lemon juice on top of corn salsa then remove and flake it apart with a fork once the fish is cooked fully.
5. Now place each tortilla on a plate and add fish and then top it with the corn salsa. Now place each tortilla next to each other in the Ninja Foodi Deluxe XL Pressure Cooker Cook & Crisp Basket.
6. Give it a cooking spray, for 5 minutes Air Crisp it at 390° F with tongs, remove it carefully, and serve it.
Nutritional Values Per Serving:
Calories: 294; Fat: 7.3g; Carbs: 49.2g; Protein: 7g

Mixed Seafood Platter

Prep Time: 9 Minutes
Cook Time: 6 Minutes
Servings: 6

Ingredients:
- 1 pound peeled and devein fresh shrimps
- 1 pound mussels
- 1 potato (coarsely cut)
- ½ cup fresh corn
- 340 g of sausage (2-inch pieces)
- 2-3 cups water
- 2 tablespoons old bay seasoning
- 2 teaspoons oil flakes
- ¼ cup fresh chopped parsley
- Butter melted 1 cup
- Garlic powder 1 tsp

Directions:
1. Add potatoes, corn, sausages, water, and oil flakes in the Ninja Foodi Deluxe XL Pressure Cooker Pot. Give it a good stir.
2. Now on the High Pressure, cook it for 4 minutes and do a quick release.
3. Once the one-timer is completed and pressure is released, open the lid carefully.
4. Now add shrimps and mussels and old bay seasoning. Mix it well and cook it on High Pressure setting in Ninja Foodi Deluxe XL Pressure Cooker for 1 minute. Allow for natural release of pressure for 2 minutes, after 1 minute of cooking in Ninja Foodi Deluxe XL Pressure Cooker High Pressure setting.
5. Then add butter and garlic powder to a small bowl. Mix it well and top up with parsley. Drizzle all over the platter.

Nutritional Values Per Serving:
Calories: 521; Fat: 39.9g; Carbs: 22.6g; Protein: 19.3g

Fish Skewers

Prep Time: 3 Minutes
Cook Time: 8-10 Minutes
Servings: 4

Ingredients:
- 1 pound frozen fish cubes
- 6-8 skewers
- Salt to taste
- Pepper to taste
- 2 tablespoon ginger garlic paste
- ½ teaspoon paprika
- 1 tablespoon lemon juice
- 1 teaspoon oregano
- ½ teaspoon liquid charcoal
- 1 tablespoon olive oil

Directions:
1. Oil spray the Ninja Foodi Deluxe XL Pressure Cooker Cook & Crisp Basket. Combine the fish cubes with all the seasonings in a bowl. Set aside for one to two hours.
2. Align the cubes on the skewers. Now place the fish sticks in an even manner into the Ninja Foodi Deluxe XL Pressure Cooker Basket.
3. For 10 minutes, cook at 390° F in Air Crisp Mode. Flip it if needed and the skewers are ready to be served!

Nutritional Values Per Serving:
Calories: 182; Fat: 8.5g; Carbs: 3g; Protein: 23.3g

Bay Crab Legs

Prep Time: 6 Minutes
Cook Time: 5-6 Minutes
Servings: 1

Ingredients:
- 1 pound crab legs
- 1-2 cups water

- 2 tablespoon bay seasoning
- 1 teaspoon lime juice
- 1 tablespoon garlic infused butter

Directions:
1. Marinate the crab legs with bay seasoning and lime juice. Let it marinate for 30-40 minutes.
2. Pour in water inside the Ninja Foodi Deluxe XL Pressure Cooker. Any other seasonings can also be used here. Place the rack in Ninja Foodi Deluxe XL Pressure Cooker and place the crab legs on top.
3. Seal the Pressure Lid of the Ninja Foodi Deluxe XL Pressure Cooker for 5 minutes.
4. Cook on High Pressure by moving the nozzle to Vent quickly, release the steam, and serve it with garlic-infused butter on top!

Nutritional Values Per Serving:
Calories: 272; Fat: 4g; Carbs: 1.1g; Protein: 43.4g

Crumbed Tilapia

Prep Time: 12 Minutes
Cook Time: 6 Minutes
Servings: 4

Ingredients:
- 4 frozen tilapia fillets
- 1 cup bread crumbs
- 2 tbsp seafood seasoning
- 1 egg
- Olive oil spray

Directions:
1. At 390° F, preheat the Ninja Foodi Deluxe XL Pressure Cooker at Air Crisp Mode for 5 minutes.
2. To pat dry the fillet, use paper towels and dry the moisture.
3. Add salt and pepper to the egg in a bowl and whisk it well. First, dip the fillet in the whisked egg.
4. Combine bread crumbs with seafood seasoning on a plate and press the fillet from both sides into that mixture to coat generously.
5. Place the fillets in the Ninja Foodi Deluxe XL Pressure Cooker Cook & Crisp Basket and close the lid and cook depending on the thickness of the tilapia and in most cases, 4 minutes have been a good amount of time for

a good result. Take out the golden crispy fillets and eat a proteinaceous meal!

Nutritional Values Per Serving:
Calories: 212; Fat: 4.5g; Carbs: 15.9g; Protein: 27.5g

White Fish with Garlic Lemon Pepper Seasoning

Prep Time: 5 Minutes
Cook Time: 10-12 Minutes
Servings: 2

Ingredients:
- 2 whitefish fillets
- 1 teaspoon garlic powder
- 1 tablespoon olive oil
- 2 tablespoons lemon pepper seasoning
- Salt to taste
- 2 tablespoons fresh chopped coriander
- 1 lemon (rings)

Directions:
8. Preheat the Ninja Foodi Deluxe XL Pressure Cooker at Air Crisp Mode to 390° F for 5 minutes.
9. Drizzle olive oil on the fillets and season it with garlic powder, lemon pepper seasoning, and salt. Now repeat the step for both the sides.
10. Inside the base of the Ninja Foodi Deluxe XL Pressure Cooker Cook & Crisp Basket, lay the perforated bay paper. Spray the paper lightly with olive oil.
11. Place fish fillets on the paper and add lemon veggies to it.
12. Air Crisp it for about 10 to 12 minutes at 390° F or until fish can be flaked with the help of a fork. Keep in mind the timings depend on how thick the fillet is.
13. Sprinkle chopped parsley and serve it warm with the toasted lemon wedges!

Nutritional Values Per Serving:
Calories: 146; Fat: 7.4g; Carbs: 3.7g; Protein: 17.2g

Lemon Garlic Scallops

Prep Time: 8-10 Minutes
Cook Time: 15-20 Minutes
Servings: 2

Ingredients
- 1 pound scallops
- ½ teaspoon pepper
- ½ teaspoon salt
- 1 tablespoon extra-virgin olive oil
- 2 tablespoons chopped parsley
- ¼ teaspoon lemon zest
- 1 teaspoon chopped garlic

Directions:
1. Season scallops with pepper and salt. Give the Ninja Foodi Deluxe XL Pressure Cooker Cook & Crisp Basket a generous oil spray.
2. Set the Ninja Foodi Deluxe XL Pressure Cooker at Air Crisp at 390° F, cook the scallops for about 6 minutes.
3. Now take a small bowl and add oil, parsley, lemon zest, and garlic.
4. Once scallops are seared well, drizzle this mixture over the scallops!

Nutritional Values Per Serving:
Calories: 320; Fat: 10.2g; Carbs: 14.4g; Protein: 35.4g

Garlic Red Bell Pepper Mix

Prep Time: 5 minutes
Cook Time: 16 minutes
Serves: 4

Ingredients:
- 1 lb. red bell peppers, cut into wedges
- ½ tsp curry powder
- ½ cup tomato sauce
- Salt and black pepper, to the taste
- 1 tbsp olive oil
- 2 garlic cloves, minced
- 1 tbsp parsley, chopped

Preparation:
1. Set the Foodi to BAKE/ROAST mode at 380°F for 5 minutes and preheat.
2. Put the reversible rack in the Foodi. Place the baking pan on top, and grease it with the oil.
3. Add the peppers, curry powder, and the other ingredients except for the parsley to the pan. Toss to combine.
Cook on BAKE mode at 380° F for 16 minutes.
4. When done, divide between plates and serve with the parsley sprinkled on top.

Nutritional Information Per Serving:
Calories 150; Fat: 3.5g; Carbs: 3.1g; Protein: 1.2g

Crispy Balsamic Cabbage

Prep Time: 5 minutes
Cook Time: 15 minutes
Serves: 4

Ingredients:
- 1 green cabbage head, shredded
- 2 endives, trimmed and sliced lengthwise
- Salt and black pepper, to taste
- 1 tbsp olive oil
- 2 shallots, chopped
- ½ cup chicken stock
- 1 tbsp sweet paprika
- 1 tbsp balsamic vinegar

Preparation:
1. Set the Foodi to SEAR/SAUTÉ mode on MD:HI temperature setting. Add the oil, heat it up, then add the shallots and sauté for 2 minutes.
2. Add the cabbage, endives, and the other ingredients. Stir to combine.
3. Put the Pressure Lid on. Set to PRESSURE mode and cook on HI for 13 minutes.
4. Quick-release the pressure for 5 minutes, then divide the mixture between plates and serve.

Nutritional Information Per Serving:
Calories 120; Fat: 2g; Carbs: 3.3g; Protein: 4g

Ninja Foodi Brown Rice

Prep Time: 5 minutes
Cook Time: 15 minutes
Serves: 4
Ingredients:
- 2 cups brown rice
- 1 tsp salt
- 1 tsp cumin
- Cooked chicken chunks (optional)
- Cooked veggies (optional)

Preparation:
1. Add 2 cups of brown rice along with the salt and cumin to your Ninja Foodi.
2. Add 2¼ cups of water. Put the Pressure Lid on and seal the steam valve.
3. Press PRESSURE mode, set it to HI, and adjust the timing to 15 minutes.
4. When done, allow it to naturally release pressure for 5 minutes, and then release the rest quickly.

Nutritional Information Per Serving:
Calories 337; Fat: 12g; Carbs: 73g; Protein: 6g

Pumpkin Chili

Prep Time: 10 minutes
Cook Time: 4 minutes
Serves: 8
Ingredients:
- 1 lb. lean ground beef
- 2 (16 oz each) cans chili beans
- 1 (14½ oz) can beef broth
- 1 (10 oz) can diced tomatoes
- 1 cup pureed pumpkin
- 2 tsp pumpkin pie spice
- ¼ cup yellow or white onion, chopped
- 1 clove garlic, crushed
- 1 tsp chili powder
- ½ cup natural ketchup

Toppings (optional)
- Cornbread
- Fritos
- Shredded cheese
- Sour cream
- Green onions

Preparation:
1. Set the Ninja Foodi to SEAR/SAUTÉ mode on MD:HI temperature setting. Add the ground beef and brown it.
2. Drain the ground beef if necessary and then return it to the pot.
3. Add in all the remaining chili ingredients, then stir.
4. Close the Pressure Lid securely, ensuring the steam vent is closed.
5. Select PRESSURE mode and cook on HI for 4 minutes.
6. Quickly release the steam.

Nutritional Information Per Serving:
Calories 345; Fat: 12g; Carbs: 35g; Protein: 25g

Low-Carb Italian Wedding Soup

Prep Time: 13 minutes
Cook Time: 15 minutes
Serves: 6
Ingredients:
Meatballs
- 1 lb. ground sausage
- ¼ cup parmesan cheese, shredded
- ½ cup pork rinds, crushed
- ¼ cup heavy cream

- 1 egg, beaten
- ½ tbsp Italian seasoning
- Salt and pepper, to taste

Soup
- 6 cups chicken broth
- 1 garlic, minced
- 1 tbsp Italian seasoning
- 1 carrot, chopped
- 3 green onions, chopped
- 3 ribs celery, chopped
- 10 oz frozen riced cauliflower
- 3 oz baby spinach
- Parmesan cheese, shredded, for garnish

Preparation:
1. Mix the meatball ingredients together in a bowl. Form into 12 meatballs and spread them across the base of the Ninja Foodi pot.
2. Select AIR CRISP mode at 350°F for 13 minutes. Close with the Crisping Lid and start cooking.
3. When done, open the lid, pour the broth over the top of the meatballs, and gently stir.
4. Add all the remaining ingredients except the spinach and garnish.
5. Select PRESSURE mode and close the Pressure Lid. Cook on HI for 15 minutes and then do a quick release. Stir in the spinach.

Nutritional Information Per Serving:
Calories 345; Fat: 27.9g; Carbs: 5g; Protein: 18g

Chives, Beets, and Carrots

Prep Time: 5 minutes
Cook Time: 20 minutes
Serves: 4

Ingredients:
- 1 lb. beets, peeled and roughly cubed
- 1 lb. baby carrots, peeled
- Salt and black pepper, to taste
- 2 tbsp olive oil
- 1 tbsp chives, minced

Preparation:
1. In a bowl, mix the beets with the carrots and the other ingredients and toss well.
2. Select AIR CRISP mode. Put the beets and carrots in the Foodi's Cook & Crisp Basket and place it in the Foodi. Close the Crisping Lid and cook at 390°F for 20 minutes. Divide between plates and serve.

Nutritional Information Per Serving:
Calories 150; Fat: 4.5g; Carbs: 7.3 g; Protein: 3.6g

Mexican Rice

Prep Time: 5 minutes
Cook Time: 3 minutes
Serves: 6

Ingredients:
- 2 tbsp canola or vegetable oil
- 1 cup basmati rice
- ½ green peppers, diced into ¼-inch
- 1 onion (about 1 cup), diced into ¼-inch
- 1 carrot, diced into ¼-inch
- ½ red bell pepper, diced into ¼-inch
- 1 jalapeño pepper, diced into ¼-inch
- 2 tbsp tomato paste
- 2 cups water

Spice blend
- 1½ tsp fine-grind sea salt
- 1½ tsp cumin
- 1½ tsp smoked paprika

Preparation:
1. Place the oil in the inner pot of the Ninja Foodi. Select SEAR/SAUTÉ mode and put it on HI.
2. When the oil is hot, add the rice and sauté for 3–5 minutes, stirring constantly.
3. When the rice starts to brown, add in the vegetables and the spice blend. Stir and sauté for 3–5 minutes. Add in the tomato paste and stir to combine.
4. Pour in the 2 cups of water and put the Pressure Lid on. Turn the seal to VENT and select the STEAM function for 8 minutes.
5. When finished, remove the lid and stir the rice.

Nutritional Information Per Serving:
Calories 178; Fat: 5g; Carbs: 30g; Protein: 3g

Vegetable Soup

Prep Time: 20 minutes
Cook Time: 4 minutes
Serves: 8

Ingredients:
- 1 lb. ground turkey
- 1 (14½ oz) can of beef broth
- 4 cups water
- 1 (15 oz) can tomato sauce
- 1 cup frozen corn
- 2 potatoes, halved and quartered
- 2 large carrots, sliced
- 2 stalks celery, diced
- 1 medium tomato, sliced
- ½ cup white onion, diced
- ½ cup white cooking wine
- ½ tsp parsley
- 1 cup elbow macaroni

Preparation:
1. Set the Foodi to SEAR/SAUTÉ mode on MD temperature setting. Cook the meat in the pot, then add in the remaining ingredients.
2. Select PRESSURE mode. Add the Pressure Lid. Cover and lock the lid in place.
3. Set to cook on HI for 4 minutes.
4. Quick-release the steam and remove the lid.

Nutritional Information Per Serving:
Calories 314; Fat: 13g; Carbs: 26g; Protein: 20g

Kale Stir Fry

Prep Time: 5 minutes
Cook Time: 15 minutes
Serves: 4

Ingredients:
- 1 lb. kale, torn
- 2 leeks, sliced
- 2 tbsp balsamic vinegar
- 1 tbsp fresh parsley, chopped
- Salt and black pepper, to the taste
- 2 shallots, chopped
- ½ cup tomato sauce

Preparation:
1. In your Foodi's inner pot, combine the kale with the leeks and the other ingredients.
2. Put the Pressure Lid on, set it to PRESSURE mode, and cook on HI for 15 minutes.
3. Quick-release the pressure for 5 minutes, divide the mix between plates, and serve.

Nutritional Information Per Serving:
Calories 100; Fat: 2g; Carbs: 3.4g; Protein: 4g

Zucchini and Spinach Mix

Prep Time: 5 minutes
Cook Time: 17 minutes
Serves: 4

Ingredients:
- 2 zucchinis, sliced
- 1 lb. baby spinach
- ½ cup tomato sauce
- Salt and black pepper
- 1 tbsp avocado oil
- 1 red onion, chopped
- 1 tbsp sweet paprika
- ½ tsp garlic powder
- ½ tsp chili powder

Preparation:
1. Set the Foodi to SEAR/SAUTÉ mode on MD:HI temperature setting. Add the oil, heat it up, and then add the onion and sauté for 2 minutes.
2. Add the zucchinis, spinach, and other ingredients. Stir to combine.
3. Adjust the setting to PRESSURE mode. Put the Pressure Lid on and cook on HI for 15 minutes.
4. Quick-release the pressure for 5 minutes, then divide everything between plates and serve.

Nutritional Information Per Serving:
Calories 130; Fat: 5.5g; Carbs: 3.3g; Protein: 1g

Southern Fried Cabbage with Bacon

Prep Time: 5 minutes
Cook Time: 20 minutes
Serves: 4
Ingredients:
- 4 cups red cabbage, shredded
- ¼ cup veggie stock
- A pinch of salt and black pepper
- 1 tbsp olive oil
- 1 cup crushed canned tomatoes
- 1 lime, grated zest
- 2 oz cooked bacon, crumbled

Preparation:
1. Put the reversible rack in the Foodi, add the baking pan, and grease it with the oil.
2. Add the cabbage, the stock, and the other ingredients to the pan.
3. Set the Foodi to BAKE/ROAST mode at 380°F for 20 minutes.
4. When done, divide the mixture between plates and serve.

Nutritional Information Per Serving:
Calories 144; Fat: 3g; Carbs: 4.5g; Protein: 4.4g

Black-Eyed Peas

Prep Time: 5 minutes
Cook Time: 35 minutes
Serves: 10

Ingredients:
- 1 tsp olive oil
- 1 cup white onion, chopped
- 3 garlic cloves
- 6 cups chicken broth
- 1 lb. bag dried black-eyed peas, rinsed
- 1 fully-cooked smoked turkey leg (about 1–1½ lbs.)
- 1 tsp Creole seasoning
- 1 bay leaf

Preparation:
1. Set the Ninja Foodi to SEAR/SAUTÉ mode on MD:HI temperature setting and add the olive oil.
2. When hot, add the onions and garlic. Sauté until translucent and fragrant.
3. Add the chicken broth, black-eyed peas, smoked turkey leg, Creole seasoning, and bay leaf. Stir.
4. Place on the Pressure Lid and seal. Select PRESSURE mode and cook for 30 minutes on HI.
5. When the pot indicates that the cooking time is over, allow the steam to release naturally for 10 minutes.
6. Open the pot and remove the bay leaf and smoked turkey leg. Use 2 forks to shred the turkey. Return it to the pot. Taste it and add salt and pepper if needed.
7. Serve the black-eyed peas using a slotted spoon.

Nutritional Information Per Serving:
Calories 248; Fat: 10.8g; Carbs: 40.7g ; Protein: 2.5g

Potatoes and Lemon Sauce

Prep Time: 5 minutes
Cook Time: 15 minutes
Serves: 4

Ingredients:
- 1 lb. Yukon Gold potatoes, peeled and cut into wedges
- 1 tbsp fresh dill, chopped
- 1 tbsp grated lemon zest
- ½ lemon, juiced
- 2 tbsp butter, melted
- Salt and black pepper, to the taste

Preparation:
1. Set the Foodi to SEAR/SAUTÉ mode on MD:HI temperature setting. Add the butter,

melt it, then add the potatoes and brown for 5 minutes.

2. Add the lemon zest and the other ingredients. Stir to combine.

3. Set the Foodi to AIR CRISP mode and cook at 390°F for 10 minutes.

4. Divide everything between plates and serve.

Nutritional Information Per Serving:
Calories 122; Fat: 3.3g; Carbs: 3g; Protein: 2g

Italian Potatoes

Prep Time: 6 Minutes
Cook Time: 10-12 Minutes
Servings: 4

Ingredients:
- 4 potatoes
- 1 tablespoon olive oil
- 2 lemons
- ½ teaspoon salt
- 1 tablespoon Italian Seasoning
- 1 teaspoon mixed herbs

Directions:

1. Wash off the potatoes and cut them into wedges.

2. In the Ninja Foodi Deluxe XL Pressure Cooker, set the inner pot and then pour in half a cup of water. Now add the Ninja Foodi Deluxe XL Pressure Cooker Cook & Crisp Basket into the inner pot and dump in wedges to it.

3. Preheat Ninja Foodi Deluxe XL Pressure Cooker, Pressure Cook on Low temperature setting for 20 minutes.

4. Pressure Cook potatoes at High temperature for 4 minutes.

5. Meanwhile, prepare your seasoning mixture by combining Italian seasoning, lemon juice, herbs, salt, and olive oil in a mixing bowl and put its side.

6. Once the potatoes are cooked, release the pressure by setting the valve to vent. After the pressure has been released remove the lid, take one tablespoon of olive oil, and spread evenly on the potatoes.

7. Now for an additional three to 5 minutes, cook wedges in the Ninja Foodi Deluxe XL Pressure Cooker, until the desired crispiness is achieved. Sprinkle some more seasoning and serve!

Nutrition Information per Serving:
Calories: 70; Fat: 4.1g; Carbs: 11g; Protein: 1.2g

Ninja Foodi Cauliflower Fried Rice

Prep Time: 10 minutes
Cook Time: 15 minutes
Servings: 4

Ingredients:
- 4 cups riced cauliflower
- ¼ cup diced green onion
- ½ teaspoon garlic powder
- ½ teaspoon ground ginger
- 2 tablespoons low-sodium soy sauce
- 1 egg, beaten
- ½ cup peas
- ¼ cup shredded carrots
- 2 tablespoons olive oil

Directions:

1. Add olive oil in Ninja Foodi Deluxe XL Pressure Cooker. Select to sauté mode.

2. Press the "Start/Stop" button and sauté peas, carrot and onion in it.

3. Add in egg, garlic powder, and ginger. Stir properly.

4. Stir in cauliflower rice and close the pressure Lid.

5. Cook for about 5 minutes and open the lid.

6. Add in soy sauce and mix well.

7. Take out, serve and enjoy!

Nutritional Values Per Serving:
Calories: 130; Fat: 8.2g; Carbs: 9.8g; Protein: 5.1g

Zucchinis Spinach Fry

Prep Time: 5 minutes
Cook Time: 17 minutes
Servings: 4
Ingredients:
- 2 zucchinis, sliced
- 1-pound baby spinach
- ½ cup tomato sauce
- Black pepper and salt
- 1 tablespoon avocado oil
- 1 red onion, chopped
- 1 tablespoon sweet paprika
- ½ teaspoon garlic powder
- ½ teaspoon chilli powder

Directions:
1. Set the Foodi on Sauté, stir in the oil, heat it up, add the onion and sauté for 2 minutes.
2. Add the zucchinis, spinach, and the other ingredients Put the Ninja Foodi's lid on and cook on High for 15 minutes.
3. Release the pressure quickly for 5 minutes, divide everything between plates and serve.

Nutritional Values Per Serving:
Calories: 130; Fat: 5.5g; Carbs: 3.3g; Protein: 1g

Cabbage with Carrots

Prep Time: 5 minutes
Cook Time: 20 minutes
Servings: 4
Ingredients:
- 1 Napa cabbage, shredded

- 2 carrots, sliced
- 2 tablespoons olive oil
- 1 red onion, chopped
- Black pepper and salt to the taste
- 2 tablespoons sweet paprika
- ½ cup tomato sauce

Directions:
1. Set the Foodi on Sauté mode, stir in the oil, heat it up, add the onion and sauté for 5 minutes.
2. Add the carrots, the cabbage and the other ingredients, toss.
3. Put the Ninja Foodi's lid on and cook on High for 15 minutes.
4. Release the pressure quickly for 5 minutes, divide everything between plates and serve.

Nutritional Values Per Serving:
Calories: 140; Fat: 3.4g; Carbs: 1.2g; Protein: 3.5 g

Saucy Kale

Prep Time: 5 minutes
Cook Time: 15 minutes
Servings: 4
Ingredients:
- 1-pound kale, torn
- 2 leeks, sliced
- 2 tablespoons balsamic vinegar
- 1 tablespoon parsley, chopped
- Black pepper and salt to the taste
- 2 shallots, chopped
- ½ cup tomato sauce

Directions:
1. In your Ninja Foodi, combine the kale with the leeks and the other ingredients.
2. Put the Ninja Foodi's lid on and cook on High for 15 minutes.
3. Release the pressure quickly for 5 minutes, divide the mix between plates and serve.

Nutritional Values Per Serving:
Calories: 100; Fat: 2g; Carbs: 3.4g; Protein: 4g

Broccoli Cauliflower

Prep Time: 10 minutes
Cook Time: 15 minutes
Servings: 4
Ingredients:
- 2 cups broccoli florets
- 1 cup cauliflower florets
- 2 tablespoons lime juice
- 1 tablespoon avocado oil
- ⅓ cup tomato sauce
- 2 teaspoons ginger, grated
- 2 teaspoons garlic, minced
- 1 tablespoon chives, chopped

Directions:
1. Set the Foodi on Sauté mode, stir in the oil, heat it up, add the garlic and the ginger and sauté for 2 minutes.
2. Stir in the broccoli, cauliflower and the rest of the ingredients.
3. Put the Ninja Foodi's lid on and cook on High for 13 minutes.
4. naturally Release the pressure for 10 minutes, divide everything between plates and serve.
Nutritional Values Per Serving:
Calories: 118; Fat: 1.5g; Carbs: 4.3g; Protein: 6g

Eggplant with Kale

Prep Time: 5 minutes
Cook Time: 15 minutes
Servings: 4
Ingredients:
- Juice of 1 lime
- 1-pound eggplant, roughly cubed
- 1 cup kale, torn
- A pinch of black pepper and salt
- ½ teaspoon chilli powder
- ½ cup chicken stock
- 3 tablespoons olive oil

Directions:
1. Set the Foodi on Sauté mode, stir in the oil, heat it up, add the eggplant and sauté for 2 minutes.
2. Stir in the kale and the rest of the ingredients.
3. Put the Ninja Foodi's lid on and cook on and cook on High for 13 minutes.
4. Release the pressure quickly for 5 minutes, divide the mix between plates and serve.
Nutritional Values Per Serving:
Calories: 110; Fat: 3g; Carbs: 4.3g; Protein: 1.1g

Leeks and Carrots

Prep Time: 5 minutes
Cook Time: 15 minutes
Servings: 4
Ingredients:
- 2 leeks, roughly sliced
- 2 carrots, sliced
- 1 teaspoon ginger powder
- 1 teaspoon garlic powder
- ½ cup chicken stock
- Black pepper and salt to the taste
- 2 tablespoons lemon juice
- 2 tablespoons olive oil
- ½ tablespoon balsamic vinegar

Directions:
1. In your Ninja Foodi, combine the leeks with the carrots and the other ingredients.
2. Put the Ninja Foodi's lid on and cook on High for 15 minutes.
3. Release the pressure quickly for 5 minutes, divide the mix between plates and serve.
Nutritional Values Per Serving:
Calories: 133; Fat: 3.4g; Carbs: 5g; Protein: 2.1g

Creamy Kale

Prep Time: 5 minutes
Cook Time: 15 minutes
Servings: 4
Ingredients:
- 1 tablespoon lemon juice
- 2 tablespoons balsamic vinegar
- 1-pound kale, torn
- 1 tablespoon ginger, grated
- 1 garlic clove, minced
- 2 tablespoons olive oil
- 1 cup heavy cream
- A pinch of black pepper and salt
- 2 tablespoons chives, chopped

Directions:
1. Set the Foodi on Sauté mode, stir in the oil, heat it up, add the garlic and the ginger and sauté for 2 minutes.
2. Stir in the kale, lemon juice and the other ingredients.
3. Put the Ninja Foodi's lid on and cook on High for 13 minutes.
4. Release the pressure quickly for 5 minutes, divide between plates and serve.

Nutritional Values Per Serving:
Calories: 130; Fat: 2g; Carbs: 3.4g; Protein: 2g

Pomegranate Radish Mix

Prep Time: 5 minutes
Cook Time: 8 minutes
Servings: 4
Ingredients:
- 1-pound radishes, roughly cubed
- Black pepper and salt to the taste
- 2 garlic cloves, minced
- ½ cup chicken stock
- 2 tablespoons pomegranate juice

- ¼ cup pomegranate seeds

Directions:
1. In your Ninja Foodi, combine the radishes with the stock and the other ingredients.
2. Put the Ninja Foodi's lid on and cook on High for 8 minutes.
3. Release the pressure quickly for 5 minutes, divide everything between plates and serve.

Nutritional Values Per Serving:
Calories: 133; Fat: 2.3g; Carbs: 2.4g; Protein: 2g

Bell Peppers Mix

Prep Time: 5 minutes
Cook Time: 16 minutes
Servings: 4
Ingredients:
- 1-pound red bell peppers, cut into wedges
- ½ teaspoon curry powder
- ½ cup tomato sauce
- Black pepper and salt to the taste
- 1 tablespoon olive oil
- 2 garlic cloves, minced
- 1 tablespoon parsley, chopped

Directions:
1. Put the reversible rack in the Foodi, add the baking pan inside and grease it with the oil.
2. Add the peppers, curry powder and the other ingredients except for the parsley, toss a bit and
3. Cook on Baking mode at 380 degrees F for 16 minutes.
4. Divide cooked peppers between plates and serve with the parsley sprinkled on top.

Nutritional Values Per Serving:
Calories: 150; Fat: 3.5g; Carbs: 3.1g; Protein: 1.2g

Minty Radishes

Prep Time: 5 minutes
Cook Time: 15 minutes
Servings: 4
Ingredients:
- 1-pound radishes, halved
- black pepper and salt
- 2 tablespoons balsamic vinegar
- 2 tablespoons mint, chopped
- 2 tablespoons olive oil

Directions:
1. In your Ninja Foodi's basket, combine the radishes with the vinegar and the other ingredients, and
2. Cook on Air Crisp at 380 degrees F for 15 minutes.
3. Divide the radishes between plates and serve.
Nutritional Values Per Serving:
Calories: 170; Fat: 4.5g; Carbs: 7.4g; Protein: 4.6g

Okra Stew

Prep Time: 5 minutes
Cook Time: 12 minutes
Servings: 4
Ingredients:
- 1-pound okra, trimmed
- 2 leeks, sliced
- Black pepper and salt to the taste
- 1 cup tomato sauce
- ¼ cup pine nuts, toasted
- 1 tablespoon cilantro, chopped
Directions:

1. In your Ninja Foodi, mix the okra with the leeks and the other ingredients except the cilantro,
2. Put the Ninja Foodi's lid on and cook on High for 12 minutes.
3. Release the pressure quickly for 5 minutes, divide the okra mix into bowls and serve with the cilantro sprinkled on top.
Nutritional Values Per Serving:
Calories: 146; Fat: 3g; Carbs: 4g; Protein: 3g

Beets and Carrots

Prep Time: 5 minutes
Cook Time: 20 minutes
Servings: 4
Ingredients:
- 1-pound beets, peeled and roughly cubed
- 1-pound baby carrots, peeled
- Black pepper and salt to the taste
- 2 tablespoons olive oil
- 1 tablespoon chives, minced
Directions:
1. In a suitable, mix the beets with the carrots and the other ingredients and toss.
2. Put the beets and carrots in the Foodi's basket.
3. Cook on Air Crisp at 390 degrees F for 20 minutes, divide between plates and serve.
Nutritional Values Per Serving:
Calories: 150; Fat: 4.5g; Carbs: 7.3g; Protein: 3.6g

Cauliflower chunks with Lemon Sauce

Prep Time: 5 minutes
Cook Time: 15 minutes
Servings: 4
Ingredients:
- 1-pound cauliflower, cut into chunks
- 1 tablespoon dill, chopped
- 1 tablespoon lemon zest, grated
- Juice of ½ lemon
- 2 tablespoons butter, melted
- Black pepper and salt to the taste

Directions:
1. Set the Foodi on Sauté mode, stir in the butter, melt it, add the cauliflower chunks and brown for 5 minutes.
2. Add the lemon zest and the other ingredients set the machine on Air Crisp and cook at 390 degrees F for 10 minutes.
3. Divide everything between plates and serve.
Nutritional Values Per Serving:
Calories: 122; Fat: 3.3g; Carbs: 3g; Protein: 2g

Radish Apples Salad

Prep Time: 5 minutes
Cook Time: 15 minutes
Servings: 4
Ingredients:
- 1-pound radishes, roughly cubed
- 2 apples, cored and cut into wedges
- ¼ cup chicken stock
- 2 spring onions, chopped

- 3 tablespoons tomato paste
- Juice of 1 lime
- Cooking spray
- 1 tablespoon cilantro, chopped

Directions:
1. In your Ninja Foodi, combine the radishes with the apples and the other ingredients
2. Put the Ninja Foodi's lid on and cook on High for 15 minutes.
3. Release the pressure quickly for 5 minutes, divide everything between plates and serve.
Nutritional Values Per Serving:
Calories: 122; Fat: 5g; Carbs: 4.5g; Protein: 3g

Balsamic Cabbage with Endives

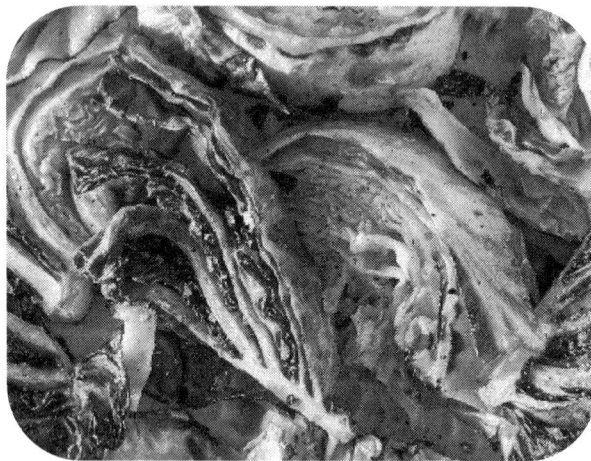

Prep Time: 5 minutes
Cook Time: 15 minutes
Servings: 4
Ingredients:
- 1 green cabbage head, shredded
- 2 endives, trimmed and sliced lengthwise
- Black pepper and salt to the taste
- 1 tablespoon olive oil
- 2 shallots, chopped
- ½ cup chicken stock
- 1 tablespoon sweet paprika
- 1 tablespoon balsamic vinegar

Directions:
1. Set the Foodi on Sauté mode, stir in the oil, heat it up, add the shallots and sauté for 2 minutes.
2. Add the cabbage, the endives and the other ingredients.
3. Put the Ninja Foodi's lid on and cook on High for 13 minutes.
4. Release the pressure quickly for 5 minutes, divide the mix between plates and serve.
Nutritional Values Per Serving:
Calories: 120; Fat: 2g; Carbs: 3.3g; Protein: 4

Sesame Radish

Prep Time: 5 minutes
Cook Time: 15 minutes
Servings: 4
Ingredients:
- 2 leeks, sliced
- ½ pound radishes, sliced
- 2 scallions, chopped
- 2 tablespoons black sesame seeds
- ⅓ cup chicken stock
- 1 tablespoon ginger, grated
- 1 tablespoon chives, minced

Directions:
1. In your Ninja Foodi, combine the leeks with the radishes and the other ingredients.
2. Put the Ninja Foodi's lid on and cook on High for 15 minutes more.
3. Release the pressure quickly for 5 minutes, divide everything between plates and serve.
Nutritional Values Per Serving:
Calories: 112; Fat: 2g; Carbs: 4.2g; Protein: 2g

Kale and Parmesan

Prep Time: 5 minutes
Cook Time: 15 minutes
Servings: 4
Ingredients:
- 1-pound kale, torn
- 2 tablespoons parmesan, grated
- 1 red onion, sliced
- 1 cup bacon, cooked and chopped
- ½ cup chicken stock
- 1 tablespoon olive oil
- A pinch of black pepper and salt
- 1 tablespoon balsamic vinegar

Directions:
1. Set the Foodi on Sauté mode, stir in the oil, heat it up, add the onion and sauté for 2 minutes.
2. Stir in the kale and the other ingredients except the parmesan.
3. Sprinkle the cheese at the end, set the machine on Baking mode.
4. Cook at 380 degrees F for about 12 minutes.
5. Divide everything into bowls and serve.
Nutritional Values Per Serving:
Calories: 130; Fat: 5g; Carbs: 3.4g; Protein: 6g

Carrots Walnuts Salad

Prep Time: 5 minutes
Cook Time: 15 minutes
Servings: 4
Ingredients:
- 4 carrots, roughly shredded
- ½ cup walnuts, sliced
- 3 tablespoons balsamic vinegar
- 1 cup chicken stock
- Black pepper and salt to the taste
- 1 tablespoon olive oil

Directions:
1. In your Ninja Foodi, mix the carrots with the vinegar and the other ingredients except for the walnuts
2. Put the pressure cooking lid on and cook on High for 15 minutes.
3. Release the pressure quickly for 5 minutes, divide the mix between plates and serve with the walnuts sprinkled on top.
Nutritional Values Per Serving:
Calories: 120; Fat: 4.5g; Carbs: 5.3g; Protein: 1.3g

Maple Dipped Kale

Prep Time: 5 minutes
Cook Time: 15 minutes
Servings: 4
Ingredients:
- 2 pounds kale, torn
- ½ cup soy sauce
- 1 teaspoon choc zero maple syrup
- 2 teaspoons olive oil
- ½ teaspoon garlic powder
- Black pepper and salt

Directions:
1. In your Ninja Foodi, combine the kale with the soy sauce and the other ingredients.
2. Put the Ninja Foodi's lid on and cook on High for 15 minutes.
3. Release the pressure quickly for 5 minutes, divide everything between plates and serve.
Nutritional Values Per Serving:
Calories: 120; Fat: 3.5g; Carbs: 3.3g; Protein: 1.1g

Ninja Foodi Spinach and Onion Soup

Prep Time: 10 minutes
Cook Time: 20 minutes
Servings: 6
Ingredients:
- 4 chicken bouillon cubes
- 6 celery stalks, chopped
- ½ cup spinach, chopped
- ½ cup chopped onion
- 1 cup water
- Salt and black pepper, to taste

Directions:
1. Add water and chicken bouillon cubes in the pot of Ninja Foodi Deluxe XL Pressure Cooker and press the "Broil" button.
2. Close the Crisping Lid and press the "Start/Stop" button.
3. Cook for about 5 minutes and open the lid.
4. Stir in vegetables and simmer the mixture for 15 minutes.
5. Take out, serve and enjoy!
Nutritional Values Per Serving:
Calories: 13; Fat: 0.3g; Carbs: 2.1g; Protein: 0.7g

Ninja Foodi Asparagus Soup

Prep Time: 10 minutes
Cook Time: 40 minutes
Servings: 3
Ingredients:
- 1 pound asparagus, chopped
- 3 cups vegetable broth
- 1½ tablespoons lemon juice
- 2 scallions, chopped
- 1 tablespoon olive oil
- Salt and black pepper, to taste

Directions:
1. Heat oil in Ninja Foodi Deluxe XL Pressure Cooker and select "Pressure".
2. Sauté scallions in it for about 5 minutes and stir in broth and asparagus.
3. Cook for about 5 minutes and let the mixture simmer for about 25 minutes.
4. Take out, place it in a food-processor and pulse to form a smooth mixture.
5. Pour it again in the pot of Ninja Foodi Deluxe XL Pressure Cooker and close the lid.
6. Select "pressure" and press the "Start/Stop" button.
7. Cook for 5 minutes at HIGH pressure and open the lid.
8. Stir in salt, lemon juice and pepper and take out.
9. Serve hot and enjoy!
Nutritional Values Per Serving:
Calories: 119; Fat: 6.5g; Carbs: 8.1g; Protein: 8.6g

Ninja Foodi Broccoli Soup

Prep Time: 15 minutes
Cook Time: 40 minutes
Servings: 6

Ingredients:
- 2 broccoli, cut into florets
- 1½ garlic cloves, minced
- ¼ tablespoons red pepper flakes, crushed
- ½ cup chopped onion
- 6 cups vegetable broth
- 1½ tablespoons chopped thyme
- ¼ teaspoon ground cumin

Directions:
1. Heat half cup vegetable broth in Ninja Foodi Deluxe XL Pressure Cooker and press the "Broil" button.
2. Sauté onion in it and add in garlic, thyme, cumin and red pepper flakes after 5 minutes. Mix well.
3. Sauté for 1 minute and stir in half cup broth and broccoli.
4. Cook for about 4 minutes and stir in remaining the broth.
5. Close the Crisping Lid and simmer the mixture for half an hour.
6. Open the lid and take out.
7. Pour it in the blender and blend until a smooth mixture is formed.
8. Take out, serve and enjoy!

Nutritional Values Per Serving:
Calories: 65; Fat: 1.7g; Carbs: 6.5g; Protein: 6.3g

Ninja Foodi Vegetables Smoothie

Prep Time: 10 minutes
Cook Time: 5 minutes
Servings: 4

Ingredients:
- ½ cup chopped spinach
- 1 cup broccoli florets, chopped
- 1 cup chopped green bell peppers
- 3 cups chilled water
- 1 cup green cabbage, chopped
- 2 teaspoons sugar

Directions:
1. Add spinach, broccoli, bell peppers, cabbage, sugar and water in the pot of Ninja Foodi Deluxe XL Pressure Cooker.
2. Select "Pressure" and close the pressure Lid.
3. Press the "Start/Stop" button and cook for 5 minutes at LOW pressure.
4. Open the lid, take out and refrigerate for 2 to 3 hours.
5. Pour in serving glasses and serve.

Nutritional Values Per Serving:
Calories: 30; Fat: 0.2g; Carbs: 6.9g; Protein: 1.3g

Cabbage with Bacon

Prep Time: 5 minutes
Cook Time: 20 minutes
Servings: 4

Ingredients:
- 4 cups red cabbage, shredded
- ¼ cup veggie stock
- A pinch of black pepper and salt
- 1 tablespoon olive oil
- 1 cup canned tomatoes, crushed
- Zest of 1 lime, grated
- 2 ounces bacon, cooked and crumbled

Directions:
1. Put the reversible rack in the Foodi, add the baking pan inside and grease it with the oil.
2. Add the cabbage, the stock and the other ingredients into the pan.
3. Cook on Baking mode at 380 degrees F for 20 minutes.
4. Divide the mix between plates and serve.

Nutritional Values Per Serving:
Calories: 144; Fat: 3g; Carbs: 4.5g; Protein: 4.4g

Ninja Foodi Tomato Olive Salad

Prep Time: 10 minutes
Cook Time: 2 minutes
Servings: 4
Ingredients:
- 4 tablespoons red wine vinegar
- 5 cucumbers, chopped
- ½ red onion, thinly sliced
- 5 tomatoes, chopped
- ½ cup green olives, chopped
- 1 cup black olives, halved

Directions:
1. Add every ingredient in the pot of Ninja Foodi Deluxe XL Pressure Cooker and select "Steam".
2. Close the pressure Lid and press the "Start/Stop" button.
3. Cook for 2 minutes and open the lid.
4. Take out and toss to coat well.
5. Serve and enjoy!
Nutritional Values Per Serving:
Calories: 133; Fat: 4.5g; Carbs: 23.3g; Protein: 4.3g

Ninja Foodi Roasted Red Pepper Gazpacho

Prep Time: 10 minutes
Cook Time: 5 minutes
Servings: 2
Ingredients:
- 1 cup cherry tomatoes
- 2 roasted red sweet peppers
- ½ red onion, chopped
- 1 garlic clove, minced
- 1 cucumber, chopped
- 2 tablespoons diced mild green chilies
- 1 tablespoon apple cider vinegar
- 1 tablespoon olive oil

Directions:
1. Add everything in a Ninja Foodi Deluxe XL Pressure Cooker and select "pressure".
2. Close the pressure Lid and press the "Start/Stop" button.
3. Cook for 5 minutes at HIGH pressure and open the lid.
4. Take out, serve and enjoy!
Nutritional Values Per Serving:
Calories: 131; Fat: 7.5g; Carbs: 15.7g; Protein: 2.7g

Ninja Foodi Kale Salad

Prep Time: 10 minutes
Cook Time: 5 minutes
Servings: 4
Ingredients:
- 2 tomatoes, sliced
- 2 tablespoons fresh lemon juice
- 2 red onions, sliced
- 2 scallions, chopped
- 8 cups fresh kale, trimmed and chopped
- 4 tablespoons fresh orange juice

Directions:
1. Add all the ingredients in the pot of Ninja Foodi Deluxe XL Pressure Cooker and select "Steam".
2. Close the pressure Lid and press the "Start/Stop" button.
3. Cook for 5 minutes and open the lid.
4. Take out and refrigerate for about 8 hours.
5. Serve and enjoy!
Nutritional Values Per Serving:
Calories: 110; Fat: 0.3g; Carbs: 23.9g; Protein: 5.5g

Ninja Foodi Vegetable Curry

Prep Time: 10 minutes
Cook Time: 27 minutes
Servings: 6

Ingredients:
- 1 tablespoon olive oil
- 1 onion, chopped
- 1 teaspoon fresh thyme, chopped
- 3 cups fresh spinach
- 1 pound Brussel sprouts
- 1 cup sliced mushrooms
- Salt and black pepper, to taste

Directions:
1. Heat oil in a Ninja Foodi Deluxe XL Pressure Cooker and select "pressure".
2. Press the "Start/Stop" button and sauté onion in it for about 4 minutes.
3. Add in garlic and thyme and sauté for about 1 minute.
4. Stir in mushrooms and cook for about 15 minutes.
5. Then, add in Brussel sprouts and spinach and close the pressure lid.
6. Cook for 7 minutes at HIGH pressure and open the lid.
7. Stir in salt and pepper and take out.
8. Serve and enjoy!

Nutritional Values Per Serving:
Calories: 66; Fat: 2.7g; Carbs: 9.6g; Protein: 3.6g

Ninja Foodi Citrus Carrots

Prep Time: 5 minutes
Cook Time: 5 minutes
Servings: 2

Ingredients:
- 1 tablespoon fresh ginger, minced
- 1 teaspoon olive oil
- ¼ cup fresh orange juice
- 1½ cups carrots, peeled and chopped
- Salt and black pepper, to taste

Directions:
1. Add ginger, carrots and oil in a Ninja Foodi Deluxe XL Pressure Cooker and press the "Sear" button.
2. Close the pressure Lid and press the "Start/Stop" button.
3. Cook for 2 minutes and open the lid.
4. Add in salt, pepper and orange juice. Stir well.
5. Simmer for about 3 minutes and take out.
6. Serve and enjoy!

Nutritional Values Per Serving:
Calories: 167; Fat: 2.6g; Carbs: 34.9g; Protein: 3g

Flavored Fries

Prep Time: 12 Minutes
Cook Time: 15 Minutes
Servings: 2

Ingredients:
- 2 medium-sized sweet potatoes
- 1 tablespoon butter
- 1 teaspoon salt
- 1 teaspoon cinnamon
- 2 teaspoons brown sugar
- ½ teaspoon chili flakes

Directions:
1. Preheat the Ninja Foodi Deluxe XL Pressure Cooker at Air Crisp Mode at 390° F and cut sweet potatoes into thick strips. Rinse the fries, then let them dry.
2. Take a bowl and add fries, butter, cinnamon salt, and chili flakes in it. Mix it well.
3. In the Ninja Foodi Deluxe XL Pressure Cooker, place fries in a single layer, it is recommended to work in batches.
4. Cook it at 390° F for 3 to 7 minutes and then shake the Ninja Foodi Deluxe XL Pressure Cooker Cook & Crisp Basket.
5. Again, cook it for another 7 minutes and sprinkle brown sugar on top of it.

Nutritional Values Per Serving:
Calories: 89; Fat: 6.1g; Carbs: 4.2g; Protein: 4.4g.

Hawaiian Fried Rice

Prep Time: 6 Minutes
Cook Time: 12-15 Minutes
Servings: 3-4
Ingredients:
- ½ cup rice
- 1 cup water
- 1 tablespoon cooking oil
- ½ cup frozen peas
- ½ cup corn
- ½ cup diced carrots
- 1 tablespoon soya sauce
- ¼ cup chopped green onions
- 1 scrambled egg
- 1 cup shredded chicken
- Salt according to taste

Directions:
1. Combine rice, water, and oil in the inner pot of the Ninja Foodi Deluxe XL Pressure Cooker.
2. Set on High pressure for 1 minute and put the pressure lid on and set the back of the valve to Seal. Release the pressure immediately.
3. Cut the vegetables while the rice is being cooked. Then except for the eggs and green onions, add all the remaining ingredients.
4. Put on the Ninja Foodi Deluxe XL Pressure Cooker Crispy lid and set to 390° F, set the Ninja Foodi Deluxe XL Pressure Cooker to Air Crisp Mode Timer for 10 minutes, and keep stirring occasionally.
5. Make a well in the center pushing the rice to the edges, pour the egg, and scramble it.
6. Turn on the Ninja Foodi Deluxe XL Pressure Cooker Mode at Medium temperature on High and add the green onion to it. Cook it for 2 to 3 minutes and dish out the refreshing rice!

Nutrition Information per Serving:
Calories: 187; Fat: 10.5g; Carbs: 14.6g; Protein: 9.3.

Buttered cabbage

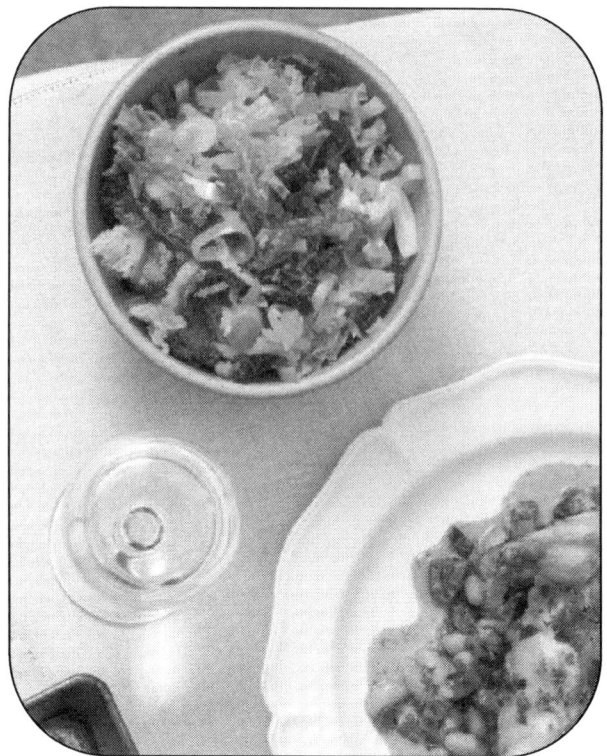

Prep Time: 5 Minutes
Cook Time: 12-15 Minutes
Servings: 4
Ingredients:
- 1 finely cut cabbage head
- ½ cup unsalted butter
- 1 cup chicken broth
- Salt to taste
- Pepper to taste
- ½ teaspoon chili flakes

Directions:
1. Take the Ninja Foodi Deluxe XL Pressure Cooker Pot and add chicken broth and butter to it. Then add chopped cabbage and make sure the lid is closed tightly and set the pressure lid on the Seal. Cook on High Pressure for 6 minutes.
2. Slowly move the valve to the Vent for a quick release. Open the lid once the pressure is released.
3. Stir the cabbage and sprinkle salt, pepper, and chili flakes to season it!

Nutritional Values Per Serving:
Calories: 291; Fat: 22.3g; Carbs: 10.5g; Protein: 5.3g

Veggie Pot Pie

Prep Time: 8-10 Minutes
Cook Time: 20-25 Minutes
Servings: 4

Ingredients:
- 2 tablespoon butter
- 1 small onion
- 1 cup diced carrots
- 1 teaspoon ginger garlic paste
- ½ cup sliced potatoes
- ½ cup vegetable broth.
- ⅛ cup pie
- 4 tablespoons corn
- 1 tablespoon parsley
- 2 tablespoon flour
- ½ cup cream
- Salt to taste
- Pepper to taste
- Pie crust (pre-prepared)

Directions:
1. Start the Ninja Foodi Deluxe XL Pressure Cooker and set to Medium-High temperature, then press the Start/Stop button and let the Ninja Foodi Deluxe XL Pressure Cooker Pot preheat. It would take about 5 minutes. Now put melted butter in the pot. Add carrots, onions in it for about 3 minutes on Sauté Mode.
2. Now add ginger garlic paste to the veggies and cook. Make sure to keep stirring it constantly for about 30 seconds.
3. Then add potatoes and broth to the pot. Put on the Pressure Lid after stirring a little and close the lid to Seal.
4. Now cook on High Pressure Cook Ninja Foodi Deluxe XL Pressure Cooker setting for 5 minutes.
5. Do a quick release, when done and remove the lid now. Add the pies, parsley, and corn to the Ninja Foodi Deluxe XL Pressure Cooker Pot. Then put in flour and mix well. Then stir in cream (heavy cream is preferred) and give it a good mix.
6. Select Sear, and set to High temperature, press Start/Stop to cook it and keep stirring it constantly, until the sauce thickens up, do this for 2 to 3 minutes, and then press the Start/Stop button.
7. Add in salt and pepper to season. Now comes the interesting part, place the pie crust on top of the vegetable mixture and hold the edges of the crust to fit the Ninja Foodi Deluxe XL Pressure Cooker Pot.
8. Make a little vent in the center of the crust, now close the Crisping Lid and select the Broil Mode, set the timer for about 10 minutes, and press the Start/Stop button.
9. Transfer the Ninja Foodi Deluxe XL Pressure Cooker Inner Pot to any heatproof surface, after time is up. Let it sit for about four to 5 minutes and it's ready to be served!

Nutritional Values Per Serving:
Calories: 404; Fat: 22.5g; Carbs: 19.4g; Protein: 4g

Air Crisped Brussels Sprouts

Prep Time: 6 Minutes
Cook Time: 12-15 Minutes
Servings: 2-3

Ingredients:
- ¼ pound brussels sprouts
- 2 slices of bacon
- 1 onion
- Salt to taste
- Pepper to taste

Directions:
1. Preheat the Ninja Foodi Deluxe XL Pressure Cooker by selecting Air Crisp Mode at 390° F for about 5 minutes.
2. Cut off the ends of brussels sprouts and slice them in half. Cut the bacon into small pieces and cut the onions into slices.
3. Put all the ingredients including brussels sprouts, onions, and bacon in Ninja Foodi Deluxe XL Pressure Cooker.
4. Season it with salt and pepper. Let it cook for 15 minutes and mix occasionally. Keep a check and make sure it does not burn!

Nutritional Values Per Serving:
Calories: 90; Fat: 2.3g; Carbs: 14.5g; Protein: 7.1g

Seasoned Beets

Prep Time: 5 Minutes
Cook Time: 25-30 Minutes
Servings: 2
Ingredients:
- 5 -6 beets
- ¼ cup water
- Salt to taste
- Black pepper to taste
- ½ teaspoon paprika

Directions:
1. Trim the beets well. It's suggested to leave about half an inch of stem and roots, this way these can easily be peeled after cooking and then wash and scrub the beets thoroughly. Pour in the water and place the rack in the Ninja Foodi Deluxe XL Pressure Cooker Pot. Align the prepared beets on the rack.
2. Now in place, put the Ninja Foodi Deluxe XL Pressure Cooker Pressure Lid on and lock it well.
3. Set the Ninja Foodi Deluxe XL Pressure Cooker Pressure Lid to Seal, push the Start/Stop button and set to Ninja Foodi Deluxe XL Pressure Cooker High Pressure, and cook for 30 minutes. After the time, release pressure and take it out.
4. Use a sharp knife to pierce the beets. If the knife easily pierces the flesh without much resistance, it means they are done, and if the beets seem a little hard or firm, cook for another two to 5 minutes under High Pressure.
5. Now let the beets cool down to handle them easily. Once they are cool, trim off both of its ends to peel off, use your hands under running water, slice it up, season it with salt, pepper, paprika, and serve!

Nutritional Values Per Serving:
Calories: 74; Fat: 0.4g; Carbs: 16.6g; Protein: 2.8g

Steak and Veggie Bowl

Prep Time: 6 Minutes
Cook Time: 12-15 Minutes
Servings: 1
Ingredients:
- 2 steak strips
- ½ coarsely cut red bell pepper
- ½ coarsely cut green bell pepper
- ½ coarsely cut summer squash
- 10 sliced olives
- ½ cup diced onion
- 2 tablespoons barbecue sauce
- Salt to taste
- Black pepper to taste
- Olive oil spray

Directions:
1. Start by cutting the steak into smaller chunks. Spray olive oil in the Ninja Foodi Deluxe XL Pressure Cooker Cook & Crisp Basket.
2. Now put the steak chunks and cut vegetables in the Ninja Foodi Deluxe XL Pressure Cooker Cook & Crisp Basket. Sprinkle salt, pepper, and barbecue sauce evenly and make sure the seasoning is sprinkled generously.
3. Again, spray with olive oil and cook for seven minutes at 375° F on Bake/Roast option. Open the lid carefully and toss the ingredients.
4. Spray some more olive oil and cook for an additional 8 minutes. Serve it in a bowl!

Nutritional Values Per Serving:
Calories: 19.4g; Fat: 5.2g; Carbs: 12g; Protein: 21g.

Gluten-free Taco Beans

Prep Time: 5 Minutes
Cook Time: 20-25 Minutes
Servings: 1
Ingredients:
- ½ cup Albi beans
- 2 cloves minced garlic
- 1 diced onion
- ½ teaspoon of salt and pepper
- 1 tablespoon taco seasoning mix
- 5-7 cups water

Directions:
1. In the pot of Ninja Foodi Deluxe XL Pressure Cooker, place your beans, garlic, onions, and the seasonings together.
2. Add water and secure the Ninja Foodi Deluxe XL Pressure Cooker Lid and set its valve to Seal.
3. Let it cook for 25 minutes on High Pressure of Ninja Foodi Deluxe XL Pressure Cooker setting, but keep in mind if the beans have been soaked already, then cook for 3 minutes only.
4. When the cooking is over do nothing for 10 minutes and let them naturally release and your taco beans are ready!

Nutritional Values Per Serving:
Calories: 126; Fat: 0.5g; Carbs: 20.9g; Protein: 6.6g

Mac & Cheese

Prep Time: 4-5 Minutes
Cook Time: 3-4 Minutes
Servings: 4
Ingredients:
- 1 tablespoon salted and melted butter
- 1 tablespoon flour
- 4 ounces milk
- 1 cup water
- 4 ounces elbow macaroni
- 2 ounces cheddar cheese

Directions:
1. In a pan combine butter and flour and keep stirring until a smooth paste is formed.
2. Now add milk and stir continuously to avoid the lumps.
3. Add one cup water and macaroni to the inner pot of the Ninja Foodi Deluxe XL Pressure Cooker and stir to mix well.
4. Make sure pasta is fully drenched in the water. Place the wrap in Ninja Foodi Deluxe XL Pressure Cooker and seal the pressure lid.
Cook for 3 minutes on Ninja Foodi Deluxe XL Pressure Cooker High Pressure setting. When time is up, let Ninja Foodi Deluxe XL Pressure Cooker naturally release pressure for 2 minutes and then manually release the leftover pressure.
5. Meanwhile, grate the cheese. After that remove the rack and stir that mixture and pour into the macaroni and mix well.
6. Add grated cheese and stir to melt it!

Nutritional Values Per Serving:
Calories: 297; Fat: 17.7g; Carbs: 22.4g; Protein: 12g

Blackberry Cake

Prep Time: 15 minutes
Cook Time: 3 hours
Serves: 10
Ingredients:
* 2 cups almond flour
* 1 cup unsweetened coconut, shredded
* ½ cup erythritol
* ¼ cup unsweetened protein powder
* 2 tsp baking soda
* ¼ tsp salt
* 4 large eggs
* ½ cup heavy cream
* ½ cup unsalted butter, melted
* 1 cup fresh blackberries
* 1/3 cup 70% dark chocolate chips

Preparation:
1. Grease the Ninja Foodi pot.
2. Mix together the flour, coconut, erythritol, protein powder, baking soda, and salt in a bowl.
3. In another large bowl, add the eggs, cream, and butter and beat until well combined.
4. Add the flour mixture to the wet mixture and mix until well combined.
5. Fold in the blackberries and chocolate chips.
6. Place the mixture in the prepared pot of the Ninja Foodi.
7. Close the Foodi with the Crisping Lid and select SLOW COOK.
8. Set to LO for 3 hours.
9. Press START/STOP to begin cooking.
10. When done, transfer the pot onto a wire rack to cool for about 10 minutes.
11. Carefully invert the cake onto the wire rack to cool completely.

Nutritional Information Per Serving:
Calories 305; Fat: 27.9g; Carbs: 7.7g; Protein: 10.6g

Cinnamon Sugar Biscuit Donuts

Prep Time: 5 minutes
Cook Time: 10 minutes
Serves: 8
Ingredients:
* 1 tube (16 oz) Grands™ Flaky Layers Original Biscuits
* ½ cup unsalted butter, melted
* ½ cup sugar
* ¼ cup brown sugar
* ¼ tsp salt
* 1 tbsp ground cinnamon

Preparation:
1. Combine the sugar, brown sugar, salt, and cinnamon in a small bowl and then set aside.
2. Lay the biscuit dough out on a flat surface. Use a clean bottle cap or similar-sized cookie/biscuit cutter to press into the center of each biscuit, creating a donut-like hole. Repeat this until all the biscuit holes are made. Don't discard the dough, as you can use it to make more donut holes.
3. Mist the Cook & Crisp Basket with olive oil and use a paper towel to wipe the surface down. Place four donuts in the basket, put it in the Foodi, and close the Crisping Lid.
4. Press AIR CRISP, set the temperature to 360°F and set the time for 10 minutes. Press the START/STOP button. A couple of times during the cooking process, check to make sure the donuts don't overbake.
5. After 10 minutes, open the Foodi and remove your finished donuts. They should be golden brown and crisp on the outside. Repeat this process until all the donuts and holes are cooked.
6. Once all the donuts are done, dredge them one at a time in the melted butter, letting the excess drip off. Then place them into the bowl of the cinnamon-sugar mix and coat on all sides. Repeat until all the donuts are coated.

Nutritional Information Per Serving:
Calories 297; Fat: 7.9g; Carbs: 42.6g; Protein: 3.1g

Chocolate Lava Cake

Prep Time: 10 minutes
Cook Time: 10 minutes
Serves: 4

Ingredients:
- 7 tbsp butter
- 1 cup chocolate chips
- 2 eggs
- 3½ tbsp sugar
- 1½ tbsp self-rising flour

Preparation:
1. Melt the chocolate chips and butter together in the microwave. (Put in for 30 seconds, stir, then heat for another 30 seconds until it's melted and smooth.)
2. Whisk together the eggs and sugar in a separate bowl. Then whisk the egg mixture and chocolate together until combined and smooth.
3. Then mix in the flour until smooth.
4. Pour the batter equally into 4 oven-safe ramekins. Fill each ¾ full.
5. Put in the ramekins in the Ninja Foodi pot. Select AIR CRISP mode for 10 minutes at 370°F.
6. Allow the ramekins to cool for 2 minutes before flipping over onto plates.

Nutritional Information Per Serving:
Calories 297| Fat 33g; Carbs: 43g; Protein: 5g

Yogurt Cheesecake

Prep Time: 10 minutes.
Cook Time: 40 minutes
Servings: 8

Ingredients:
- 4 cups plain Greek Yogurt
- 1 cup Erythritol
- ½ teaspoon vanilla extract

Directions:
1. Line a cake pans with Parchment paper.
2. In a suitable, stir in the yogurt and Erythritol and with a hand mixer, mix well.
3. Stir in vanilla extract and mix to combine.
4. Add the mixture into the prepared pan and cover with a paper kitchen towel.
5. Then with a piece of foil, cover the pan tightly.
6. In the Ninja Foodi's insert, place 1 cup of water.
7. Set a "Reversible Rack" in the Ninja Foodi's insert.
8. Place the ramekins over the "Reversible Rack".
9. Close the Ninja Foodi's lid with a pressure lid and place the pressure valve to the "Seal" position.
10. Select "Pressure" mode and set it to "High" for 40 minutes.
11. Press the "Start/Stop" button to initiate cooking.
12. Switch the pressure valve to "Vent" and do a "Quick" release.
13. Place the pan onto a wire rack and remove the foil and paper towel.
14. Again, cover the pan with a new paper towel and refrigerate to cool overnight.

Nutritional Values Per Serving:
Calories: 88; Fats: 1.5g; Carbs: 8.7g; Proteins: 7g

Chocolate Cheesecake

Prep Time: 15 minutes.
Cook Time: 20 minutes
Servings: 10
Ingredients:
For Crust
- ¼ cup coconut flour
- ¼ cup almond flour
- 2½ tablespoons cacao powder
- 1½ tablespoons Erythritol
- 2 tablespoons butter, melted

For Filling
- 16 ounces cream cheese, softened
- ⅓ cup cacao powder
- ½ teaspoon powdered Erythritol
- ½ teaspoon stevia powder
- 1 large egg
- 2 large egg yolks
- 6 ounces unsweetened dark chocolate, melted
- ¾ cup heavy cream
- ¼ cup sour cream
- 1 teaspoon vanilla extract

Directions:
1. For the crust: in a suitable, mix together flours, cacao powder and Erythritol.
2. Stir in the melted butter and mix until well combined.
3. Stir in the mixture into a parchment paper-lined 7-inch springform pan evenly, and with your fingers, press evenly.
4. For filling: in a food processor, add the cream cheese, cacao powder, monk fruit powder and stevia and pulse until smooth.
5. Stir in the egg and egg yolks and pulse until well combined.
6. Add the rest of the ingredients and pulse until well combined.
7. Place the prepared filling mixture on top of the crust evenly and with a rubber spatula, smooth the surface.
8. With a piece of foil, cover the springform pan loosely.
9. In the Ninja Foodi's insert, place 2 cups of water.
10. Set a "Reversible Rack" in the Ninja Foodi's insert.
11. Place the springform pan over the "Reversible Rack".
12. Close the Ninja Foodi's lid with a pressure lid and place the pressure valve in the "Seal" position.
13. Select "Pressure" mode and set it to "High" for 20 minutes.
14. Press the "Start/Stop" button to initiate cooking.
15. Switch the pressure valve to "Vent" and do a "Natural" release.
16. Place the pan onto a wire rack to cool completely.
17. Refrigerate for about 6-8 hours before serving.
Nutritional Values Per Serving:
Calories: 385; Fats: 35.6g; Carbs: 9.8g; Proteins: 8.9g

Raspberry Cobbler

Prep Time: 15 minutes.
Cook Time: 2 hours
Servings: 8
Ingredients:
- 1 cup almond flour
- ¼ cup coconut flour
- ¾ cup Erythritol
- 1 teaspoon baking soda
- ¼ teaspoon ground cinnamon
- ⅛ teaspoon salt
- ¼ cup unsweetened coconut milk
- 2 tablespoons coconut oil
- 1 large egg, beaten lightly
- 4 cups fresh raspberries

Directions:
1. Grease the Ninja Foodi's insert.
2. In a large bowl, mix together flours, Erythritol, baking soda, cinnamon and salt.
3. In another bowl, stir in the coconut milk, coconut oil and egg and beat until well combined.
4. Add the prepared egg mixture into the flour mixture and mix until just combined.
5. In the pot of the prepared Ninja Foodi, add the mixture evenly and top with raspberries.
6. Close the Ninja Foodi's lid with a pressure lid and select "Slow Cook".
7. Set on "Low" for 2 hours.
8. Press the "Start/Stop" button to initiate cooking.
9. Place the pan onto a wire rack to cool slightly.
10. Serve warm.
Nutritional Values Per Serving:
Calories: 164; Fats: 12.5g; Carbs: 10.9g; Proteins: 4.7

Chocolate Blackberry Cake

Prep Time: 15 minutes.
Cook Time: 3 hours
Servings: 10
Ingredients:
- 2 cups almond flour
- 1 cup unsweetened coconut, shredded
- ½ cup Erythritol
- ¼ cup unsweetened Protein: powder
- 2 teaspoons baking soda
- ¼ teaspoon salt
- 4 large eggs
- ½ cup heavy cream
- ½ cup unsalted butter, melted
- 1 cup fresh blackberries
- ⅓ cup 70% dark chocolate chips

Directions:
1. Grease the Ninja Foodi's insert.
2. In a suitable, mix together the flour, coconut, Erythritol Protein: powder, baking soda and salt.
3. In another large bowl, stir in the eggs, cream and butter and beat until well combined.
4. Stir in the dry flour mixture and mix until well combined.
5. Fold in the blackberries and chocolate chips.
6. In the prepared Ninja Foodi's insert, add the mixture.
7. Close the Ninja Foodi's lid with a pressure lid and select "Slow Cook".
8. Set on "Low" for 3 hours.
9. Press the "Start/Stop" button to initiate cooking.
10. Transfer the pan onto a wire rack about 10 minutes.
11. Flip the baked and cooled cake onto the wire rack to cool completely.
12. Cut into desired-sized slices and serve.
Nutritional Values Per Serving:
Calories: 305; Fats: 27.5g; Carbs: 7.7g; Proteins: 10.6g

Mocha Cake

Prep Time: 15 minutes.
Cook Time: 3 hours 37 minutes
Servings: 6
Ingredients:
- 2 ounces 70% dark chocolate, chopped
- ¾ cup butter, chopped
- ½ cup heavy cream
- 2 tablespoons instant coffee crystals
- 1 teaspoon vanilla extract
- ⅓ cup almond flour
- ¼ cup unsweetened cacao powder
- ⅛ teaspoon salt
- 5 large eggs
- ⅔ cup Erythritol

Directions:
1. Grease the Ninja Foodi's insert.
2. In a microwave-safe bowl, stir in the chocolate and butter and microwave on High for about 2 minutes or until melted completely, stirring after every 30 seconds.
3. Remove from the microwave and stir well.
4. Set aside to cool.
5. In a small bowl, stir in the heavy cream, coffee crystals, and vanilla extract and beat until well combined.
6. In a suitable bowl, mix the flour, cacao powder and salt.
7. In a large bowl, stir in the eggs and with an electric mixer, beat on high speed until slightly thickened.
8. Slowly, stir in the Erythritol and beat on high speed until thick and pale yellow.
9. Stir in the chocolate mixture and beat on low speed until well combined.
10. Stir in the dry flour mixture and mix until just combined.
11. Slowly stir in the cream mixture and beat on medium speed until well combined.
12. In the prepared Ninja Foodi's insert, add the mixture.
13. Close the Ninja Foodi's lid with a pressure lid and select "Slow Cook".
14. Set on "Low" for 2½-3½ hours.
15. Press the "Start/Stop" button to initiate cooking.
16. Transfer the pan onto a wire rack for about 10 minutes.
17. Flip the baked and cooled cake onto the wire rack to cool completely.
18. Cut into desired-sized slices and serve.
Nutritional Values Per Serving:
Calories: 407; Fats: 39.7g; Carbs: 6.2g; Proteins: 9g

Lemon Cheesecake

Prep Time: 15 minutes.
Cook Time: 4 hours
Servings: 12
Ingredients:
For Crust:
- 1½ cups almond flour
- 4 tablespoons butter, melted
- 3 tablespoons sugar-free peanut butter
- 3 tablespoons Erythritol
- 1 large egg, beaten

For Filling:
- 1 cup ricotta cheese
- 24 ounces cream cheese, softened
- 1½ cups Erythritol
- 2 teaspoons liquid stevia
- ⅓ cup heavy cream
- 2 large eggs
- 3 large egg yolks
- 1 tablespoon fresh lemon juice
- 1 tablespoon vanilla extract

Directions:
1. Grease the Ninja Foodi's insert.
2. For crust: in a suitable, add all the ingredients and mix until well combined.
3. In the pot of prepared of Ninja Foodi, place the crust mixture and press to smooth the top surface.
4. With a fork, prick the crust at many places.
5. For filling: in a food processor, stir in the ricotta cheese and pulse until smooth.
6. In a large bowl, add the ricotta, cream cheese, Erythritol and stevia and with an electric mixer, beat over medium speed until smooth.
7. In another bowl, stir in the heavy cream, eggs, egg yolks, lemon juice and vanilla extract and beat until well combined.
8. Stir in the egg mixture into cream cheese mixture and beat over medium speed until just combined.
9. Place the prepared filling mixture over the crust evenly.
10. Close the Ninja Foodi's lid with a pressure lid and select "Slow Cook".
11. Set on "Low" for 3-4 hours.
12. Press the "Start/Stop" button to initiate cooking.

13. Place the pan onto a wire rack to cool.
14. Refrigerate to chill for at least 6-8 hours before serving.
Nutritional Values Per Serving:
Calories: 410; Fats: 37.9g; Carbs: 6.9g; Proteins: 13g

Mini Chocolate Cheesecakes

Prep Time: 15 minutes.
Cook Time: 18 minutes
Servings: 4
Ingredients:
- 1 egg
- 8 ounces cream cheese, softened
- ¼ cup Erythritol
- 1 tablespoon powdered peanut butter
- ¾ tablespoon cacao powder

Directions:
1. Grease the Ninja Foodi's insert.
2. In a blender, stir in the eggs and cream cheese and pulse until smooth.
3. Add the rest of the ingredients and pulse until well combined.
4. Transfer the mixture into 2 8-ounce mason jars evenly.
5. In the Ninja Foodi's insert, place 1 cup of water.
6. Set a "Reversible Rack" in the Ninja Foodi's insert.
7. Place the mason jars over the "Reversible Rack".
8. Close the Ninja Foodi's lid with a pressure lid and place the pressure valve in the "Seal" position.
9. Select "Pressure" mode and set it to "High" for 18 minutes.
10. Press the "Start/Stop" button to initiate cooking.
11. Switch the pressure valve to "Vent" and do a "Natural" release.
12. Open the Ninja Foodi's lid and place the ramekins onto a wire rack to cool.
13. Refrigerate to chill for at least 6-8 hours before serving.
Nutritional Values Per Serving:
Calories: 222; Fats: 28.4g; Carbs: 2.9g; Proteins: 6.5g

Double Chocolate Cake

Prep Time: 15 minutes.
Cook Time: 1 hour
Servings: 12
Ingredients:
- ½ cup coconut flour
- 1½ cups Erythritol
- 5 tablespoons cacao powder
- 1 teaspoon baking powder
- ½ teaspoon salt
- 3 eggs
- 3 egg yolks
- ½ cup butter, melted and cooled
- 1 teaspoon vanilla extract
- ½ teaspoon liquid stevia
- 4 ounces 70% dark chocolate chips
- 2 cups hot water

Directions:
1. Grease the Ninja Foodi's insert.
2. In a large bowl, stir in the flour, 1¼ cups of Erythritol, 3 tablespoons of cacao powder, baking powder and salt.
3. In a suitable bowl, add the eggs, egg yolks, butter, vanilla extract and liquid stevia and beat until well combined.
4. Stir in the egg mixture into the flour mixture and mix until just combined.
5. In a small bowl, add hot water, remaining cacao powder and Erythritol and beat until well combined.
6. In the prepared Ninja Foodi's insert, stir in the mixture evenly and top with chocolate chips, followed by the water mixture.
7. Close the Ninja Foodi's lid with a pressure lid and select "Slow Cook".
8. Set on "Low" for 3 hours.
9. Press the "Start/Stop" button to initiate cooking.
10. Transfer the pan onto a wire rack for about 10 minutes.
11. Flip the baked and cooled cake onto the wire rack to cool completely.
12. Cut into desired-sized slices and serve.

Nutritional Values Per Serving:
Calories: 169; Fats: 15.4g; Carbs: 4.4g; Proteins: 3.9g

Chocolate Brownie Cake

Prep Time: 15 minutes.
Cook Time: 35 minutes.
Servings: 6
Ingredients:
- ½ cup 70% dark chocolate chips
- ½ cup butter
- 3 eggs
- ¼ cup Erythritol
- 1 teaspoon vanilla extract

Directions:
1. In a microwave-safe bowl, stir in the chocolate chips and butter and microwave for about 1 minute, stirring after every 20 seconds.
2. Remove from the microwave and stir well.
3. Set a "Reversible Rack" in the pot of the Ninja Foodi.
4. Close the Ninja Foodi's lid with a crisping lid and select "Air Crisp".
5. Set its cooking temperature to 350 degrees F for 5 minutes.
6. Press the "Start/Stop" button to initiate preheating.
7. In a suitable, add the eggs, Erythritol and vanilla extract and blend until light and frothy.
8. Slowly add in the chocolate mixture and beat again until well combined.
9. Add the mixture into a lightly greased springform pan.
10. After preheating, Open the Ninja Foodi's lid.
11. Place the springform pan into the "Air Crisp Basket".
12. Close the Ninja Foodi's lid with a crisping lid and select "Air Crisp".
13. Set its cooking temperature to 350 degrees F for 35 minutes.
14. Press the "Start/Stop" button to initiate cooking.
15. Place the hot pan onto a wire rack to cool for about 10 minutes.
16. Flip the baked and cooled cake onto the wire rack to cool completely.
17. Cut into desired-sized slices and serve.

Nutritional Values Per Serving:
Calories: 302; Fats: 28.2g; Carbs: 5.6g; Proteins: 5.6g

Strawberry Crumble

Prep Time: 15 minutes.
Cook Time: 2 hours
Servings: 5
Ingredients:
- 1 cup almond flour
- 2 tablespoons butter, melted
- 10 drops liquid stevia
- 4 cups fresh strawberries, hulled and sliced
- 1 tablespoon butter, chopped

Directions:
1. Lightly, grease the Ninja Foodi's insert.
2. In a suitable, stir in the flour, melted butter and stevia and mix until a crumbly mixture form.
3. In the pot of the prepared Ninja Foodi, place the strawberry slices and dot with chopped butter.
4. Spread the flour mixture on top evenly
5. Close the Ninja Foodi's lid with a pressure lid and select "Slow Cook".
6. Set on "Low" for 2 hours.
7. Press the "Start/Stop" button to initiate cooking.
8. Place the pan onto a wire rack to cool slightly.
9. Serve warm.

Nutritional Values Per Serving:
Calories: 233; Fats: 19.2g; Carbs: 10.7g; Proteins: 0.7g

Mini Vanilla Cheesecakes

Prep Time: 15 minutes.
Cook Time: 10 minutes
Servings: 4
Ingredients:
- ¾ cup Erythritol
- 2 eggs
- 1 teaspoon vanilla extract
- ½ teaspoon fresh lemon juice
- 16 ounces cream cheese, softened
- 2 tablespoon sour cream

Directions:
1. Set the "Air Crisp Basket" in the Ninja Foodi's insert.
2. Close the Ninja Foodi's lid with a crisping lid and select "Air Crisp".
3. Set its cooking temperature to 350 degrees F for 5 minutes.
4. Press the "Start/Stop" button to initiate preheating.
5. In a blender, stir in the Erythritol, eggs, vanilla extract and lemon juice and pulse until smooth.
6. Stir in the cream cheese along with sour cream and pulse until smooth.
7. Stir in the mixture into 2- 4-inch spring-form pans evenly.
8. After preheating, Open the Ninja Foodi's lid.
9. Place the pans into the "Air Crisp Basket".
10. Close the Ninja Foodi's lid with a crisping lid and select "Air Crisp".
11. Set its cooking temperature to 350 degrees for 10 minutes.
12. Press the "Start/Stop" button to initiate cooking.
13. Place the pans onto a wire rack for 10 minutes.
14. Refrigerator overnight before serving.

Nutritional Values Per Serving:
Calories: 436; Fats: 21g; Carbs: 3.2g; Proteins: 13.1g

Lime Blueberry Cheesecake

Prep Time: 15 minutes.
Cook Time: 30 minutes
Servings: 6
Ingredients:
- ¼ cup 1 teaspoon Erythritol
- 8 ounces cream cheese, softened
- ⅓ cup Ricotta cheese
- 1 teaspoon fresh lime zest, grated
- 2 tablespoons fresh lime juice
- ½ teaspoon vanilla extract
- 1 cup blueberries
- 2 eggs
- 2 tablespoons sour cream

Directions:
1. In a suitable, stir in ¼ cup of Erythritol and remaining ingredients except for eggs and sour cream and with a hand mixer, beat on high speed until smooth.
2. Stir in the eggs and beat on low speed until well combined, then fold in blueberries.
3. Transfer the mixture into a 6-inch greased springform pan evenly.
4. With a piece of foil, cover the pan.
5. In the Ninja Foodi's insert, place 2 cups of water.
6. Set a "Reversible Rack" in the Ninja Foodi's insert.
7. Place the springform pan over the "Reversible Rack".
8. Close the Ninja Foodi's lid with a pressure lid and place the pressure valve in the "Seal" position.
9. Select "Pressure" mode and set it to "High" for 30 minutes.
10. Press the "Start/Stop" button to initiate cooking.
11. Switch the pressure valve to "Vent" and do a "Natural" release.
12. Place the pan onto a wire rack to cool slightly.
13. Meanwhile, in a small bowl, stir in the sour cream and remaining erythritol and beat until well combined.

14. Spread the cream mixture on the warm cake evenly.
15. Refrigerate for about 6-8 hours before serving.
Nutritional Values Per Serving:
Calories: 182; Fats: 16.6g; Carbs: 2.1g; Proteins: 6.4g

Chocolate Walnut Cake

Prep Time: 15 minutes.
Cook Time: 20 minutes
Servings: 6
Ingredients:
- 3 eggs
- 1 cup almond flour
- ⅔ cup Erythritol
- ⅓ cup heavy whipping cream
- ¼ cup butter softened
- ¼ cup cacao powder
- ¼ cup walnuts, chopped
- 1 teaspoon baking powder

Directions:
1. In a suitable bowl, mix all the ingredients and with a mixer, beat until fluffy.
2. Add the mixture into a greased Bundt pan.
3. With a piece of foil, cover the pan.
4. In the Ninja Foodi's insert, place 2 cups of water.
5. Set a "Reversible Rack" in the Ninja Foodi's insert.
6. Place the Bundt pan over the "Reversible Rack".
7. Close the Ninja Foodi's lid with a pressure lid and place the pressure valve to the "Seal" position.
8. Select "Pressure" mode and set it to "High" for 20 minutes.
9. Press the "Start/Stop" button to initiate cooking.
10. Switch the pressure valve to "Vent" and do a "Quick" release.
11. Place the pan onto a wire rack to cool for about 10 minutes.
12. Flip the baked and cooled cake onto the wire rack to cool completely.
13. Cut into desired-sized slices and serve.
Nutritional Values Per Serving:
Calories: 270; Fats: 25.4g; Carbs: 7g; Proteins: 8.9g

Ninja Foodi Vanilla Shake

Prep Time: 7 minutes
Cook Time: 2 minutes
Servings: 2
Ingredients:
- 1 cup water
- 1 cup almond milk
- ½ cup vanilla ice cream
- 2 teaspoons sugar

Directions:
1. Add every ingredient in the Ninja Foodi Deluxe XL Pressure Cooker and select "Pressure".
2. Close the pressure Lid and press the "Start/Stop'" button.
3. Cook for 2 minutes and open the lid.
4. Take out and set aside.
5. Refrigerate overnight, serve and enjoy!
Nutritional Values Per Serving:
Calories: 325; Fat: 30.4g; Carbs: 14.7g; Protein: 3.3g

Ninja Foodi Mocha Cake

Prep Time: 2 minutes
Cook Time: 2 minutes
Servings: 4
Ingredients:
- ½ cup water
- 2 tablespoons beaten egg
- 4 teaspoons chocolate chips
- ½ teaspoon baking powder
- 4 teaspoons Splenda
- 4 teaspoons coffee

Directions:
1. Add all the ingredients to a large bowl and mix well.
2. Place the bowl in Ninja Foodi Deluxe XL Pressure Cooker, press the "Bake" button and close the lid.
3. Press the "Start/Stop" button and bake for 2 minutes.
4. Open the lid and take out.
5. Serve and enjoy!
Nutritional Values Per Serving:
Calories: 46; Fat: 1.5g; Carbs: 6.4g; Protein: 0.8g

Ninja Foodi Chia Seed Smoothie

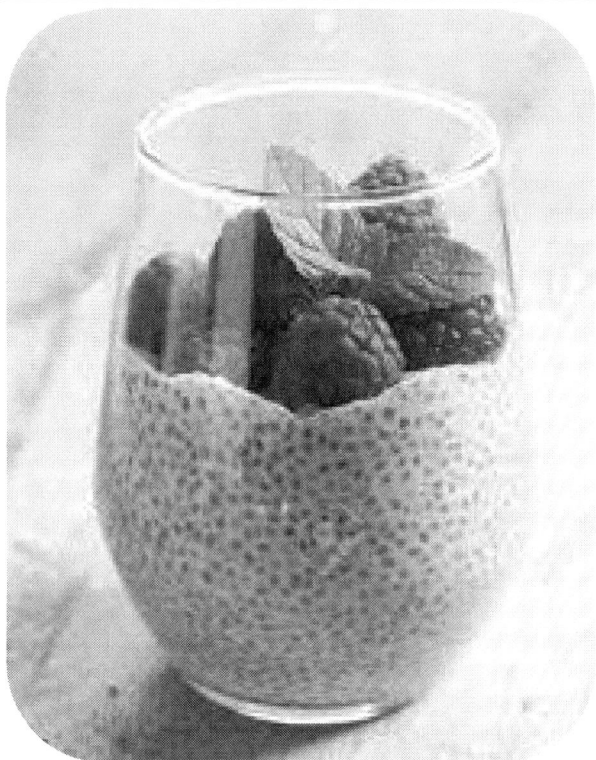

Prep Time: 10 minutes
Cook Time: 2 minutes
Servings: 2
Ingredients:
- 2 cups unsweetened almond milk
- ½ cup chia seeds
- 2 teaspoons sugar

Directions:
1. Add almond milk, chia seeds and sugar in a Ninja Foodi Deluxe XL Pressure Cooker and select "Pressure".
2. Close the pressure lid and press the "Start/Stop" button.
3. Cook for 2 minutes and open the lid.
4. Take out and refrigerate overnight.
5. Serve and enjoy!
Nutritional Values Per Serving:
Calories: 89; Fat: 5.7g; Carbs: 9g; Protein: 2.2g

Ninja Foodi Fruity Frozen Treat

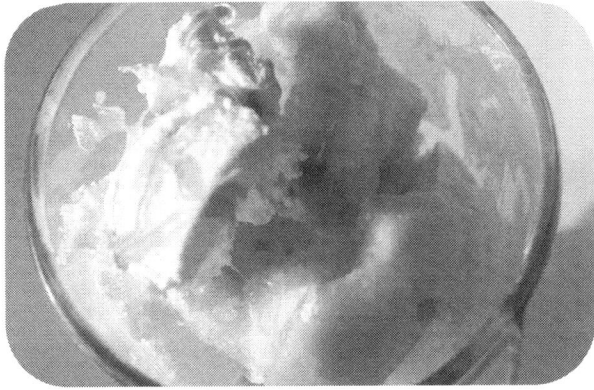

Prep Time: 5 minutes
Cook Time: 3 minutes
Servings: 3

Ingredients:
- ½ cup frozen pineapple chunks
- 1 cup almond milk
- 4 tablespoons fresh lime juice
- 2 cups banana slices

Directions:
1. Add pineapple slices, almond milk, lime juice and banana slices in a Ninja Foodi Deluxe XL Pressure Cooker and select "Pressure".
2. Close the pressure Lid and press the "Start/Stop" button.
3. Cook for about 3 minutes and open the lid.
4. Dish out and freeze for about 1 hour.
5. Take out, serve and enjoy!

Nutritional Values Per Serving:
Calories: 464; Fat: 31.4g; Carbs: 45.2g; Protein: 5.4g

Ninja Foodi Ricotta Mousse

Prep Time: 10 minutes
Cook Time: 2 minutes
Servings: 2

Ingredients:
- 2½ cups water
- 2 teaspoons stevia powder
- ½ teaspoon vanilla extract
- 1 cup ricotta cheese
- 2 teaspoons cocoa powder

Directions:
1. Add everything to a Ninja Foodi Deluxe XL Pressure Cooker and select "pressure".
2. Close the pressure Lid and press the "Start/Stop" button.
3. Cook for about 2 minutes and open the lid.
4. Pour the mixture in serving glasses and refrigerate for about 6 hours.
5. Serve and enjoy!

Nutritional Values Per Serving:
Calories: 178; Fat: 10.1g; Carbs: 7.5g; Protein: 14.5g

Ninja Foodi Chickpea Fudge

Prep Time: 10 minutes
Cook Time: 1 hour 5 minutes
Servings: 3

Ingredients:
- ½ cup cooked chickpeas
- 2 dates, pitted and chopped
- ½ tablespoon cocoa powder
- 2 tablespoons almond butter
- 2 tablespoons almond milk
- ¼ teaspoon vanilla extract

Directions:
1. Add everything except cocoa powder in the Ninja Foodi Deluxe XL Pressure Cooker and select "Pressure".
2. Close thepressure Lid and press the "Start/Stop" button.
3. Cook for about 5 minutes and open the lid.
4. Transfer the mixture to a bowl and stir in cocoa powder.
5. Pour the mixture in Ninja Foodi Deluxe XL Pressure Cooker and press the "Bake" button.
6. Bake for about an hour and take out.
7. Refrigerate, slice and serve.

Nutritional Values Per Serving:
Calories: 228; Fat: 10.5g; Carbs: 27.4g; Protein: 9.2g

Ninja Foodi Blackberry Crumble

Prep Time: 10 minutes
Cook Time: 45 minutes
Servings: 6
Ingredients:
Blackberries Filling:
- ¼ cup coconut flour
- 3 tablespoons water
- ¼ cup arrowroot flour
- 2 tablespoons melted butter
- ¼ cup mashed banana
- 1½ cups fresh blackberries
- ¾ teaspoon baking soda
- ½ tablespoon lemon juice

Crumble Topping
- ½ cup old fashioned oats
- ½ cup coconut flour
- ½ cup brown sugar, packed
- ⅛ tsp baking powder
- ⅛ tsp baking soda
- ¼ cup butter, softened

Directions:
1. Add all the ingredients for filling except blackberries in a bowl and mix well.
2. Combine the ingredients for crumble topping in another bowl.
3. Arrange blackberries in the bottom of Ninja Foodi Deluxe XL Pressure Cooker and pour the filling batter on them.
4. Top with the crumble topping.
5. Press the "Bake" button and close the lid.
6. Press the "Start/Stop" button and bake for 40 minutes at 300 degrees F.
7. Open the lid and take out.
8. Serve and enjoy!

Nutritional Values Per Serving:
Calories: 292; Fat: 10.7g; Carbs: 45.7g; Protein: 5.9g

Ninja Foodi Yogurt Cheesecake

Prep Time: 15 minutes
Cook Time: 30 minutes
Servings: 10
Ingredients:
- 6 drops liquid stevia
- 1 teaspoon vanilla extract
- 4 egg whites
- ½ cup cocoa powder
- 3 cups low-fat Greek yogurt
- ¼ cup arrowroot starch
- Pinch of salt

Crust
- ¼ cup white sugar
- 7 graham crackers
- ¼ cup brown sugar
- 1 pinch salt
- 6 tablespoons butter, melted

Directions:
1. Gather all the crust ingredients and dump into the blender.
2. Blend until all the ingredients are well combined and form the sand like consistency.
3. Combine all crust ingredients in a blender and blend until mixture becomes the consistency of damp sand.
4. Shift the crust mixture into a 7-inch springform pan and pat it down with spatula.
5. Add all the ingredients of cheesecake filling in a large bowl and mix well.
6. Pour the mixture in the springform pan over the top of the crust and place it in the pot of Ninja Foodi Deluxe XL Pressure Cooker.
7. Press the "Bake" button and close the Crisping Lid.
8. Press the "Start/Stop" button and bake for about 30 minutes at 350 degrees F.
9. Open the lid and take out.
10. Slice and serve.

Nutritional Values Per Serving:
Calories: 236; Fat: 9.3g; Carbs: 35.1g; Protein: 5.9g

Ninja Foodi Banana Custard

Prep Time: 10 minutes
Cook Time: 25 minutes
Servings: 4
Ingredients:
- 1 banana, mashed
- 1 cup almond milk
- ¼ teaspoon vanilla extract
- 2 eggs

Directions:
1. Add all the ingredients in a large bowl and mix well.
2. Pour the batter evenly in custard cups and place them in Ninja Foodi Deluxe XL Pressure Cooker.
3. Press the "Bake" button and close the Crisping Lid.
4. Press the "Start/Stop" button and bake for 25 minutes at 350 degrees F.
5. Open the lid and take out.
6. Serve and enjoy!

Nutritional Values Per Serving:
Calories: 196; Fat: 16.6g; Carbs: 10.3g; Protein: 4.5g

Ninja Foodi Chocolate Tofu Mousse

Prep Time: 10 minutes
Cook Time: 1 minute
Servings: 2
Ingredients:
- 1 banana, peeled and sliced
- ¾ cup firm tofu, drained
- 1 teaspoon cocoa powder
- 1 teaspoon chopped almonds

Directions:
1. Add all the ingredients in a Ninja Foodi Deluxe XL Pressure Cooker and select "Pressure".
2. Close the lid and press the "Start/Stop" button.
3. Cook for 1 minute and open the lid.
4. Pour the mixture in serving glasses and refrigerate for about 3 hours.
5. Take out, serve and enjoy!

Nutritional Values Per Serving:
Calories: 264; Fat: 2.7g; Carbs: 51.7g; Protein: 14.2g

Ninja Foodi Raspberry Ice Cream

Prep Time: 20 minutes
Cook Time: 2 minutes
Servings: 4
Ingredients:
- 1 cup fresh raspberries
- ½ banana, sliced
- 2 tablespoons shredded coconut
- ½ cup coconut cream

Directions:
1. Add all the ingredients in a Ninja Foodi Deluxe XL Pressure Cooker and select "Pressure".
2. Close the lid, press the "Start/Stop" button and cook for about 2 minutes.
3. Open the lid and transfer the mixture to an ice-cream maker.
4. Process according to manufacturer's directions and take out.
5. Pour the mixture into an air-tight container and freeze for about 4 hours. Stir after every half an hour.
6. Take out and serve.

Nutritional Values Per Serving:
Calories: 107; Fat: 8.2g; Carbs: 9.1g; Protein: 1.3g

Rocky Road Fudge

Prep Time: 5 Minutes
Cook Time: 5 hours
Servings: 6
Ingredients:
- 8 ounces pretend condensed milk
- 9 ounces chocolate chips
- 1 teaspoon vanilla extract
- ¼ teaspoon sea salt
- ½ cup almonds
- 2 ounces marshmallows

Directions:
1. On Broil, preheat the Ninja Foodi Deluxe XL Pressure Cooker for 10 minutes with the Basket inside. Now add almonds to the Basket and Broil it for 3 to 5 minutes. Take out the almonds and let them cool.
2. Line the square pan with parchment paper, add in chocolate chips and sweetened condensed milk, and then cover it again with the foil.
3. Place the pan in Ninja Foodi Deluxe XL Pressure Cooker. Add two cups of water in it and cook at Steam setting for 5 minutes.
4. Set the valve to the Vent position while the chocolate mixture is steaming.
5. Meanwhile, crush the almonds coarsely and cut marshmallows if you're using large ones.
6. Remove the pan from Ninja Foodi Deluxe XL Pressure Cooker and add vanilla, marshmallows, salt, and chopped almonds. Give it a good mix.
7. Then the fudge will start to thicken up as it cools down. Let it cool down for two to four hours in the refrigerator and cut it into bite-size squares!

Nutritional Values Per Serving:
Calories: 328; Fat: 18.7g; Carbs: 38.1g; Protein: 7.1g

Chocolate Brownies

Prep Time: 5 Minutes
Cook Time: 4 hours
Servings: 8
Ingredients:
- ½ cup butter
- 4 ounces dark chocolate chips
- 4 ounces milk chocolate chips
- 1 cup sugar
- 2 tablespoon canola oil
- 3 beaten eggs
- ½ teaspoon vanilla extract
- ¼ cup unsweetened cocoa powder
- ¼ cup all-purpose flour

Directions:
1. Turn the Ninja Foodi Deluxe XL Pressure Cooker on and select the Pressure Cook option on High, then add in the butter.
2. Once it's half-melted, add chocolate chips on one side and keep melting the chips until 75% are melted.
3. Turn off the Ninja Foodi Deluxe XL Pressure Cooker and continue to cool down the chocolate. When it reaches room temperature, add in oil and sugar and stir it well.
4. Beat eggs lightly in a bowl and add in the eggs slowly in the chocolate batter and keep stirring it, then add vanilla extract. Now add in cocoa powder and stir it to incorporate well.
5. Add in flour gradually. Make sure to add ⅓ portions at a time and then mix it well to avoid any lumps.
6. Now put the Ninja Foodi Deluxe XL Pressure Cooker Pressure Lid back on and turn the valve to Vent. And then select the Slow Cook function on Low for 4 hours. Scoop out brownies if you want them gooey. And if you want to achieve that flaky top then for 8 to 20 minutes put the lid.
7. Serve warm with your coffee!

Nutritional Values Per Serving:
Calories: 458; Fat: 27.7g; Carbs: 50.5g; Protein: 6.9g

Pineapple Chunks

Prep Time: 3 Minutes

Cook Time: 10-12 Minutes

Servings: 6

Ingredients:
- 1 stick melted butter
- ½ cup brown sugar
- ½ teaspoon cinnamon
- 1 sliced pineapple

Directions:
1. Combine melted butter, cinnamon, and brown sugar in a low-sided dish. Mix it well.
2. Put in your pineapple pieces to allow it to soak in the flavors for a bit.
3. Select the Bake option, and set the temperature to 375° F. Add pineapple pieces and let them Bake for 12 minutes.
4. Flip the pineapple slices gently halfway through.
5. Serve immediately when ready!

Nutritional Values Per Serving:
Calories: 455; Fat: 22.4g; Carbs: 39g; Protein: 4.5g

Banana Bread

Prep Time: 10 Minutes

Cook Time: 30 Minutes

Servings: 4

Ingredients
- 2 large ripe bananas
- ¾ cup all-purpose flour
- 1 egg
- 3 teaspoons brown sugar
- 2 teaspoons butter
- ¼ cup sour cream
- ½ teaspoon baking soda
- ½ teaspoon salt

Directions:
1. Preheat the Ninja Foodi Deluxe XL Pressure Cooker at Bake Mode at 375° F.
2. Now grease the mini loaf and set it aside.
3. Take all ingredients in a medium bowl and combine them and stir until combined well.
4. Put the batter evenly in a butter paper-lined loaf pan. Dump the pan and Bake it for 25 to 30 minutes.
5. To check the doneness, make sure that when a toothpick is inserted in the center, it comes out clean. Check the banana bread with a toothpick and serve it warm!

Nutritional Values Per Serving:
Calories: 271; Fat: 10.4g; Carbs: 40.8g; Protein: 4.8g

Honey Almond Scones

Prep Time: 5 Minutes

Cook Time: 6 Minutes

Servings: 6

Ingredients:
- 2 cups all-purpose flour
- 3 tablespoons brown sugar
- 1 egg
- 1 teaspoon baking powder
- ½ teaspoon salt
- 1 cup milk
- 1 teaspoon almond extract
- ¼ cup butter
- Cinnamon to sprinkle

Directions:
1. Combine the dried ingredients in a large bowl. Melt butter in a pan, then adds it to dry ingredients.
2. Now combine all the wet ingredients with the dry ones and stir it. Make sure to not overwork with the dough mixture.
3. Place on parchment paper in Ninja Foodi Deluxe XL Pressure Cooker Cook & Crisp Basket. Scoop out the dough with a rounded spoon on the Ninja Foodi Deluxe XL Pressure Cooker Basket. Set your Ninja Foodi Deluxe XL Pressure Cooker to an Air Crisp function and set the temperature at 390° F for 8 minutes until it's golden brown.
4. Let the cones cool down and then sprinkle a little bit of cinnamon!

Nutritional Values Per Serving:
Calories: 267; Fat: 9.9g; Carbs: 37.4g; Protein: 6.5g

Chocolate Chip Cookies

Prep Time: 4 Minutes
Cook Time: 10 Minutes
Servings: 8
Ingredients:
- ½ cup butter
- ½ cup sugar
- 1 egg
- 1 teaspoon vanilla essence
- ¼ cup light brown sugar
- ½ teaspoon baking soda
- ¼ teaspoon salt
- ¾ cup all-purpose flour
- 1 cup chocolate chips or chocolate chunks

Directions:
1. Preheat the Ninja Foodi Deluxe XL Pressure Cooker at Air Crisp Mode at 390° F then grease a metal cookie pan that fits the Ninja Foodi Deluxe XL Pressure Cooker. You can use the cookie cutter and place it in a baking tray.
2. Combine butter, brown sugar, and sugar, and cream.
3. Now add vanilla essence and egg. Mix it well until combined.
4. Add in baking soda, flour, and salt. Now stir in chocolate chips. Give it a good mix.
5. Flatten the cookie dough and press it in the bottom of the greased pan. Dump it in the Ninja Foodi Deluxe XL Pressure Cooker and bake for ten to 12 minutes until it becomes slightly brown around the edges!

Nutritional Values Per Serving:
Calories: 364; Fat: 20.3g; Carbs: 42.8g; Protein: 4g

Air Crisped Cake

Prep Time: 10 Minutes
Cook Time: 20 Minutes
Servings: 6
Ingredients:
- 4 tablespoons self-rising flour
- 7 tablespoons butter
- 1 cup chocolate chips
- 3 tablespoons sugar
- 2 eggs

Directions:
1. Melt the butter and chocolate chips. Mix until the chocolate is completely melted.
2. Beat eggs and sugar together in a bowl for 2 minutes. Make sure that sugar is beaten well. Pour this egg mixture into the chocolate mix and fold it to make a smooth batter.
3. Then mix in flour until smooth. Fold it well.
4. Take four oven-safe ramekins, and pour the batter equally in them. Fill it ¾ th of the ramekin and Air Crisp it for 10 minutes at 390° F in Ninja Foodi Deluxe XL Pressure Cooker.
5. Let it cool for 2 minutes before you flip it onto the plate!

Nutritional Values Per Serving:
Calories: 370; Fat: 25.8g; Carbs: 34g; Protein: 5.3g

Crispy Apple Delight

Prep Time: 6 Minutes
Cook Time: 10 Minutes
Servings: 4

Ingredients:
- 5 medium-sized apples
- ½ cup water
- ½ teaspoon nutmeg powder
- 1 teaspoon cinnamon
- 4 tablespoons butter
- ¼ cup flour
- ¾ cup rolled oats
- ¼ cup brown sugar
- ½ teaspoon salt
- 1 teaspoon maple syrup

Directions:
1. Cut apples in bite sizes and place them on the bottom of your Ninja Foodi Deluxe XL Pressure Cooker.
2. Now sprinkle cinnamon, maple syrup, and nutmeg on it. Then pour water over this mixture.
3. Melt butter in a separate bowl then adds flour, brown sugar, butter, oats, and salt to the bowl. Mix it well.
4. Pour this butter mix over the apple layer.
5. Seal the Ninja Foodi Deluxe XL Pressure Cooker Pressure Lid and secure the Valve. Cook for 10 minutes on Ninja Foodi Deluxe XL Pressure Cooker Pressure Cook at High setting. Then manually release pressure for 5 minutes.
6. Lower Ninja Foodi Deluxe XL Pressure Cooker Crisper Lid and let this combination sit for a few minutes before serving!

Nutritional Values Per Serving:
Calories: 322; Fat: 12.5g; Carbs: 54.2g; Protein: 2g

Blueberry Buttermilk Cake

Prep Time: 10 Minutes
Cook Time: 15-20 Minutes
Servings: 8

Ingredients:
- 8 tablespoons unsalted butter
- 1 cup sugar (keep 1 tbsp aside)
- 1 egg
- 1 teaspoon vanilla
- 2 cups all-purpose flour (¼ cup aside)
- 1 teaspoon baking powder
- ¼ teaspoon salt
- ½ cup buttermilk
- 2 cups blueberries

Directions:
1. Beat the butter with one cup of sugar for four to 5 minutes, until it's light and fluffy.
2. Now add vanilla and eggs into it and beat it well.
3. Put in ¼ cup of flour, one tablespoon sugar, and blueberries together in a bowl to coat them and set aside.
4. Mix the remaining flour, salt, and baking powder in another bowl.
5. Add this dry mixture to batter and mix it with a spatula, then add buttermilk.
6. Beat until flour is mixed in and add remaining flour. Now fold in the blueberries and remove the excess flour from the blueberry bowl behind it.
7. Spray the Ninja Foodi Deluxe XL Pressure Cooker Pot with canola oil. Pour this batter into the Ninja Foodi Deluxe XL Pressure Cooker Pot at 390° F. Select Air Crisp, and set it for 25 minutes then close the Ninja Foodi Deluxe XL Pressure Cooker Crisping Lid. Now select the Start/Stop button for about 15 minutes. Check it with a toothpick and extend the time if it's raw. Enjoy the berrylicious flavor!

Nutritional Values Per Serving:
Calories: 344; Fat: 12.4g; Carbs: 33.4g; Protein: 4.5g

Biscuit Donuts

Prep Time: 5 Minutes
Cook Time: 8-10 Minutes
Servings: 8
Ingredients:
- 16 ounces flaky layers biscuits
- ½ cup butter unsalted
- ¼ cup brown sugar
- ½ cup sugar
- 1 teaspoon grounded cinnamon
- ¼ teaspoon salt

Directions:
1. Take sugar, brown sugar, cinnamon, and salt in a small bowl and mix well to combine the ingredients.
2. Now, on a flat surface, align the flaky biscuits. Take a clean bottle cap and press it in the center of the biscuit creating the hole of the donuts.
3. Spray the Ninja Foodi Deluxe XL Pressure Cooker Cook & Crisp Basket with olive oil. Place four donuts in the Basket of the Ninja Foodi Deluxe XL Pressure Cooker and close the lid. Press the option Start/Stop then Air Crisp it at 390° F for about 10 minutes then press the Start/Stop button again. Keep in mind to check a couple of times to make sure they don't overbake.
4. Open the Ninja Foodi Deluxe XL Pressure Cooker after 10 minutes and take out your fresh donuts.
5. The second batch of donuts usually takes 7 to 8 minutes for Bake.
6. Drench the donuts one at a time in the melted butter once all the donuts are air-fried.
7. Then invert them into the dry ingredients to coat them generously.
8. Repeat this process until all donuts are coated, enjoy them warm and appropriately store the leftovers!

Nutritional Values Per Serving:
Calories: 341; Fat: 16.8g; Carbs: 34.3g; Protein: 3.3g

Pumpkin Pie

Prep Time: 10 Minutes
Cook Time: 8-9 Minutes
Servings: 24
Ingredients:
- 18" mini pie crust
- 1 can pumpkin
- 1 can evaporate milk
- ¾ cup sugar
- ½ teaspoon salt
- ½ teaspoon cinnamon
- ½ teaspoon ground ginger
- ½ teaspoon ground cloves
- 2 eggs

Directions:
1. Preheat the Ninja Foodi Deluxe XL Pressure Cooker at Air Crisp Mode at 390° F for 5 minutes.
2. Whisk all ingredients together until a smooth mixture is formed. Make sure the pumpkin is mixed well.
3. Take mini pie tins and set the crust on the bottom of them.
4. Then use a measuring cup to scoop filling in the tins until there is a bit of space at the top.
5. Now for 8 minutes, cook at Air Crisp Mode at 390° F and close the lid and seal valve. Now take tongs and remove them carefully from Ninja Foodi Multi-Cooker and then let them cool aside.
6. Add another batch of mixture and continue cokking same like above at Air Crisp mode until all is done!

Nutritional Values Per Serving:
Calories: 651; Fat: 36.6g; Carbs: 73.2g; Protein: 1.3g

Vanilla Cheesecake

Prep Time: 15 minutes.
Cook Time: 2 hours
Servings: 6

Ingredients:

For Crust:
- 1 cup almonds, toasted
- 1 egg
- 2 tablespoons butter
- 4-6 drops liquid stevia

For Filling:
- 2 8-ounce packages of cream cheese, softened
- 4 tablespoons heavy cream
- 2 eggs
- 1 tablespoon coconut flour
- 1 teaspoon liquid stevia
- 1 teaspoon vanilla extract

Directions:
1. For the crust: in a high-speed food processor, stir in almonds and pulse until a flour-like consistency is achieved.
2. In a suitable, add ground almond, egg, butter and stevia and mix until well combined.
3. In the bottom of a 1½-quart oval pan, place the crust mixture and press to smooth the top surface, leaving a little room on each side.
4. For the filling: in a suitable, stir in all ingredients and with an immersion blender, blend until well combined.
5. Place the prepared filling mixture over the crust evenly.
6. In the Ninja Foodi's insert, place 1 cup of water.
7. Carefully set the pan in the Ninja Foodi's insert.
8. Close the Ninja Foodi's lid with a pressure lid and select "Slow Cook".
9. Set on "Low" for 2 hours.
10. Press the "Start/Stop" button to initiate cooking.
11. Place the pan onto a wire rack to cool.
12. Refrigerate to chill for at least 6-8 hours before serving.

Nutritional Values Per Serving:
Calories: 446; Fats: 42.9g; Carbs: 7.2g; Proteins: 10.6g

4 Weeks Meal Plan

Week 1

Day 1
Breakfast: Cheesy Eggs with Tomatoes
Lunch: Beets and Carrots
Dinner: Shrimp Zoodles
Snack: Ninja Foodi Popcorn
Dessert: Chocolate Walnut Cake

Day 2
Breakfast: Ninja Foodi Arugula Omelet
Lunch: Ninja Foodi Kale Salad
Dinner: Ninja Foodi Ginger Cod
Snack: Ninja Foodi Spicy Peanuts
Dessert: Ninja Foodi Chickpea Fudge

Day 3
Breakfast: Cashew Porridge
Lunch: Zucchinis Spinach Fry
Dinner: Ninja Foodi Spinach Chicken
Snack: Ninja Foodi Spicy Cashews
Dessert: Ninja Foodi Banana Custard

Day 4
Breakfast: Broccoli Egg Scramble
Lunch: Buttered cabbage
Dinner: Braised Lamb Shanks
Snack: Shallot Pepper Pancakes
Dessert: Pumpkin Pie

Day 5
Breakfast: All Cheese Egg Bites
Lunch: Carrots Walnuts Salad
Dinner: Ninja Foodi Plum & Beef Salad
Snack: Ninja Foodi Spicy Popcorns
Dessert: Ninja Foodi Chia Seed Smoothie

Day 6
Breakfast: Swiss Bacon Frittata
Lunch: Cabbage with Carrots
Dinner: Beef Onion Pattie Burgers
Snack: Chicken Pork Nuggets
Dessert: Pineapple Chunks

Day 7
Breakfast: Hashbrown Casserole
Lunch: Italian Potatoes
Dinner: Ninja Foodi Salmon
Snack: Ninja Foodi Cod Sticks
Dessert: Air Crisped Cake

Week 2

Day 1
Breakfast: Ninja Foodi Coconut Cereal
Lunch: Vanilla Banana Bread
Dinner: Ninja Foodi Basil Pesto Chicken
Snack: Herbed Cauliflower Fritters   38
Cheesy Egg Bombs
Dessert: Mocha Cake

Day 2
Breakfast: Morning Pancakes
Lunch: Ninja Foodi Tomato Olive Salad
Dinner: Shredded Chicken Salsa
Snack: Shallots with Mushrooms
Dessert: Chocolate Brownie Cake

Day 3
Breakfast: Chicken Omelet
Lunch: Ninja Foodi Citrus Carrots
Dinner: Veggies & Beef Stew
Snack: Ninja Foodi Lemon Scones
Dessert: Ninja Foodi Yogurt Cheesecake

Day 4
Breakfast: Breakfast Oats Bowl
Lunch: Veggie Pot Pie
Dinner: Ham-Stuffed Turkey Rolls
Snack: Dried Tomatoes
Dessert: Chocolate Brownies

Day 5
Breakfast: Deviled Eggs
Lunch: Radish Apples Salad
Dinner: Ninja Foodi Lamb & Kale Stew
Snack: Loaded Zucchini Chips
Dessert: Honey Almond Scones

Day 6
Breakfast: Breakfast pizza
Lunch: Pomegranate Radish Mix
Dinner: Fish Broccoli Stew
Snack: Chicken Wings
Dessert: Blackberry Cake

Day 7
Breakfast: Ninja Foodi Cinnamon Tea
Lunch: Eggplant with Kale
Dinner: Taiwanese Chicken
Snack: Air Crisped Chicken Nuggets
Dessert: Rocky Road Fudge

Week 3

Day 1
Breakfast: Spinach Casserole
Lunch: Ninja Foodi Cauliflower Fried Rice
Dinner: Beef Sirloin Steak
Snack: Avocado Deviled Eggs
Dessert: Ninja Foodi Ricotta Mousse

Day 2
Breakfast: Cowboy Casserole
Lunch: Maple Dipped Kale
Dinner: Parmesan Chicken
Snack: Ninja Foodi Spiced Almonds
Dessert: Mini Vanilla Cheesecakes

Day 3
Breakfast: Brussels Sprouts Bacon Hash
Lunch: Gluten-free Taco Beans
Dinner: Beef Stew
Snack: Ninja Foodi Banana Cookies
Dessert: Ninja Foodi Raspberry Ice Cream

Day 4
Breakfast: Nutmeg Pumpkin Porridge
Lunch: Hawaiian Fried Rice
Dinner: Sweet and Sour Fish
Snack: Garlic Pretzels with Ranch Dressing
Dessert: Chocolate Chip Cookies

Day 5
Breakfast: Bell Pepper Frittata
Lunch: Broccoli Cauliflower
Dinner: Chicken Tortilla
Snack: Cheesy Stuffed Mushroom
Dessert: Chocolate Blackberry Cake

Day 6
Breakfast: Chorizo Omelet
Lunch: Crispy Balsamic Cabbage
Dinner: Garlic Turkey Breasts
Snack: Crispy Chicken Skin
Dessert: Ninja Foodi Vanilla Shake

Day 7
Breakfast: Ninja Foodi Baked Eggs
Lunch: Cabbage with Bacon
Dinner: Maple Lamb Chops
Snack: Zucchini Muffins
Dessert: Lime Blueberry Cheesecake

Week 4

Day 1
Breakfast: Almond Quinoa Porridge
Lunch: Air Crisped Brussels Sprouts
Dinner: Coconut Curry Salmon with Zucchini Noodles
Snack: Zucchini Egg Tots
Dessert: Chocolate Cheesecake

Day 2
Breakfast: Pepperoni Omelets
Lunch: Steak and Veggie Bowl
Dinner: Beef Prime Roast
Snack: Cauliflower Nuggets
Dessert: Double Chocolate Cake

Day 3
Breakfast: Apricot Oatmeal
Lunch: Eggplant with Kale
Dinner: Ninja Foodi Broiled Mahi-Mahi
Snack: Buffalo Cauliflower Platter
Dessert: Ninja Foodi Fruity Frozen Treat

Day 4
Breakfast: Flaxseeds Granola
Lunch: Gluten-free Taco Beans
Dinner: Paprika Chicken
Snack: Cauliflower Gratin
Dessert: Ninja Foodi Blackberry Crumble

Day 5
Breakfast: Omelets in the Jar
Lunch: Pumpkin Chili
Dinner: Korean Ribs
Snack: Parmesan Breadsticks
Dessert: Yogurt Cheesecake

Day 6
Breakfast: Ninja Foodi Eggs with Spinach
Lunch: Southern Fried Cabbage with Bacon
Dinner: Air Fried Scallops
Snack: Japanese Eggs
Dessert: Raspberry Cobbler

Day 7
Breakfast: Glazed Carrots
Lunch: Balsamic Cabbage with Endives
Dinner: Ninja Foodi Turkey Stew
Snack: Instant Cheesy Broccoli
Dessert: Mini Chocolate Cheesecakes

Conclusion

The Ninja Foodi is the best 9-in-1 kitchen appliance available today. This is a user-friendly, multi-purpose appliance suitable for all types of cooking. Rather than fiddling with numerous gadgets, you can manage several cooking appliances in just one device, clearing your kitchen countertop from unnecessary products.

And the Foodi isn't just convenient. You can enjoy healthy, oil-free (or less oily) food without compromising taste or flavor. You can create delicious, nutritious air-fried food and baked items. There's even the option of using the pressure cooking and crisping modes at the same time. And with the Foodi's large cooking capacity, you can cook as much food as you desire in one go.

If you're planning to start eating more healthily but while enjoying filling and yummy meals, then the Ninja Foodi will help you on your way. A Ninja Foodi, together with this cookbook's tasty recipes, will kick start your new healthy lifestyle. You'll no longer have to worry about excess fat or calories in your food, but still eat your favorite foods such as fries, pies, and cookies. This comprehensive cookbook will help you unlock endless cooking possibilities when using the Ninja Foodi. You can start cooking like a pro—even if you're a complete beginner.

So, folks, let's start some healthy cooking—today!

Appendix 1 Measurement Conversion Chart

VOLUME EQUIVALENTS(DRY)

US STANDARD	METRIC (APPROXIMATE)
1/8 teaspoon	0.5 mL
1/4 teaspoon	1 mL
1/2 teaspoon	2 mL
3/4 teaspoon	4 mL
1 teaspoon	5 mL
1 tablespoon	15 mL
1/4 cup	59 mL
1/2 cup	118 mL
3/4 cup	177 mL
1 cup	235 mL
2 cups	475 mL
3 cups	700 mL
4 cups	1 L

VOLUME EQUIVALENTS(LIQUID)

US STANDARD	US STANDARD (OUNCES)	METRIC (APPROXIMATE)
2 tablespoons	1 fl.oz.	30 mL
1/4 cup	2 fl.oz.	60 mL
1/2 cup	4 fl.oz.	120 mL
1 cup	8 fl.oz.	240 mL
1 1/2 cup	12 fl.oz.	355 mL
2 cups or 1 pint	16 fl.oz.	475 mL
4 cups or 1 quart	32 fl.oz.	1 L
1 gallon	128 fl.oz.	4 L

TEMPERATURES EQUIVALENTS

FAHRENHEIT(F)	CELSIUS(C) (APPROXIMATE)
225 °F	107 °C
250 °F	120 °C
275 °F	135 °C
300 °F	150 °C
325 °F	160 °C
350 °F	180 °C
375 °F	190 °C
400 °F	205 °C
425 °F	220 °C
450 °F	235 °C
475 °F	245 °C
500 °F	260 °C

WEIGHT EQUIVALENTS

US STANDARD	METRIC (APPROXIMATE)
1 ounce	28 g
2 ounces	57 g
5 ounces	142 g
10 ounces	284 g
15 ounces	425 g
16 ounces (1 pound)	455 g
1.5 pounds	680 g
2 pounds	907 g

Printed in Great Britain
by Amazon